POLITICAL ALIENATION
AND POLITICAL BEHAVIOR

WITH STUDIES BY

the author and,
under his direction, by:

SUZANNE DI VINCENZO

PETER SHUBS

STANLEY RENSHON

KENT EKLUND

STEVEN GOLDBERG

WILLIAM NELSEN

FRED SWAN

DON J. VOGT

GERALD T. WEST

CONRAD WINN

CRAIG WYNN

POLITICAL ALIENATION AND POLITICAL BEHAVIOR

DAVID C. SCHWARTZ
LIVINGSTON COLLEGE
AND GRADUATE FACULTY
RUTGERS UNIVERSITY

ALDINE PUBLISHING COMPANY
CHICAGO

ABOUT THE AUTHOR

David C. Schwartz is presently Associate Professor of Political Science
at Livingston College and in the Graduate Faculty of Rutgers University.
He is an Associate Editor of *Society* magazine and a consultant in research to several public institutions, foundations, and agencies. In addition to his work on political alienation, violence, and revolution, Dr.
Schwartz is now working in two interdisciplinary areas of research:(1)
The impact of people's health, physical development and body images
on their political attitudes and behavior; and (2) the relationships among
folklore, popular culture, and politics.

CONSULTING EDITOR

Martin Landau
University of California
Berkeley

*First published 1973 by
Aldine Publishing Company
529 South Wabash Avenue
Chicago, Illinois 60605*

*ISBN-202-24121-1
Library of Congress Catalog Number 70-169518*

Printed in the United States of America

*To the memory of my father, to my mother, to Todd,
and especially to Sandra*

CONTENTS

PREFACE

Why do people adopt attitudes of political alienation, attitudes of estrangement from or lack of identification with the political system? Why do some politically alienated people react to their alienation by engaging in revolutionary behavior while others, similarly alienated, become reformers or ritualists or just drop out of political activity? In this book, I attempt to answer these questions, to develop and test a theory of the causes and consequences of political alienation. In this Preface, I indicate some of the concerns that make these questions important and some of the strategies of explanation and research experiences that have shaped my answers to them.

Political alienation is a phenomenon of fundamental importance in political processes. Recent empirical research, employing a variety of measures, has found alienation to be significantly associated with a wide range of political behaviors, including revolutionary behavior, reformism, support for demagogues, nonvoting, protest voting, participation in radical political movements, and vicarious use of mass media. Given these behavioral consequences, it is now widely accepted that the magnitude and distribution of political alienation are significantly related to the stability, integration, and development of political systems. Alienation, then, appears to be a fundamental human political orientation. It seems clear that an understanding of the causes and consequences of that orientation is basic to the practice and hence to the study of politics.

The importance of alienation, and the need to understand its causes and consequences, are perhaps nowhere more clear than in the contemporary America where this book was conceived, researched and written. Our time and place are marked by substantial alienation, evidenced and exacerbated by daylight murders of Presidents and public leaders, by political riots with snipers, armed troops and blood in the streets, by student strikes, and bombings that have shut down schools, colleges and public buildings and by a mounting number of protests, demonstrations, confrontations and crises. Even in recent moments of relative calm, our awareness of the substantial alienation in our midst has given American politics a brooding, foreboding, anxious quality; a nervous, "anything might happen" mood. These anxieties are themselves alienating, and they produce divergent, incongruent, oscillatory reactions across different social sectors and groups, which further expand public disaffection. The result, even when not violent, is not social peace either; it is a quiet, but very real, crisis.

Social crises are always the objects of speculation; continuing crises are inevitably the objects of myth. Accordingly, it is perhaps not surprising that much of our current scholarly and popular thinking about American politics is concerned with interpretations of our alienated era, interpretations that often begin as speculations and end as new dogmas.

Virtually all recent interpretations of American public affairs recognize the importance of alienation. The early reactions to the manifest alienation of the 1960s were shock and puzzlement; most social scientists and other professional observers of the polity were unprepared for the new politics of ethnic, racial, student and female radicalism. The puzzlement gave way to intensely human and emotional expressions of alienation. One thinks, for example, of Claude Brown, Kenneth Clark, Piri Thomas, Eldridge Cleaver, Jerry Rubin and James Simon Kunen, not to mention the moviemakers and the musicians, as having contributed highly successful descriptive expressions that made American alienation first visible and then fashionable (and even profitable).

Once it is fashionable, a "concern" becomes a "problem," and the putative explanations begin to flow. So we have had the poverty explanations of the government reports, the anti-riot answers of the police, the single-issue panaceas (end the war, change the schools, wave the flag) and the response of the revolutionaries (scrap the whole show, burn, drop out). As proponents of these views roam the land in abundance purveying their wares (often to the same buyers), the importance of alienation becomes increasingly clear and the myths grow.

The importance of political alienation can also be seen in the fact that major public policies aimed at reversing it and political strategies aimed at exploiting it have been formulated. To get funding, each new proposed public policy program has had to rehearse the whole range of evils (poverty, racism, pollution, etc.) and to promise to stop them all. This process rehearses and reinforces alienation and oversells the policies. In part because the policies are based on inadequate or partial understandings of alienation, they regularly fail, and this failure acts as an alienation multiplier. The fears that are generated and reinforced in overselling the policies, and the frustrations caused by the failure of these policies, go far to create still more alienation.

Political strategies aimed at exploiting alienation to build electoral or radical movements also abound. Mobilization of the alienated (whether they be the silent majority that is silent because withdrawn in passive alienation or the strident minority that has passed over into active alienation) has become a major effort and tactic of American politics. Such tactics have met with generally indifferent or limited success, for they, too, are based upon partial explanations. Both the "establishment" and the radicals regularly give evidence of the importance of alienation, and both of them seem to need a better theory of that phenomenon.

Scholars have also recognized the importance of alienation. Recent years have witnessed a burgeoning and diffusion of social science interest in the phenomenon. Scholarly articles and books on the subject have increased of late, and, where these once were mostly written by sociologists, now political scientists and others are involved in alienation research. But the social science studies have thus far managed to explain rather little of the observed variance in political alienation. The authors of these studies seem to have great difficulty in predicting the behavioral consequences of alienation as well. Social science, like the societies it studies, appears to need a better theory of alienation.

In sum, the importance of the phenomenon of political alienation derives not only from its increasing scope and magnitude, not only from the many fundamental behaviors that are the consequences of alienation, but from the present and pressing need for more effective explanations of the causes and consequences of the phenomenon. This book represents my effort to provide some better explanations of alienation and to facilitate the development of still more satisfying ones.

The social science study of political alienation has been dominated by a single strategy of explanation. This is the idea that "a specified social-cultural condition gives rise to specified feelings [alienation] in individuals which in turn give rise to specified behaviors."[1] In practice, this has meant that virtually all of the studies on the causes of political alienation have concentrated on the correlation of socio-economic status (SES) and alienation, and that most of the studies on the consequences of alienation have concentrated on the correlation of alienation and specific political behaviors. This simple social conditons ➤ political attitudes ➤ political behavior notion is so pervasive in the research literature that "different writers have worked variations on this theme but nobody has challenged the scheme it-self or attempted a fundamental revision of it."[2]

In this book, I seek to build upon our existing knowledge but also offer several fundamental challenges to, and revisions of, the prevailing strategy of explanation. First, I argue, and adduce evidence indicating, that peo-ple's social positions and cultural orientations do not now bear sig-nificant causal relationship to the attitude of alienation. Then, I ad-vance a three-variable, psychological model to account for political alienation and present data from studies in American cities, suburbs and campuses, and from specialized national samples and laboratory experiments which indicate that the model has considerable explana-tory utility. Third, I state and apply an attitude-to-behavior model intended to help explain three basic processes that intervene between the adoption of a political attitude and the outplay of behavior relevant to that attitude. Specifically, the attitude-to-behavior model includes: (1) a chart-ing of the process by which different basic behavioral orientations toward politics are adopted by alienated people; (2) an explanation of the differ-ential political-communications preferences among alienated people that make these people available to hear radical, reformist and revolutionary messages (political stimuli); and (3) an analysis of the evaluation processes by which alienated people are likely to accept or reject com-munications (and behavior suggestions) from various leaders, groups, in-stitutions and systems. As these communications arouse and channel alien-ated people into specific political behaviors, the model predicts to the probability and direction of political behaviors that issue from the attitude of alienation. Although all of the theoretical and empirical material in this book relates specifically to political alienation, it seems clear that the four basic features of the models advanced in the book—(1) attitude acquisi-tion, (2) adoption of basic behavioral orientations to politics, (3) differen-tial amenability to political influence, (4) arousal and channelling of be-havior by stimuli from political leaders, groups, systems, etc.—are relevant to the development of a general theory of political behavior.

This effort to develop better theories of alienation should serve some important practical purposes, because the absence of an integrated, vali-dated theory of alienation has had profound and deleterious effects on the development and orchestration of public policies and political strategies designed to affect alienation.

Many of the most important American public policy programs of the present era have had the aim of affecting alienation. These policies, of course, are based on the explanation of alienation believed valid by public policy-makers. There are, however, a multiplicity of unintegrated popular explanations. We have heard it argued, for example, that economic disadvantage is at the heart of alienation (and unrest), and therefore programs of economic relief and opportunity are needed. We have also been told that governmental inefficiency is a cause of alienation, so that we ought to embark on governmental streamlining reforms. Others contend that government is too distant from the people, and suggest programs of decentralization, neighborhood control of governmental functions, revenue-sharing, and the like. Still others argue that alienation is primarily caused by a loss of belief in American political myths and therefore exhortation (that is, symbol manipulation) toward patriotism is needed. Without knowing the relative importance of socio-economic statuses, perceptions of systemic inefficacy, perceptions of personal political inefficacy and political ideology and myths, and because of confusion as to how these variables fit together, we have embarked on a wide variety of somewhat uncoordinated public policy programs—oscillating in our emphasis on different approaches, unclear on how these programs should or do fit together, expecting short-run successes but inadequately funding most of the programs.

Similarly, uncertainty about the consequences of political alienation has given rise to considerable confusion about appropriate political strategies among "establishment" leaders, reformers and radicals alike. For example, those who see revolutionary violence as the inevitable or highly likely result of alienation are most inclined either to advocate or use violence themselves as a means of social control or social change, or to be immobilized by fears of such violence. Alternatively, those who believe that alienation leads primarily to withdrawal may advocate "benign neglect," the politics of normalcy or, worse, they may mistake quiescence for acquiescence or assent. Reformers and radicals who believe that withdrawal is the main result of alienation have become disheartened or hysterical, with unfortunate consequences for their efforts to foster social change.

This book is primarily an effort to explain political alienation, not an attempt to derive public policies and political strategies as implications of that explanation. Still, the relative importance and meshing of economic, inefficacy and ideological variables as causes of alienation are explored. Thus, the studies reported in this book do deal with the variables that major public policy programs are designed to manipulate. Accordingly, the explanations of alienation advanced here should have substantial relevance for the evaluation, planning, conduct and orchestration of public policy. Similarly, the charting of the processes by which political behaviors issue from the attitude of alienation should have considerable utility for the derivation and implementation of political strategies.

The explanations of alienation and the data intended to test and refine those explanations are couched in terms of recent American political experiences. I believe, however, that the validity and utility of these explana-

tions are not unique to this time and place. Some of my students and I
have begun to examine the cross-cultural, cross-temporal utility of the ex-
plantations, but these very preliminary efforts are not represented in this
book.

The organization of the book

I have tried to organize the book, and each of the chapters, with the busy
reader in mind. In the first chapter, I define and discuss the concept of
political alienation, review and critique the relevant scholarly and popular
literature and advance a theoretical explanation of the causes and consequences of alienation. In Chapters 2 and 3, I present data from studies
testing the adequacy of previous explanations of the causes of alienation.
Chapters 4 through 7 include research reports of investigations intended to
test my own explanation of political alienation. Chapters 8 through 13 are
tests of my effort to model the processes whereby different kinds of political
behavior issue from the attitude of political alienation. The conclusion
(Chapter 14) summarizes the major findings of the research, indicates some
of the directions future research might profitably take and seeks to apply
and expand the explanations developed in this book in an interpretive essay
on contemporary American politics: "From the Lonely Crowd to the
Strident Society." Readers who are especially interested in the new theoretical statements advanced in this book should consult Chapters 1, 4, 8 and
14 in particular.

Each of the individual data chapters (Chapters 2 through 13) is also
organized for the convenience of the busy reader. The standardized format
of these chapters is: (1) a statement of the intellectual problem addressed
in the chapter; (2) the derivation of hypotheses; (3) a description of the
context of the research (cities, campuses, etc.); (4) a discussion of the
methods of research; and (5) a presentation of the findings and their
implications.

This organization of the research chapters was also selected to permit the
reader to obtain a feeling for the powerful emotional aspects of alienation
in the communities we studied. Such an appreciation of the emotional side
of political alienation is not sought here as human interest or as "local
color," laudable as these qualities may be. Rather, awareness and compre-
hension of the emotional correlates of alienation are basic to an understanding of the phenomenon. Political alienation is often associated with strong
emotions—pain, fear, loneliness and rage—and these emotions have profound effects on human motivation and arousal. Hence, emotional reactions to alienation predict to the political behaviors in which alienated
people are likely to engage. Therefore, the variables in our theories and

hypotheses include emotional factors (that is, we seek to discover the "actor-meaning" of politics and political alienation). Also, our descriptions of both research contexts and the implications of our findings centrally include the emotional aspects of people and their politics.

Of course, a book on political alienation in America could hardly be unconcerned with the emotions, for these are passionate times in American politics, and the people whose political attitudes and behaviors are studied in this book have been profoundly touched by the passions of our alienated period. I, too, have been deeply moved by some of the political and research experiences reported in this book: by long days and nights in Newark and receiving the black power salute from twenty-three magnificent young black people there; by crisis committee meetings in Philadelphia while police sirens screamed and influential men voiced fears that went beyond riots and repressions; by sit-ins and student strikes and peace marches (not all of them reported herein). Most of all, I have been touched by the people I studied, the people with whom I have been privileged to work and talk during the last few years, and by the dreams, joys, fears, tears and ideas they shared with me. Some of these people are thanked in this Preface. Whether or not they are individually identified here, these people are the real subjects of this book. The abstract concepts we employ are aspects of their concrete experiences, the tables and statistics are summarized reflections of their feelings, and, as I remind myself in arrogant moments, any truths we discover in those tables are the truths that they have taught us.

Acknowledgments

I am profoundly indebted to a great number of people whose teachings, advice, assistance and love made it both possible and fun for me to write this book. Martin Landau inspired me to want to be a political scientist in the first place, taught and advised me wonderfully and encouraged me to write the book. While I was at M.I.T., Lucian Pye and Robert Melson commented usefully on the very earliest statements of the ideas expressed here.

In the period of research and writing, the following people were most helpful. First, I am especially grateful to William R. Kintner, Director of the Foreign Policy Research Institute, who encouraged the writing of the book and commented helpfully on it. Indeed, special thanks are due to the F.P.R.I. and its staff, which supported much of the research and selected the book to be a part of its series. Suzanne DiVincenzo handled the enormous tasks of data management for the book and it quite literally could not have been written without her outstanding efforts. Peter Shubs, co-author of one of the chapters of this book, was very helpful in connection with several of the drafts. Neal Cutler, Will Keim, James C. Davies, Robert Strausz-Hupé (former Director of the F.P.R.I.), Daniel Dolan, Robert Frank and Harvey Sicherman also made invaluable suggestions. My sincere gratitude is extended to Teresa Torelli and the secretarial and administrative staff of the F.P.R.I. who transformed my nearly illegible notes into typed manuscripts.

In many of the chapters of this book, I have drawn upon studies conducted by my students or jointly by my students and myself. I consider these students the authors or co-authors of these studies. Their names are, of course, given in the text of the chapters in which their work is utilized. Nonetheless, I am pleased to acknowledge here the assistance and advice of Ignatius DeCola, Kent Eklund, Steven Goldberg, Sarah Moore, William Nelsen, Stanley Renshon, Fred Swan, Don Vogt, Gerald West, Conrad Winn and Craig Wynn.

Libby J. Goldstein made it possible for me to conduct the large-scale interview study in Newark, New Jersey, which is reported in several chapters, and her advice was important to several other chapters as well. I am also grateful to James Becker of Research for Better Schools, Inc., and to the North City Congress, both of Philadelphia, for cooperation in the use of data initially generated by or for them.

My wife, Sandra Kenyon Schwartz, helped most. Her insightful professional counsel immeasurably improved the book, and in countless personal ways she made the period of writing the book a magnificently happy one for me.

I

Introduction

1

A THEORY OF
POLITICAL ALIENATION

The purpose of this book is to explain the causes and consequences of political alienation: to account for men's identification with, or estrangement from, political systems and to chart the behavioral consequences that flow from different levels of political identification. In this introductory chapter, I advance a theory of political alienation that builds upon some of our present understandings about the phenomenon but is at the same time radically different from much of what is now assumed to be true.

The need for a theory of political alienation is clear, for alienation has been shown to be a phenomenon of fundamental importance to political systems and their study. At the individual level of analysis, recent empirical research has found alienation to be significantly associated with a wide range of important political attitudes and behaviors, including revolutionary activities,[1] innovative reformism,[2] support for demagogues,[3] rioting,[4] nonvoting and protest voting,[5] low or withdrawn political interest and participation,[6] vicarious use of the mass media,[7] participation in radical right-wing activities,[8] political party identification[9] and negative attitudes toward such political objects as metropolitan governmental organization and school desegregation.[10] In several studies reported below, I will indicate that alienation is significantly related to such "new politics" phenomena as campus sit-ins and national anti-war protest demonstrations as well.

More generally, it is now widely accepted that identification and alienation are of basic importance to the functioning of political systems as a whole and to a broad range of public institutions and processes. For example, Easton regards "diffuse support," which certainly includes the positive identification of individuals with the polity, as a prerequisite for the integration and persistence of political systems,[11] and Almond and Verba also suggest that a "long-run political stability may be . . . dependent on a more . . . diffuse sense of attachment or loyalty to the political system."[12]

3

In the study of political development, too, the idea that individual identification with a national polity is a precondition for development is now widespread.[13]

If alienation affects individual attitudes and behavior and impacts on the polity as a whole, it will certainly also be important to the institutions and processes of politics that constitute the locus of much contemporary research (for example, parties, Congress, etc.). Recently, large-scale national studies of American political parties,[14] for example, have recognized that alienation from parties and from the polity *is* an important area of investigation. Such recognition seems bound to grow in a period like the present when national presidential election campaigns centrally include overt appeals to alienated populations, when meetings of alienated youth, organized in movements for a new Congress, attract a long list of candidates seeking endorsement and help,[15] when foreign policy formation involves mass demonstrations, violence and death, and when public services that used to seem routine, such as fire control, education and law enforcement, are daily disrupted over political matters.

The need for a more comprehensive and more precise explanation of political alienation is intensified by the unpredicted increase in American alienation, which has raised fundamental questions about the models of man and paradigms of the polity that currently prevail in social science. In general, social scientists did not predict the political instability of the 1960s in America. "Not a single observer of the campus scene, as late as 1959, anticipated the emergence of the organized disaffection, protest and activism which was to take shape early in the 1960s."[16] As late as 1962 Kenneth Kenniston, one of the most respected observers of the campus scene, noted increases in alienation but said of American youth, "They will assure a highly stable political and social order, for few of them will be enough committed to politics to consider revolution, subversion or even radical change."[17] Seven years later a national government study found that 76 percent of the American colleges sampled and 75 percent of the high schools studied had experienced some form of unrest during 1968-1969 alone, 60 percent of this unrest involved police action.[18] During the first five months of 1969, there were 260 civil disorders in American schools.[19]

The same decade in which prominent social scientists concluded that the potential for radical movements in America had all but disappeared[20] witnessed an unprecedented radicalization in the black community (and widespread white radicalization as well). This development resulted in hundreds of riots and riot-connected deaths, political injuries in the thousands, political arrests in the tens of thousands and property damage in the hundreds of millions of dollars.[21] In an era of sniper attacks on police, of growing vigilante groups in urban ethnic communities, of widespread arms purchases in the suburbs, of dissident rifle clubs as well as of riots, violent protests and bombings—many of which were "unexpected in particular by social scientists who are professionals responsible for locating and understanding such phenomena"[22]—our understanding of American political motivations, behavior and processes has been called into question.

Understandably, perhaps, some social scientists have reacted to this situation with almost wholesale rejection of previous social science theories. One scholar concluded, for example, that "all of our fondest theories of economic development and political stability totter and collapse in the face of riots, guerrilla warfare, assassinations."[23] Understandable, too, is a scholarly reaction that moves from thesis to antithesis, holding that just the opposite of what we previously believed must be true. So if Riesman argued in 1949 that in politics Americans tend to desire "not power but adjustment,"[24] Nieburg in 1969 contended that "in an important sense, all individuals, groups and nations desire to 'rule the world' " and that "*all* individuals, groups or nations make a continuous effort to exploit *any* favorable opportunity to improve their roles or to impose a greater part of their own value structures upon a larger political system."[25]

In my view, neither a wholesale rejection nor outright reversal of social science theories seems warranted, but obviously our explanations at the individual level of political analysis and therefore our aggregation of individual behavior to make system-level statements, are in need of intensive scrutiny and very probably of considerable revision. If the need for a theory of political alienation derives from the importance of alienation to the behavior of individuals and of political systems, the need for a revised theory of political alienation derives from the limitations of existing theories.

Concept clarification

One of the major limitations of our present understanding of political alienation is the massive confusion surrounding the use of the term. Historically, some of the confusion derived from the fact that "alienation" had different but sometimes overlapping meanings in religious thought, law and Marxism and hence has had such diverse referents as religio-mystical ecstasy, spiritual death, sales of property and lack of relationship to the product of one's work or to the means of production.[26] There was also considerable confusion as to whether the term was to be used as a description of a social condition or as an evaluation of that condition.[27]

More recently, the confusions tend to flow from the derivation of the concept of alienation from the sociological concept of *anomie*. Anomie, as originally described by Durkheim and adapted by Merton, referred to a condition of society—a state of normlessness or confusion of norms in the culture. Merton refers to man's responses to this social condition— reformism, ritualism, rebelliousness and conformity—as "adaptations to anomie";[28] but he does not consistently distinguish between attitudinal and behavioral responses. Accordingly, one conceptual confusion concerns the use of alienation to mean both attitudes and behavior.

When Srole[29] and others sought to employ Merton's notions in empirical research, they employed the terms *anomia, anomy* and *anomie* in a social-psychological sense, referring to the psychological state of the individual. The same word is thus used often to refer both to a state of society *and* to a state of the individual.

In the empirical literature, alienation has come to be used almost exclusively in the social-psychological sense, but the ambiguities of the concept have not diminished. Although individuals rather than societies are now seen as alienated, the object from which the individual is alienated remains confused and so does the operational meaning of the term. Let us consider these problems in order.

People have been depicted as alienated from a great variety of things—from the society, culture, self, mankind, God and politics.[30] This has given rise to the assumption that if one is alienated from any of these referents one need be (or tends to be) alienated from all of them. For example, the best known and most widely used measure of social alienation, the Srole scale,[31] includes references to politics, other people in general, the present state of man, the future state of self. The Nettler scale[32] of cultural alienation also lumps references to politics together with attitudes toward cars, TV, spectator sports, media, etc. These scales have been used in several studies of political attitudes and behavior[33] under the apparent if generally implicit assumption that the scales either include or constitute political alienation. *But the degree of relationship between political and sociocultural alienation is an empirical question of enormous significance; the existence of such a relationship must be demonstrated, not simply assumed. If social or cultural alienation is the same thing as or explains political alienation, then there is little reason for the separate modeling of political alienation.* These conceptual problems have had a seriously deleterious effect on our substantive understanding. By confusing political with social and cultural alienation, scholars have tended to assume that there is a necessary or at least typically significant association between socio-cultural and political alienation—a proposition which we challenge below.

But even if we render clear *who* is alienated and from *what* he is alienated, even if we refer to the individual as alienated from the political system, the central question remains: What is alienation? What meaning or meanings can be given to the concept? Melvin Seeman's "On the Meaning of Alienation"[34] has been generally accepted as the classic clarification of the concept. Seeman's review of the literature revealed five analytically separable usages of the word: normlessness, meaninglessness, powerlessness, social isolation and self-estrangement. Some writers have argued that these five constitute a generally integrated network of negative attitudes toward society, that they tend to occur together. The empirical investigations of the subject show very mixed results,[35] however, and in general different scholars have concerned themselves with different dimensions.[36] Of course, this diversity of concerns has added to the ambiguity of the concept because each scholar tends to refer to his dependent variable simply as "alienation," whatever his definitions.[37] The result is that alienation means powerlessness (to Seeman and those who use his measurements); it refers to a complex of isolation, despair and powerlessness (to Srole and those who utilize his scale); and it is defined as a cognition that politicians don't care about people and cannot be trusted (by Thompson and Horton and by Aberbach).

Despite this great variety of meanings that have been attached to the concept of political alienation, I believe that it has a "core" meaning. This meaning may be referred to as "estrangement"—a perception that one does not identify oneself with the political system. Interestingly, this meaning is often selected as the formal or general definition of alienation even by scholars who then go on to operationalize the concept to mean inefficacy, normlessness or some other dimension. Thus Olsen, who has used both the Srole scale and the Seeman inefficacy measure as indexes of alienation, writes: "Alienation might then be defined formally as an attitude of separation or estrangement between oneself and some salient aspect of the social environment.[38] Srole himself defined alienation as estrangement, as "a generalized, pervasive sense of self-to-others belongingness at one extreme compared with . . . self-to-others alienation at the other pole of the continuum.[39] Nettler refers to the alienated man as "one who has been estranged from his society."[40] In addition, the "estrangement" meaning of alienation can be traced back to Durkheim through MacIver, who defined the concept as "a breakdown in the individual sense of attachment."[41]

Of course, in defining alienation as estrangement, I am not arguing that there is some ineluctable essence to the concept of alienation that is uniquely captured by the concept of "estrangement," or that definitions have an independent truth value, such that estrangement is a "truer" definition of alienation than is inefficacy or normlessness. Estrangement would appear to be a more summative or general orientation to politics than inefficacy or normlessness or meaninglessness and does seem more directly relevant to politics than estrangement from the self. In this sense, it may be argued that estrangement should provide a more useful definition for the term *alienation*.

Kon has argued that, to be useful in research or theoretical development, the concept of alienation needs to be made specific by answering three basic questions: (1) Who is alienated? (2) From what is he alienated? (3) How is this alienation manifested?[42] For our purposes here, it is the individual who is alienated from the political system as a whole[43] as manifested in a set of attitudes of estrangement. Following Olsen, alienation is defined herein as an attitude of separation or estrangement[44] between the self and the polity. A variety of operational attitude measures of estrangement have been designed and employed in our studies.

Defining alienation as an attitude, moreover, permits us to avoid a conceptual confusion that has often seriously weakened our substantive understanding of politics: the confusion between attitudes and behaviors. This confusion has led to serious conceptual and empirical difficulties. Berger and Pullberg, for example, suggest that change-oriented behavior cannot be a consequence of the attitude of alienation because the typical result of alienation is ritualism ("social fetishism").[45] We will show, however, that ritualism and reformism and radicalism are all associated with alienated attitudes. Similarly, Koeppen contends that alienation cannot be a major determinant of radical right-wing behavior (despite the findings of Abcarian and Stanage[46]) because many people on the radical right participate in Republican party politics, whereas alienation, she believes, leads only to withdrawal or out-of-system protest behavior.[47] Again, this is a confusion: the attitude of alienation is associated with a wide range of behavior, much of which is within the system (reformist activity, protest voting, ritualistic participation, etc.). The same confusion appears in the literature on student behavior. Kenniston and other writers on student political behaviors often contrast students who withdraw from interest in politics (whom they call alienated) with those who are "activists."[48] We will show below not only that the attitude of alienation is significantly associated with both withdrawal and activism as behavior orientations but that withdrawal and activism can be understood as part of the same psycho-political process. There is a simple set of transition rules to predict which of these orientations will be chosen and when. The point to be made here is that alienation is generally manifested in an attitude set that may or may not be activated into behavior and that must include a good deal besides alienation if political behavior is to take place or to be predicted.

On the causes of alienation:
The limitation of previous approaches

A single strategy of explanation dominates the vast preponderance of empirical research on political and social alienation: "A specified social-cultural condition gives rise to specified feelings [alienation] in individuals which in turn gives rise to specified behaviors."[49] In the words of McClosky and Schaar, "different writers have worked variations on this theme, but nobody has challenged the scheme itself or attempted a fundamental revision of it."[50] Here, I will do just that: in this section I will argue that social positions and cultural orientations, as these are presently understood, bear little or no causal relationship to the attitude of political alienation in contemporary America and that our psychological approaches to alienation are also in need of revision. More I will propose such a revision. In the following section of this chapter, I will analyze our present understanding of the processes whereby political behaviors issue out of alienated attitudes, conclude that our theories in this area are also in need of major revisions and propose a set of revisions. The theoretical discussion in this chapter, and all of the data reported in this book, relate to contemporary America. The theory itself, however, is neither time- nor place-specific and preliminary efforts at cross-cultural validation have been begun.[51]

As McClosky and Schaar indicate, the overwhelming majority of studies of alienation have concerned themselves with the interrelationship between the social positions in which individuals find themselves (usually socio-economic status and social connectedness) and alienation.[52] The results of these studies are nearly always the same: however alienation is defined, however the socio-economic status (SES) measure is constructed, there is a significant inverse relationship between alienation and social status. In more than a score of such studies published between 1956 and 1970, only two cast even a modicum of doubt on this relationship. Indeed, so typical and recurrent is this finding in the literature that investigators now report it in a laconic, matter-of-fact fashion. So Templeton reports: "In the case of every piece of research bearing on this relationship, social status was found to be negatively related to alienation. This relationship held irrespective of the particular indicator of status used."[53] Similarly, McClosky and Schaar in discussing Srole's research wrote, "He also found (as all other investigators have) that anomy is inversely related to social and economic status." They go on to say that "no study has attempted to revise even in a modest way the thesis that certain objective social conditions cause anomy."[54]

The reasoning that lies behind these nearly unanimous findings is cogent. When alienation is defined as inefficacy, then certainly the poor, the less well educated, those who are not organizationally connected to the society or polity are objectively disadvantaged; they have a "diminished differential access to the achievement of life goals," and they are likely to realize this and therefore to feel inefficacious.[55] When alienation is defined by the Srole scale (as despair, inefficacy and isolation), the objective fact is that people in lower SES categories, people who are less well connected to social and political organizations, are likely to be getting fewer of the material rewards of the system. If politics is who gets what, when and how, then people who are getting little, most of the time, should value the polity (and society) correspondingly.[56]

This reasoning has also been connected, in the social science literature, to the notion of social marginality, to the idea that people in marginal or "bypassed" social strata would feel unconnected to the ever developing society and polity. Thus McClosky and Schaar describe anomic people as "outside the articulate, prosperous and successful sectors of the population. Anomic feelings appear most strongly among those who, for whatever reasons, are stranded in the backwaters of the symbolic and material main stream, those whose lives are circumscribed by isolation, deprivation and ignorance."[57] So, too, Daniel Bell describes the radical right as bypassed men; men of the "old middle class" passed over by new trends in the economy, the university, the society at large.[58] Trow's findings on the supporters of Senator Joseph McCarthy in Vermont are also to this effect.[59]

There seems, then, to be a strong urge in American social study to explain alienation as a product of something "old" (and more than a little "weird"). Right-wingers are depicted as bypassed; poor people are "stranded" in the backwaters of our society. But what is to be said of this conception today? Now it is not only the Minutemen who are arming but also the surburbanites! Now the people who are talking about and preparing for guerrilla warfare are not people who can be dismissed as "communist-chasing wierdoes" in California but often are urban, working, lower-middle-class "ethnics"—white as well as black—and more than a few upper-class and upper-middle-class students! Can these people be meaningfully described as marginal, too? And the junior faculty (and some of the senior faculty) of our great universities who feel ineffective in our polity and despairing about the future—are they marginal as well? Finally, are the public officials and political candidates marginal, whose proposed legislation, speeches and advertising stress alienation themes, suggesting that our system isn't working and requires basic reforms? Certainly not!

The long string of studies that purport to show that social status influences alienation have a variety of things in common that cast doubt on the power and generalizability of the findings. First, many more of the people in lower-SES categories are typically not alienated rather than alienated. Second, substantial proportions of upper-SES categories are alienated. Third, the correlations tend to be weak: in almost none of the studies do SES and alienation share even one-third of their variance, and most of the reported relationships are much weaker. (In the most recently published data, income, sex, race and ethnicity were unrelated to alienation defined as inefficacy, and education and age shared respectively only 14 and 13 percent of their variance with alienation; the relationships were even weaker with alienation defined as normlessness.)[60] From these facts I conclude that SES is neither a necessary nor a sufficient condition to produce alienation and that it has been a relatively weak predictor of alienation.

Moreover, almost all of the data in the studies that purport to show that SES and alienation are significantly related to each other were collected before 1966; a majority of it was gathered in the late 1950s and early 1960s. It is outdated stuff. Most of the data were collected before John Kennedy was murdered, before Robert Kennedy was murdered, before Martin Luther King and Malcolm X and Medgar Evers and scores of others in and around the civil rights movement were slain, and we know that these assassinations tended to increase public alienation.[61] The studies of alienation that stressed SES generally preceded the active phase of the civil rights movement; they took place before Birmingham and Selma and the Civil Rights Bills of 1964 and 1965; before the Vietnam War escalated and 50,000 Americans died there; before the urban riots really began; before the college campus and then the streets became places of student protest and violence. In short, the bulk of the evidence that indicates that SES tends to produce political alienation represents the politics of yesteryear.

We will show in several later chapters that perceptions of the polity are far more powerful factors in producing alienation than social background variables. This being so, we might well expect the relationship between SES and alienation (which we have already seen to be weak) to disappear altogether in an era like the 1960s in America when politics was increasingly affecting all social strata. It should also be remembered that all of the SES ⟶ alienation work was done with alienation defined differently than we are doing here. It has not been shown in the literature that SES bears significant relationship to alienation operationalized directly as estrangement.

The outdated character of the relationship between SES and alienation seems indicated in social as well as political changes in America. The relative prosperity of the 1960s in America meant that higher education became increasingly available to lower-SES populations, and more and more Americans attained at least lower-middle-class jobs and incomes. If alienation were confined largely to lower-SES categories, then the absolute number of alienated adults should have declined in the 1960s. No study has found this result and no scholar has argued for this conclusion. By any measure, alienation in America seems to have increased, not decreased, across all social sectors during the 1960s.

Moreover, the social science literature can be cited to show a downturn in the significance of SES factors, even on the older definitions of alienation. Using the data of the Survey Research Center, for example, one can compare the correlation of five SES measures (age, sex, race, education and/income) with the SRC's four-item measure of inefficacy. Between 1956 and 1960, for example, 16 of the 20 correlations declined.[62] Similarly, while data from the 1950s and 1960s (Trow's and Olsen's) did show a significant relationship between alienation and the "old middle class," subsequent data reported in 1968 by White and by Nelson[63] tend to disconfirm this relationship. I will show in Chapter 3 that social connectedness does not now typically operate to produce low levels of alienation (as earlier studies by Erbe[64] and Neal and Seeman[65] indicated). But even if a relationship between social connectedness and alienation used to obtain, findings from the middle and late 1960s show that social connectedness is increasing far more rapidly for disadvantaged populations than for white middle-class populations[66] and that social connectedness can function to alienate and mobilize people as well as to dampen alienation.[67] These findings indicate the relative weakness of social connectedness in predicting to alienation and its behavioral consequences.

The nearly obsessive concern of social scientists with the relationship of SES and alienation has probably weakened both our explanation of alienation and our understanding of the role that SES does play in the process, for the psychological mechanisms through which SES must function to affect alienation, if it affects it at all, have been relatively deemphasized. Our understanding of alienation has been more static than processual.

A better understanding will be achieved by seeking the psychological factors that bear significant direct association with alienation and then examining the impact, if any, that social and political conditions have upon these psychologically "intervening variables." What are the psychological variables that have been posited or discovered to be associated with political alienation?

The most prevalent psychological variable in the literature on political alienation is *political inefficacy*. We have seen that inefficacy is often given as a definition of alienation, but, where it is not, it is often used as an important variable that is likely to produce alienation. We now know from a variety of studies[68] that people who perceive themselves to be relatively inefficacious in politics—that is, who perceive themselves to be unable, by their own behavior, to influence or control desired political outcomes[69]— are more likely than others to withdraw their self-identification, interest, attention and participation from politics. The logic behind this finding is simple and clear: people are expected to orient to the political system because of their personal relationship to it. If someone feels he can influence politics, then he is more likely to participate, to feel that participation and governmental policy are beneficial and to give his diffuse support and identification to the polity.[70]

This reasoning seems to make sense as far as it goes, but it simply does not go far enough. An individual may feel utterly inefficacious and yet feel no estrangement because he does not believe himself to be entitled to more power. Almond and Verba might call this a "subject" political mentality and suggest that such a mentality tends to be typical in developing countries.[71] But there is certainly at least some of this prevalent in contemporary America. Using the SRC 1966 national data, 57.7 percent of the sample who gave a definite response to the question "How much political power do you think people like you have?" thought that they and their counterparts had little or no power. Yet of those stating an opinion on the question "Do you think that people like you have too little political power or just the right amount," 61.5 percent were satisfied with the amount of power they perceived themselves to have. Thus, even if every person who saw himself as having little or no power also thought that was too little power, approximately 18 percent of the sample were satisfied to be inefficacious. A comparison of the SRC data from 1964 with their 1966 results casts some further doubt on the impact of efficacy alone on alienation. While inefficacy did not significantly increase for the sample as a whole (efficacious response increased significantly on one item, decreased significantly on a second and varied insignificantly on the third and four items), political interest, political activity and trust in government all decreased significantly.[72]

A second reason that personal inefficacy alone may not predict political alienation is that a person's inefficacy may not be salient to him. If a person is satisfied with things as they are, he may just not care very much about his inefficacy. "After all," he might reason, "what does it matter if I can't influence the polity when there is nothing I want to influence it about?" If the political system already comports with his fundamental politicized values, inefficacy is unlikely to produce estrangement.

This proposition can be derived from the extant political science literature, although it is not typically stated as I have expressed it here. What is usually said is that social cohesion or political integration are based upon a fundamental consensus on values and beliefs.[73] At the level of individual analysis, one might infer that people who do not share the consensual values and beliefs ought to become alienated. This influence, however, would be rendered dubious by the operation of the efficacy variable: people who are in fundamental value conflict with the political system need not become alienated from that polity if they perceive themselves to be efficacious in changing it so as to reduce the conflict. This conclusion, too, is hinted at in the literature; Seeman, for example, notes that efficacy must be both valued and thwarted for it to produce withdrawal from politics.[74]

But let us suppose that an individual does find himself to be in a basic value conflict with the polity[75] (that is, he can neither change his values because they are too basic nor agree with the values exhibited in the polity). Let us suppose that he *does* perceive himself to be quite personally inefficacious to do anything about it. He still need not become alienated. He may believe that one or more of his reference groups will attain his values for him. If he perceives that the political system can be reformed so that his value conflict will be reduced or eliminated, he need not withdraw his identification from that system. But if in his view the system cannot be reformed (in a time period acceptable to him), if he sees no reference groups or surrogates operating in the polity that can reform the system, if he perceives that the system and not just his person is inefficacious to attain his values, then his value conflict is truly irreconcilable and alienation seems likely to result.

This idea that alienation requires the perception of the system as inefficacious, rather than merely the perception of the self as inefficacious, seems to me to be an important addition to our explanation of alienation.

Systemic inefficacy is especially likely to be important in explaining political alienation in America because many Americans seem to orient more toward the system as a whole than toward their personal participation in it. Riesman and other commentators have noted that Americans tend to orient to politics more as consumers than as participants;[76] that we tend to "let George do it," to take our politics vicariously and to assume that we have entirely fulfilled our civic duty by voting. The national survey data certainly seems to corroborate this point. In 1964, for example, 89 percent of Americans watched political news on TV and 79 percent read about politics in the newspapers, but only 31 percent talked about politics and only 9 percent attended a political meeting. In 1966, 84 percent of the Americans sampled reported that they had never tried to influence a decision of Congress, and 79 percent said they'd never tried to influence a local governmental decision.[77] Given this seemingly high level of political interest and low level of political participation, I reason that negative perceptions of the polity and of political leaders are far more likely to lead to political alienation than is personal inefficacy.

Again, the SRC survey data can be employed to show the plausibility of this reasoning. The 1964 election survey included three variables of interest: (1) personal political inefficacy; (2) a measure of inefficacy which was more systemic than personal, because the principal references were to the government rather than to the self or to "people like you"; and (3) trust in government, which has been used as an indicator of alienation. The Pearson Product-Moment Correlation coefficient of trust with systemic inefficacy was 0.33, whereas that for trust and personal political inefficacy was only 0.13.[78] The importance of the perception of systemic inefficacy to the development of the attitude of alienation is discussed further in Chapters 4-7.

A psychological explanation of political alienation

In my view, the attitude of alienation is likely to be adopted when individuals perceive a fundamental conflict between their basic politicized values and those exhibited in the polity, under the conditions that they perceive both themselves and the political system to be inefficacious to reduce this conflict.

When fundamental value conflicts between the self and the organized society are perceived, they are likely to be threatening to the individual. There are several reasons for this. First, cognitive conflict (for example, being aware of two salient, inconsistent values) is a source of tension. Second, such conflict functions as a locus for the fixation of free-floating anxiety. Finally, the individual in this situation may have to devalue the polity in order to maintain his values (a classic approach-avoidence problem), and the possible or contemplated distantiation of self from the polity may induce a "separation anxiety". To a well-socialized citizen who identifies with the polity,[79] who regards the political system as "good," a conflict between his cherished values and his political system is likely to be a most acute one. If the values are too basic to the self to be relinquished, efforts to reform the system are likely to be made. If these efforts fail and no self-surrogates are seen as capable or likely to reform the situation, then the individual will tend to withdraw his identification from the political system.

The individual may, of course, withdraw his identification from part or all of the system. Partial political alienation is likely if: (1) the individual perceives that only some of political institutions, policies or processes are incompatible with his basic political values (and hence withdraws identification only from those subsystems of the polity) or (2) he initially withdraws from the polity as a whole but later is able to cognitively differentiate between the total polity and some part of the system perceived to require and permit reform. This is especially important in a federal system of government wherein one can be quite alienated from one level of government but not alienated from other levels.

Thus, people who *can* ascribe responsibility for the value conflict to some separable political personnel or institution, and still support what they regard as the fundamental character of the polity, are likely to maintain substantial self-identification with the polity. An historical example of this was the widely prevalent notion that "the Czar would help us if he only knew our plight" by which the nineteenth-century Russian peasant differentiated between the functionaries of the political system and the basically authoritarian character of that polity. This differentiation delayed the development of widespread revolutionary support among the peasantry.

If the individual withdraws self-identification (and possibly attention) from part of the polity and finds that this is successful in reducing the threat from value conflict, or at least the salience of that threat, he is likely to remain in that orientation. If, however, the threat continues, perhaps because his basic values are still not realized in the polity, we may expect the individual to adopt attitudes and behaviors oriented toward influencing the political institutions.

Alienation from the political system as a whole often depends upon the perceived outcome of such "threat-coping" or reform efforts. If these efforts permit the individual to perceive himself as politically efficacious, at most only partial alienation will obtain. If, however, the individual's threat-coping behavior is met only by a series of perceived system blockages, then felt threat will be reinforced and a sense of both personal and systemic inefficacy will be induced. These obstacles to value attainment and threat reduction also generate frustration. *The order is important*: salient political value conflicts yield threat, and a failure to reduce threat generates threat reinforcement, perceived political inefficacy and frustration. When the individual perceives that all of the political institutions that he deems relevant to attaining his values are closed to himself and his self-surrogates, the threat and frustration generalize to the system as a whole and total withdrawal is attempted. Of course, if the individual initially perceives the system as a whole to be both in conflict with his values and unreformable, total alienation can result without any reform efforts having taken place.

In sum, adoption of the attitude of political alienation is a function of three variables: (1) perceived threat from value conflict (denoted hereinafter as TVC); (2) perceived, personal, political inefficacy (denoted PI); and (3) perceived systemic inefficacy (SI). Notationally, then: TVC + PI + SI ⟶ *Political Alienation.*

It should be noted here that the TVC, PI, SI ⟶ Alienation formulation is both similar to, and systematically different from, most political science treatments of individual dissatisfaction with politics. Most of these treatments refer to a gap between aspirations and expectations, a revolution of rising expectations, the "want-get" ratio,[80] etc. These formulations are interesting and important, and it is hoped that the notions of TVC, PI and SI are summative measures or specifications of these frustrations and gaps. It is also intended that this formulation will integrate some of the disparate strands in the political science literature. For example, Cantril and Free's operationalization of the aspiration-achievement gap, in the self-anchoring scale,[81] asks people the level of value satisfaction that they have attained, are attaining, and expect to attain, but does not explicitly include the component of value conflict (that is, what level they feel entitled to or "must have"). Gurr,[82] the Feierabends[83] and others, on the other hand, reason from the performance of the polity and economy and interpret slowdowns in performance as implying individual frustrations or producing dissatisfying reductions in individual expectations. Aside from the problems of inferring individual-level consequences from systems-level data, this approach does not include the individual's expectation of future efficacy (that is, whether he or his reference groups will or will not be able to reform the system to improve its performance). The TVC, PI, SI formulation includes both of these factors.

To be sure, I would expect other variables also to have some important impacts on alienation. Political socialization variables which influence the strength of the individual's predisposition to identify with the political system, for example, will doubtless be found to play an important role in the alienation process because: (1) *ceterus paribus,* the stronger and more complete the socialization, the less likely and more slow the process of alienation; and (2) alienation may be conceived of as the extinction of the response tendency to identify with the polity. At present, however, there is not a sufficiently precise theory of political socialization conceived in learning theoretic terms, nor a body of data related directly to this response tendency, for this hypothesis to be tested.[84] Personality variables, too, like those dealt with by McClosky and Schaar and general socio-political orientations like those discussed by Erikson,[85] Pye and Almond and Verba may ultimately be shown to affect the adoption of alienated attitudes in significant ways. It is not expected that TVC, PI and SI will constitute a comprehensive explanation of alienation. What is expected is that these variables will explain a good deal of political alienation across a wide variety of social strata and people-types, and that subsequent research and more comprehensive and precise explanation will thereby be facilitated.

Before turning from the putative causes of alienation to a charting of the political behaviors that issue from it, it may be useful to give one or two examples of the ways in which the TVC, PI, SI ⟶ Alienation notion relates to broad systems-level approaches to political alienation and identification.

First, it should be noted that the TVC, PI, SI formulation is quite consistent with, and may be an individual level operationalization of, the major competing theories of social cohesion and nation-building. The TVC variable is consistent with the theories that stress the development of a national political consensus on values[86] as a requisite for cohesion or nation-building. This variable might enable us to chart at the individual level of analysis the process whereby a national identity or value consensus competes with more parochial subcultural identifications. The PI and SI variables are quite consistent with conflict theories of social cohesion and nation-building.[87] These theories assume that men and groups will remain in the system so long as it suits their interests, so long as it is advantageous to their conflict-bargaining. PI and SI would appear to be reasonably effective operationalizations or specifications of these ideas. As all real societies and political systems are "mixed" systems,[88] organized and maintained by both consensus and conflict, all three of our variables should be necessary not only to explain alienation but to chart systemic integration. We shall indicate that this tends to be so in a variety of American contexts in Chapters 4 through 7.

Another system-level problem that can be approached via the concept of alienation is the relationship between political development and political violence or instability. Here, alienation may be an important intervening variable for it is quite clear that alienation is significantly associated with many kinds of violence and instability and that alienation is affected by development. Alienation will not typically take place if men believe that the polity is fixed and immutable. With political development, this belief, which is not typical in traditional societies, tends to change and men increasingly come to see their social worlds as man-made. In this light, development would seem inevitably to carry with it the possibility of alienation.

Accordingly, the TVC, PI, SI ⎯⎯⎯➤ Alienation proposition may be useful in understanding more precisely the conditions under which development is associated with violence. If men see the man-made polity as effectively representative of their values or that they can be among its makers (that it, that they are efficacious), the fact of development, however psychologically unsettling it may be, is unlikely to produce alienation. In this way, our formulation may be useful to researchers interested in discriminating between the rates, conditions and styles of development which are associated with violence and instability and those developmental patterns which do not have such associations. One might hypothesize that developmental variables that are associated with alienation would have far greater relationship with violence and instability than those development variables which are unrelated to alienation. In addition, the TVC, PI and SI variables may suggest the social groupings and people-types that are most likely to be involved in the instability events.

Another aspect of political development relevant here is the possible alienation impact of the widespread use of government intervention to foster political and economic development. When governments interpenetrate a variety of social spheres, politics become more relevant to more people and, in turn, this can act as an "alienation multiplier" if policies fail. Indeed, sometimes, alienation results even if such policies succeed: If group A, for example, is helped, they may only become more resentful of past wrongs, while group B becomes alienated because they are getting less of the system's rewards (whether absolutely or relatively). Again, these situations can easily be understood in terms of the TVC, PI and SI formulation. The failure of governmental policy (and the allocation of funds to group A) may or may not create a fundamental value conflict for some identifiable set of persons; this will depend upon the salience of the policy and the publicity and style given it by the government. If it does not create such a conflict, the policy—successful or not—is unlikely to create alienation. Moreover, alienation is unlikely to result even if governmental policies do create some value conflicts (as seems inevitable). if the affected sectors of the population perceive their own and the system's general efficacy. Development does not automatically mean alienation. That it also does not automatically lead to identification with the polity has of course, already been acknowledged.

On the consequences of political alienation: The limitations of previous approaches

Most of the empirical research at the individual level of analysis in political science has been more concerned with attitudes than with behaviors. Except perhaps for voting behavior, few, if any, important nonelite political behaviors have been the subject of focused, integrated, cumulative research. Accordingly, at present, we have neither an adequate explanation of alienation-linked political behaviors such as rioting, protest behavior, etc., nor even a consensual strategy for arriving at such an explanation. To be sure, these topics have been of considerable research interest of late, and some of the recent work seems quite promising,[89] but neither the speculative nor the empirical literature on alienation-linked political behaviors provides a general or comprehensive theory for predicting whether any political behavior at all will issue from the attitude of alienation and if it does, what behaviors will be exhibited.

Here, I will identify and critique the implicit strategies of explanation which have operated in the study of two types of alienated political behavior, student protest behavior and blacks' participation in urban riots. Then, I will attempt to provide a more explicit and comprehensive theoretical structure to explain why and how different political behaviors issue from the attitude of alienation. In that discussion the two central theses will be: that alienation predicts powerfully to the fundamental behavioral orientations that men adopt toward the polity; and that the causes of political alienation, TVC, PI and SI, are also importantly involved in the processes whereby these basic behavioral predispositions are activated to produce political behavior.

Broadly, there appear to be three distinct strategies of explanation operative in the study of ghetto riot and student protest behaviors. First, there is the school of thought in which the attitude of alienation alone is deemed sufficient to explain behavior, often because alienation is taken to be a behavior-specific predisposition. Second, there is a considerable body of literature which emphasizes that both the probability and character of behavior will vary with the social structural conditions in which alienated individuals find themselves—for example, the presence or absence of a distinctive or deviant subculture, the presence or absence of leaders, the overall "structural conduciveness" of the situation. Finally, much of the research on riots and student protests has been concerned with the individual's psychological states which intervene between alienation and behavior. Most of the studies in the empirical literature are focused on one or another of these three approaches to the exclusion of the others, and typically the other approaches are not even mentioned. Not surprisingly, then, our understanding of political behaviors which are importantly linked to the attitude of alienation has been inordinately fragmented.

Let us review briefly each of these disparate strategies of explanation. As indicated, some of the recent studies of urban riots and campus protests exhibit little or no effort to move beyond the study of attitudes. Two implicit assumptions seem to be behind such studies. First, there is the idea that the attitude itself is so determinative that one really needs only to know that the individual is alienated to know that he will express his alienation overtly in political behavior (that is, the more alienated, the more likely a behavioral response). Second, some scholars appear to believe that the level of alienation predicts to the specific behavior that will be exhibited—the more alienated the individual, the more extreme or violent the behavior. Thus far, the validity of neither of these assumptions has been demonstrated. Researchers *have* shown that student protesters are more politically alienated than matched samples of nonprotesters and that rioters are more alienated than random samples of the ghetto population *but they have not shown that these actors are more alienated than those politically active alienateds who are working as reformers within the system, as revolutionaries outside the system or than those who have withdrawn from the polity entirely.*

Given the wide range of political behaviors that we know to be associated with alienation, the finding that rioters and student protesters are alienated constitutes only the barest beginnings of the explanation of riot and protest behavior or of any other political behavior. Since alienation is not a behavior-specific predisposition,[90] it is a confusion to say that given alienation (or hostility or any other summative attitude) "any spark can touch it off" and believe that one has thereby explained motives for the behavior.[91] Such a statement is also highly questionable on other grounds, given what we know about the importance of stimulus properties in predicting behavior. Similarly, the statement that "the riots were spontaneous"[92] may be meaningful in a discussion of whether or not there was a conspiracy to organize them but it is a nonexplanation at the individual level of analysis. Laurence J. Gould has argued that much of the literature on alienation and student political behavior has also been of this character: "Alienation," he writes, "has been primarily used as a *post hoc* explanatory concept defined uniquely by each theorist to evoke in the reader's mind images of the individual's psychological state congruent with the behavior under discussion."[93] Perhaps it is the incomplete and therefore unsatisfying character of this kind of theorizing that prompts many observers to throw up their hands and call riots and protests "senseless," "random" or "anomic."[94] Needless to say, these are also nonexplanations.

The second strategy of explanation focuses on the structural characteristics of the situation in which riot and protest behaviors occur. The most popular of these factors is the presence or absence of a distinctive or deviant subculture. Deviant behavior, in this view, is seen as facilitated by the supportive presence of a subcultural group; the more distinctive and the more autonomous or isolated the subculture, the more extreme the behavior. So David Riesman speaks of the children of the lonely crowd:

> Adult authority or control is disappearing, leaving the kids as captives of each other. Youth culture is increasingly autonomous. . . . Massing of young people has led to a new atmosphere . . . a critical mass that can isolate it-

self. Radical movements in America come only when a group can encapsulate itself against the disintegrating tendency of the larger society.[95]

Edgar Z. Friedenberg agrees that the more isolated the community or subculture the more deviant its likely behavior.[96] In three separate studies, moreover, Friedenberg,[97] Robert E. Grinder[98] and Martin Gold[99] all demonstrate that today's youth cultures—counter-cultures—are all substantially isolated from the larger adult society. But Riesman, Friedenberg, Grinder and Gold are each talking about different subcultures—the student protesters, hippies, dropouts and juvenile delinquents! Why do some alienated students protest (that is, join or identify with the protest subculture) while other alienateds withdraw, seek traditional reform, make bombs, use their vote as a protest, etc. The presence of a distinctive subculture may tell us something about the behaviors of those who join it (namely, that because of the protection of the group, group-affiliated persons are more likely to react to their alienation actively than passively, unless the subculture is passive); but it does not explain why people accept one subculture rather than another.

This same fundamental criticism is relevant to the other structuralist strategies of explanation. The presence or absence of leaders, who either direct behavior or who act as models for imitative behavior, is certainly a variable of interest, as both Sampson and Kenniston[100] have said about student politics and as Nieburg[101] argues for riot participants; but this leaves us with the question of explaining why people accept the particular leaders that they do. Similarly, the argument for "structural conduciveness"—that certain situations have structural properties that inure toward riot or protest behaviors is both an important contribution and an incomplete one. Scott and El Assal,[102] for example, found that the size of a college or university had a strong association with the number of protest demonstrations it experienced (the larger the school, the more protests) and that the interaction affect between size, administrative complexity and social heterogeneity also had predictive power. This is extremely interesting but, of course, it does not tell us why some alienated people reacted to this structure by protesting while other alienated people didn't. The theory of alienated behavior advanced below addresses these questions, explaining, in part, the conditions under which alienation does constitute a predisposition to seek a distinctive communications subculture and the basis on which the alienated individual is likely to identify himself with a given subculture or leader.

As McClosky and Schaar point out, a large majority of the studies on alienated behavior take the approach that "specified feelings in individuals . . . result in specified behaviors.[103] What are the intervening "feelings" or, more strictly speaking, psychological states that intervene between the attitude of alienation and alienated behavior?

Undoubtedly the most important set of variables that have been discussed in the literature are basic behavioral orientations: fundamental alternative predispositions to act in specified ways. Of these, Merton's classic enumeration—conformity, ritualism, reformism, rebelliousness and retreatism[104]—has been most important, and has stimulated research on a wide variety of so-called deviant behaviors ranging from juvenile delinquency in America[105] to the revolutionary activities of the bourgeoisie in eighteenth-century France.[106]

The reasons for the popularity of this scheme, fadism aside, are intellectually compelling. To be intellectually satisfying, a theory of individual political behavior must answer at least four central questions about the attitude to behavior linkage: (1) Under what conditions will a given attitude be acted upon? (2) Under what conditions will the observed behavior be consonant with, or different from, the expressed attitude? (3) How can we explain why two or more people may share an attitude and yet behave very differently toward the attitude object? and (4) How do attitudes function to "produce" behaviors?

Knowing the individual's fundamental behavioral orientation seems to help to answer each of these questions. For example, we want to know when and where and how likely it is that men will act on their attitudes. The answer would be that they will tend to do so to the extent that, and in situations where, they perceive their preferred behavior orientation to be appropriate and effective! Similarly, we want to know why Mr. X is acting inconsistently with his attitudes. Knowing Mr. X's behavior orientation can often reveal that the seeming inconsistency is only apparent. For example, Mr. X may remain a member of discriminatory political or social clubs while expressing integrationist attitudes because he orients to political behavior as a reformer and would rather work from within the system than withdraw. The problem of two people who have the same attitude but behave differently toward the attitude object is easily solved if their behavior orientations differ.

Finally, the notion of basic behavioral orientations to the polity does help to explain the attitude-to-behavior linkage by operating as a crucial intervening variable. As we will argue below, and demonstrate in Part IV of this book, the attitude of alienation, in confluence with personality variables, predicts to the individual's basic behavioral orientation to the political system. *This orientation, in turn, interacts with arousing media, group and situational variables to produce given behaviors. The behavioral orientation is, then, a motivational element. It is an instrument for the achievement of basic values (expressed as attitudes); an instrument that is activated by specific situational stimuli. Concrete political behaviors, then, may be explained as responses to stimuli from the political system which activate the individual's predispositions to behavior.*

Unfortunately, the potential explanatory power of this approach has not yet been fully realized in the study of alienated political behaviors.

As Robert Dubin wrote in 1965, Merton's scheme was "a statement of outcome, not process" so that "theoretical models of deviant behavior which explain why and how such behaviors occur remain to be constructed."[107]

Merton's own analysis of the conditions under which different individuals adopt different behavioral orientations was couched almost exclusively in terms of social structure. In orienting to the economy, Merton theorized that there would be different proportions of ritualists, reformers, etc., in the different social strata; that there would be more ritualists in the lower middle class, more social alienation in the direction of innovation in the lower classes, etc.[108]

This approach seems to me to be particularly useful as it is a far more sophisticated approach than is simple correlation of SES with general attitudes. While I have argued above that social class is not now significantly associated with the attitude of political alienation, there is every reason to believe that the learning of styles, values and norms governing the outplay of alienated attitudes remains influenced by social class factors. Upper- and upper-middle-class individuals, for example, seem more likely to play out their alienation in active modes, such as reformism and rebelliousness, because they have the resourses and the relative economic and social invulnerability to do so and because they have learned norms of civic duty and participation that would make withdrawal, for example, a nonvalued option.

The literature on riot behavior and student protests does make use of social background analysis. The studies on student protesters find these young people to be predominantly from middle- and upper-middle-class families, families which have liberal Christian religious identification.[109] But these studies compare the protesters to the college population as a whole and generally have not controlled for the impact of alienation in order to determine the independent effect of SES on activist orientations. Black people who reported themselves as participants in urban riots have been found to be mostly unmarried males, 15-24 years old, long-time residents of the community and to be educationally and occupationally similar to the ghetto community in which they lived (or perhaps a bit better off).[110] Again, however, these studies have not typically compared the rioters to equally alienated samples, so that the independent effects of alienation and SES have not been discovered.

Another set of variables that might help in predicting the basic behavioral orientations that alienated individuals will adopt is personality variables. McClosky and Schaar have demonstrated that personality variables have a significant effect on alienation, an effect which is independent of SES, but their study concerned the causes, not the consequences, of alienation (anomy).[111] Hendrin has shown that violence among black populations is personality-related[112] (interestingly, that fear

and futility not unlike our TVC, PI, SI formulation are powerful factors),
and Kenniston, Flacks, Heist[113] and Whittaker and Watts[114] have all
independently shown that personality variables do help to predict student
protest activism. In these studies, student protesters have been found
to be higher on measures of romanticism, intellectuality, humanitarianism,
esthetics, need autonomy and impulse expression than were comparable
nonactivist students. These studies are of great utility and are highly
suggestive of additional research. Again, however, there remains the
task of comparing these samples not with general samples of the black
or student community but with people who are equally alienated but
not activists.

Probably the most typical political science approaches to alienated
behaviors involve the study of ideologies, belief systems, leadership,
mass political movements and strategies. While there are a great variety
of theories and studies on these topics a common general theme runs
through the political science literature. In this theme, the alienated individual is appealed to by an effective communication from the reference
group (political party, reform group, revolutionary cell); he is attracted
by the leadership or indoctrinated to internalize its ideology; and then
he behaves in politics as that internalized ideology or belief system directs
or as the strategy of the group demands.[115] In terms of the ideology or
strategy, the individual is often depicted in the literature as acting "rationally." Thus, Nieberg argues that riots and protest demonstrations are
touched off by the implicit promise of attention and political efficacy
in escalated risk-taking. For him, violent acts or dramatic protest behaviors are likely to be chosen in a more or less rational fashion; the
individual will behave in politics in ways he perceives to be advantageous
in his political bargaining and conflict situations.[116]

This approach is reasonable but, like all of the other approaches considered here, it is incomplete because it leaves open such questions as: How
does the appeal of the political reference group get through the perceptual
screens of people who are alienated from politics? What kinds of appeals
are likely to be "an effective communication" with the alienated person?
What kinds of leaders and groups will be most attractive to alienated men?

Before attempting a synthesis of the approaches that we have identified,
it should be made quite explicit that we have not dealt with several current
theories of violent behavior and activism. In particular, we have not considered theories of frustration-aggression-displacement,[117] of "natural human aggressivity"[118] and "aggression as defense of territory."[119] The latter
two theories are not treated here because they have not yet made their appearance in systematic, empirical social science research on alienated behavior and, therefore, it is not yet clear how the basic variables in these
theories will be operationalized and applied. Accordingly, it would seem

relatively premature to speculate about the possible applicability of these theories.

The frustration-aggression-displacement notion, however, has been the subject of voluminous social science discussion and it has been applied to the study of political violence.[120] In the theory to be advanced below, anger as a measure of the individual's response to the frustrations of TVC, PI and SI *is* employed. We do not here consider the applicability of the theory as a whole to the study of alienated behavior because it has not yet been widely applied to nonviolent alienated political behaviors.

A theory of alienated political behavior

The basic strategy of explanation to be employed here can be represented as a predisposition-activation model. Specifically I will argue here, and present evidence in Part IV below to demonstrate, that: (1) the attitude of alienation is significantly associated with the basic behavioral orientations that men adopt toward the political system—conformity, reformism, ritualism, retreatism and rebelliousness; (2) the process by which the attitude of alienation is adopted plus certain social background and personality variables predicts which of the basic behavioral orientations a given individual will adopt; (3) the attitude of alienation and certain attitudes toward being alienated constitute a predisposition to seek political information from distinctive political reference groups (thereby allowing group and media stimuli to get through the individual's perceptual screen to activate his predispositions); (4) groups, leaders and communications will be accepted by the alienated individual to the extent that these affect and/or manipulate the same variables that caused his alienation, TVC, PI and SI; and (5) these group and communications stimuli, when perceived and accepted by the alienated individual, arouse and channel him into specific political behaviors.

Why should alienation be significantly associated with the basic behavioral orientations to politics? I reason that the nonalienated individual tends to regard the political system as instrumental to the attainment of his basic politicized values and, therefore, generally accepts the limitations placed on his political behavior by the norms of the polity. In short, he tends to conform. When the individual perceives the political system to be irreconcilably inconsistent with his politicized values, and therefore withdraws his self-identification from that system, then the rationale for conforming—the link between his values and conformity—is weakened. Accordingly, alienation should bear significant negative association with conformity. As the other behavioral orientations—reformism, revolutionism, withdrawal and ritualism—tend to be alternatives to conformity, I reason that alienation should bear significant positive association with these orientations. It should be stressed, of course, that non-alienated individuals can and do orient to the polity in a reformist or ritualistic manner. The importance of basic behavioral orientations as variables in explaining human political behavior is not limited to alienated behavior. Accordingly, much of what we say below may be true of the processes whereby nonalienated individuals adopt behavior orientations and engage in political behavior as well.

But which of these orientations will a given alienated individual adopt? It seems to me that the four nonconformist orientations can be usefully distinguished on the dimension of activism (reformism, revolutionism) and passivity (ritualism, withdrawal). Therefore, variables that predict to activism or passivity should, when added to alienation, predict which set of nonconformist orientations the individual is likely to adopt. There also seems to be an activism-passivity distinction within each set such that revolutionism is typically more active than reformism and withdrawal is typically more passive than ritualistic participation in the political system. Therefore, it may well be that people who score highest on variables that produce activism should be revolutionist in their orientations, while those who are somewhat less characterized by social and personality variables that produce activism will adopt reformist orientations, etc.

The three categories of variables that are expected to mediate between alienation and basic behavioral orientations are: (1) social background factors; (2) personality variables; and (3) process variables describing the manner in which the individual became alienated. In general, people in upper-SES categories are predicted to be more active in their orientations to politics than are those in lower social strata. Also, alienated people who are high in energy level, anger, psychological comfort with their own anger, sense of social and political invulnerability to reprisals but low in need for conformity and desire to be reintegrated with the polity should be more activist in behaviorial orientation to politics than are individuals who are characterized by the opposite personality set. Individuals who become alienated as part of a group should be systematically more extreme (either more active or more passive) in their behavioral orientations than are people who become alienated without such group attachments because of the operation of group reinforcement processes. The selection of a basic political orientation is a non-Markovian process, so that how one arrives at an attitude state (here, alienation) has important effects on the individual's reaction to that attitude state.

If, using these variables, we can predict the basic behavioral orientations that a given individual is likely to adopt, what else do we need to know in order to predict his political behavior? If we know that the individual will tend to operate in politics as a reformer, for example, how can we predict whether he is likely to engage in overt reformist behavior at all and, if he does, in what contexts he is likely to be active?

The basic processes involved in predicting behavior from predispositions are arousal and channelling.[121] The more intense the individual's predisposition to behave, and the greater the strength of the stimuli, the more likely it is that some overt behavior will be exhibited, because the stimuli "arouse" the individual or activate the predisposition.[122]

In the literature on political alienation, it has been repeatedly found that alienation is associated with a low level of political interest, knowledge and attention to media. From this, one might infer that little political stimulation is likely to get through to the alienated individual and that, therefore, little alienated behavior is likely to occur. But all of these studies researched people's orientations to the very polity from which they were alienated: small wonder that alienated men show little interest in information from sources associated with the distrusted and negatively valued political system! *I reason that alienation, so far from constituting a blockage to political stimuli, is actually associated with a predisposition to seek political information from nonsystem sources.* The alienated man is threatened by a fundamental value conflict; should we not expect him to seek information on how to deal with this threat in order to reduce it? If he does not like being alienated, and many people don't, should we not expect him to seek people and groups with whom he can feel connected, "together"—a surrogate-community? I hypothesize that alienation and negative evaluation of that alienation constitute a predisposition to seek political stimuli in, and from, untraditional, nonsystem sources. The alienated man seeks the distinctive reference group whose existence facilitates alienated behavior.

In order for political behavior to issue out of a behavior orientation, there must be more than a high level of political stimulation getting through to the individual. That stimulation must facilitate rather than inhibit behavior. To predict behavior, it is not enough to know that Mr. X perceives a communication from some group leader or media; we need to know whether he identifies with the group leader or media and, therefore, is likely to be moved by that communication. In short, to facilitate behavior the stimuli must be accepted, not merely noted, by the individual.

What distinctive reference group will be identified with? When will a communication be accepted by the alienated individual? How does a revolutionary or radical or reformist group secure the support of the alienated man? What leaders, ideologies or strategies will commend themselves to alienated people? There are, of course, a multiplicity of political science answers to these questions—including explanations in terms of individual identity, the explanation of crisis, the offering of material and symbolic rewards.[123]

Here I advance a simple hypothesis, derived from our theory of alienation: communications, groups, leaders, ideologies and strategies will be accepted by the alienated individual to the extent that they manipulate the same variables that caused his alienation—TVC, PI and SI. Since political identification with a political system is associated with these variables, I reason that the individual will reinvest the identification he withdrew from the political system (and its leaders, groups, ideologies, etc.) if the counter-elites, counter-groups, counter-cultures that are bidding for his support convince him that his value conflict and his perceptions of inefficacy will thereby be reduced or reversed. In effect, these leaders and groups must successfully convey the message that they are or will be effective in realizing the alienated man's political values and that, by joining or identifying with the group, he will become politically efficacious.

I have said that political alienation is significantly associated with the basic behavioral orientations that men adopt toward the polity; that alienation plus identified social and personality variables predict which of these orientations a given individual will adopt; that alienation constitutes a predisposition to seek the very stimuli (information and groups) that are likely to activate that predisposition; and that knowing the variables that cause alienation gives us an analytic routine for assessing the likelihood that he will accept these stimuli. If this theory is correct, this process predicts whether or not political behavior will issue. The character of that behavior will be that directed by the strategies and ideologies of the reference groups with which he identifies (which identification is predicted by the theory).

The process is represented schematically in Figures 1.1 and 1.2.

 = predicts to

1. TVC + PI + SI ⟶ Alienation Level.

2. Alienation Level + SES, Personality and Process by Which Individual Becomes Alienated ⟶ Basic Behavioral Orientation.

3. Strength of TVC ⟶ Strength of Basic Behavioral Orientation.

4. Alienation + Evaluation of Being Alienated ⟶ Stimulation-Seeking in Nonsystem Sources.

5. Stimulation, Affecting TVC, PI and SI, ⟶ Acceptance of Stimuli.

6. Accepted Stimuli Arouses Behavioral Orientation ⟶ Political Behavior.

FIGURE 1.1

A SIMPLIFIED STEP DIAGRAM OF THE PROCESS OF POLITICAL ALIENATION

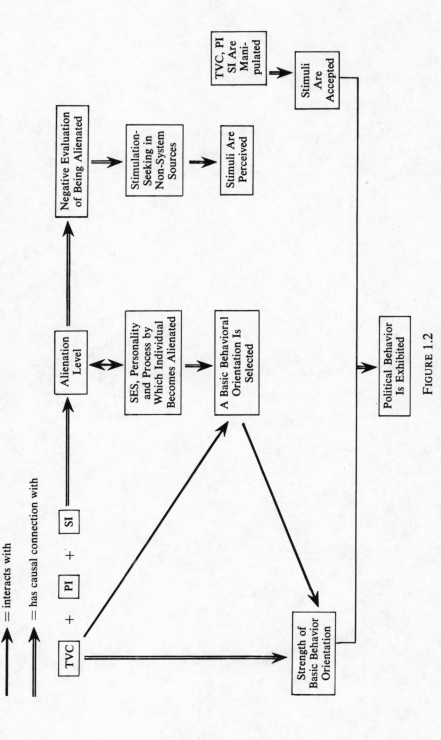

= interacts with

= has causal connection with

TVC + PI + SI

Alienation Level

Negative Evaluation of Being Alienated

Stimulation-Seeking in Non-System Sources

Stimuli Are Perceived

TVC, PI SI Are Manipulated

Stimuli Are Accepted

SES, Personality and Process by Which Individual Becomes Alienated

A Basic Behavioral Orientation Is Selected

Strength of Basic Behavior Orientation

Political Behavior Is Exhibited

FIGURE 1.2

A SIMPLIFIED FLOW DIAGRAM OF THE PROCESS OF POLITICAL ALIENATION

II

On the Limitations of Traditional Approaches to the Study of Political Alienation

INTRODUCTION

The focus of Part II

Two principal approaches to the study of the causes of political alienation were identified in Part I. First, there is the hypothesis that a person who is alienated from a political system is also likely to be alienated from the society or culture of which the polity is a part. In this view, political alienation is explained as a process of response generalization (generalizing from one domain, society, to another, the polity). The second, and even more typical, approach to the causes of political alienation is that of social position: it seeks to identify the socio-economic statuses that correlate with political alienation. There are four main variants of this approach: (1) the conception that low SES should be associated with political alienation because low status makes for political dissatisfactions; (2) the notion that higher social status should be associated with alienation because higher status people will be better able to analyze, and less inhibited from examining, socio-political injustices; (3) the idea that people whose social status is inconsistent (for example, high education but low income) should be politically alienated because such inconsistencies will be experienced as deprivation; (4) the position that people who are largely unconnected to the society, whose institutional and organizational linkages to the larger society are few or weak, will be alienated, in part because they lack the organized means to attain political goals.

In this part, these approaches are more fully explicated, critiqued and tested. In Chapter 2, the first approach is explored. Studies of urban adults, college students and political protesters are presented in an effort to determine whether people who hold attitudes of political alienation are more likely to be estranged from society or culture than are people who are not politically alienated. In Chapter 3, I provide a brief critical review of the literature on the relationship between SES and political alienation and present a series of studies designed to test the basic theoretical propositions deriving from this approach.

CONTEXTS AND METHODS OF RESEARCH: NOTES ON THE DATA CHAPTERS OF THIS BOOK

The empirical testing of the theory of political alienation which is re-ported in this book was conducted in America between the spring of 1968 and the spring of 1970. During this period, manifestations of politi-cal alienation grew and spread in America—from the burning black ghet-toes of the city to increasingly defensive and angry white urban communi-ties and on out to the suburbs as well. It was a time, too, in which evi-dences of political estrangement abounded on American college campuses, then spilled out of the academy and into the streets as mass protests, not a few of them violent recurred. Our theories were tested in all of these con-texts: in five different urban and suburban communities; among four very disparate student populations; in campus and national protest demonstra-tions; in both laboratory and field settings and in a national sample of academic social scientists.

The selection of research contexts and overall design

The intellectual objective to be achieved in the research reported here was the testing of theories at the individual level of analysis. Epistemologically, appropriate testing of the generality, parsimony and causal character of a theory at this level should involve cross-systemic comparisons. "The criteria of generality and parsimony imply that the same theories must be evaluated in different systemic settings and that social science theories can gain con-firmation only if theories formulated in terms of the common factors con-stitute the point of departure for . . . research. . . . The postulate of causal-ity implies that factors operating at different levels of analysis . . . should be incorporated into theories. . . ."[1]

In addition, several recent empirical studies have shown the importance of local or system-specific factors in explaining political attitudes and behaviors.[2] Accordingly, we sought to study individuals in as diverse a set of social and political settings as was possible within the limits of available access and resources. In this way, we were enabled to compare the effect on alienation of the individual level variables that we had identified (TVC, PI, SI) in a variety of settings. In principal, moreover, this strategy would allow us to explore the systems factors identified by other scholars (for example, size of university, differences between communities in density of population, etc.) and, ultimately, to integrate individual- and systems-level variables into a more comprehensive theory. Therefore, for reasons relevant both to our intellectual objectives and to our resources, we chose to test this theory not in one large study, but in a series of smaller sample researches.

The overall research strategy followed here has been called the "most different systems design" for comparative research.[3] Research settings which were designedly and systematically different from each other on theoretically interesting dimensions were selected in an effort to determine whether or not the process of individual political alienation is the same across all of the different samples. Thus, for example, in addition to a citywide sample of Newark, New Jersey, we chose to compare alienation in Philadelphia's black ghetto communities with alienation in a representative group of its white, lower-middle-class communities and its middle-class communities and suburbs. Also seeking diversity in our student populations, we selected a prestigious, private liberal arts college (the University of Pennsylvania), a large urban, state-related university (Temple University), a medium-sized urban engineering and technical college (Drexel Institute of Technology) and a representative two-year community college (Atlantic County Community College). Although generally restricted to the northeastern region of the United States by available resources, these diverse research sites seem to provide considerable variation on interesting dimensions.

Methods

Various aspects of our theory were tested in sixteen separate studies. Of these, three were laboratory experiments and all of the others employed some variant of sample survey methodology. Differences in access to the various communities, and in resources, prompted some differences in the methodologies employed. Of the thirteen survey studies, two were personal interview researches, seven involved direct contact with the respondent followed by a self-administered questionnaire and four were conducted via mailed questionnaire.

A LIST OF THE COMMUNITIES STUDIED BY SURVEY METHODS

Place	Type of Sample	n	Means of Contact	Period of Study
Newark	City-wide, area-probability	626	Personal interview	Summer 1968
Philadelphia Black ghettoes	Random block, random house	69	Personal interview	Summer 1969
Philadelphia White community	(a) Random block, random house-(b) purposive sample	74	In the home questionnaire	Spring 1969
Philadelphia suburbs	Random block, random house	60	Mailed questionnaire	Spring 1969
North Philadelphia Black ghetto	Random sample of participants in civic program	854	In the home questionnaire	Winter 1968
University of Pennsylvania	Random sample of all freshmen and seniors	109	Mailed questionnaire	Spring 1969
University of Pennsylvania	Random sample of University	205	Mailed questionnaire	Winter 1970
Temple University	Self-selected sample of students in a required course (representativeness tested analytically)	215	In school questionnaire	Spring 1970

		n		
Drexel Institute	Self-selected sample of students in a required course (representativeness tested analytically)	113	In school questionnaire	Spring 1969
Atlantic Community College	Same as above	49	In school questionnaire	Spring 1969
Anti-War Demonstration (Vietnam moratorium)	Random buses	50	On the bus questionnaire	Fall 1969
Matched sample non-protesters	Matched on age & sex	57	In school questionnaire	Fall 1969
College demonstration University of Pennsylvania	Random sample	49	At protest questionnaire	Spring 1969
Matched sample non-protesters	Matched on age, sex, class in school and major	49	In school questionnaire	Spring 1969
National sample of academic social scientists	Random sample	108	Mailed questionnaire	Spring 1969

Total $n = 2687$

These differences in method involve certain advantages and disadvantages. The principal disadvantage is that some questions as to the strict comparability of the studies must be raised. We know that there is considerable variation in attitudinal response tendencies by social situation and that responding to interviews, filling out a questionnaire after being contacted in the home and responding to a mailed questionnaire are quite different social situations. Accordingly, cross-method comparisons, at least on absolute levels of a variable, need to be made and interpreted quite cautiously. On the other hand, it seems clear that a relationship which is confirmed by several different methods inspires a greater degree of confidence in its validity than one that has been tested by only one technique. The convergent validity (that is, multi-method validity) of the relationships presented in this book constitute, then, a somewhat stronger degree of confirmation than would have been possible if only one method of observation had been employed. On balance, it would seem that our use of laboratory as well as field methods and of several alternative field methods does facilitate testing the accuracy and generality of the theory. While a discussion of specific methods and sampling procedures used in each study is presented in each of the data chapters, the following table summarizes the studies conducted to test our theory.

One other consideration of method that bears on the comparability of these studies should be noted. All of the survey indexes and items used to tap the relevant variables in our theory are similar in every study, and all are proffered as having acceptable face-validity as measures of the variables they purport to tap. They are not, however, identical across every study. Of course, efforts were made to measure the variables as consistently as possible but several important differences across the studies led to some differences in measurement. There were variations in the communities, in our access to them, in the survey instrument space available to us, and in our resources, and each of these operated to restrict the possibility of identical measurements. In addition, we made some modifications in our measures in later studies based upon what we learned in the earlier ones. For example, the standard item "Sometimes politics and government are too complicated for people like me to understand" seems to be a fairly good indicator of inefficacy among general adult populations but appears to be a rather poor question among college populations in that it produces little variation because almost all of the students in our studies disagreed with the statement. In our later studies of college populations, then, we tended to drop this item.

Again, this aspect of comparability has its compensating advantages. As long as there is broad comparability between measures, that is, acceptable face validity to the proposition that two indexes or items tap the same variable, moderate differences in measures may actually add strength to the confirmation of a relationship. As we saw above in the study of SES and anomy, a relationship which tends to hold despite some variation in the operational definition of the variables in the relationship is generally considered to be relatively strong and consistent.

The measures employed in our studies are presented, illustratively, in each of the data chapters and are reported in full in the Methods Appendix, where there is also included the matrix of inter-item correlation coefficients for every index constructed in each of these studies.

SOCIO-CULTURAL AND
POLITICAL ALIENATION

Are alienation from politics and alienation from society the same thing? Are they related, so that knowing the degree to which an individual feels himself estranged from society or culture helps us to predict the degree of his political alienation? These questions are clearly crucial to the study of political alienation, for, if social alienation includes or explains political alienation, then there is little need for the separate modeling of political alienation.

Many students of the subject have at least tacitly assumed an identity or strong relationship between socio-cultural and political alienation (often by using measures of alienation which lump together social and political referents). Intuitively, this assumption appears reasonable. After all, political systems are now generally conceived of in social study as subsystems of the larger society[1] so that the individual might well be expected to perceive the polity and society in similar ways and to feel similar emotions about both of them. Accordingly, much if not all of the "political culture" school of thought assumes that people orient themselves to politics in ways that are consistent with their social orientations. Riesman, for example, observes that Americans who are work-oriented, inner-directed types tend to behave very differently in politics from consumption-oriented, other-directed men;[2] and Pye finds that politicians and administrators in Burma have fundamentally different social orientations toward conflict and co-operation which are reflected in dramatically different and divisive political styles.[3] In addition, a good deal of post World War II empirical political research indicates the importance of social background factors to the explanation of political attitudes and behavior.[4] If different social experiences predict to different political consequences because of different expectations, values and styles, then it seems quite plausible to expect the individual's identification with, or alienation from, society—which is a summative evaluation of his social experience—to underly his summative response to the polity.

But there also exist theoretical and empirically based reasons to assume that just the opposite is true: that socio-cultural alienation should be essentially unrelated to political alienation. This counter-hypothesis can be derived from the notion of cognitive compartmentalization. We know, for example, that people are quite capable of holding dramatically different and conflicting attitudes at the same time, if they can keep the cognitive sets in which the conflicting attitudes are imbedded separate. Perhaps the classic examples of this are found in studies of prejudice where a general negative attitude toward blacks or Jews or some other group is expressed (for example, blacks are lazy, Jews are mercenary), but where, at the same time, Mr. X who belongs to the negatively valued group is highly regarded.[5] When the individual is confronted by the apparent inconsistency, he is likely to retort: "Oh, but X is different." The same phenomenon has been observed in Americans' political attitudes. Americans seem quite able to honor the free speech ideal as a general principle while comfortably holding the attitude that communists should not be allowed to address the local high school or teach at the state university.[6]

In these examples, the cognitive compartmentalization exists on the generality-specificity continuum; general attitudes are not applied because they are not perceived to be applicable in some concrete contexts. Other kinds of cognitive compartmentalization also exist. For example, an individual may not have a general overall reaction to a given object or situation but rather hold only context-specific attitudes toward it. It is distinctly possible, for example, that whole classes of people orient to power relationships differently in the family, the school, the Church, the work place and the polity.[7] If people can hold conflicting attitudes within the political sphere, then clearly they can hold them as between political and other social spheres.

In modern societies or social sectors, moreover, people tend to be socialized to differentiate rather sharply between society and polity. Indeed, there is evidence to suggest that, by the fourth grade, American urban school children see clear distinctions between political roles and other social-authority roles on such dimensions as importance and benevolence.[8] The well-known adult American's ambivalence toward politics, as shown for example by the status rankings Americans give to political offices in comparison with other social roles,[9] also indicates that politics is seen to be different from other social spheres.

The hypothesis with which this research was begun was that socio-cultural and political alienation are essentially unrelated to each other in contemporary America. A variety of factors accounts for this choice of hypothesis. First, there is no *logical* reason to assume a *necessary* relationship between alienation from society or culture and estrangement from politics. One can conceive of cases in which men psychologically separate themselves from the social-cultural norms and from the social arrangements in which they find themselves, without a concomitant alienation from public affairs. This can come about if the individual does not locate responsibility for socio-cultural affairs in the polity or, even if he does, if he also embraces the polity as a means of reforming the society, the culture or the self. Similarly, men may accept and enjoy their social and cultural situations and yet find the polity to be alienating.

These logical possibilities are amply reflected in history. Our immigrants certainly felt themselves to be alien from the American culture, separated from the American way of doing things by a myriad of cultural differences in tastes, language, habits, facial expressions; yet on the whole they did come to identify with the American polity. Indeed the history of minorities in America, like the recent history of the black movement, is at least partly the history of using politics to secure diminished ethnic prejudice in American society. The fact that politics has been a relatively important means of upward social mobility for ethnic and racial minorities suggests that profound dissatisfactions and estrangements from the main stream of American society may in fact have been a principal motivation for political involvement and allegiance.[10]

In addition, many men who are highly involved in American social and cultural life, men who are contributing energetically to the American scene, have been profoundly alienated from our politics. One might think perhaps of Arthur Miller or of Norman Mailer as examples. The reader who is familiar with the torrent of political alienation themes now being expressed in contemporary art, music and theatre will be aware that these are not isolated examples and that political alienation and cultural alienation can be quite distinct phenomena.

The apparently rising political alienation of upper- and middle-class individuals today—especially, but not exclusively, students—gives evidence that people can be quite turned off by the polity while maintaining most of their basic ties to the social system.

Another way of saying all of this is that we hypothesize political alienation to derive principally from the individual's evaluation of the polity and his relationship to it; not primarily from his evaluations of social or cultural conditions. Accordingly, we would expect that alienation in America today is not a general cognitive state which manifests itself across social, cultural and political domains, but rather that it tends to be domain-specific. Operationally, we hypothesize that people whose orientations to life in American society are those tapped by standard scales of social alienation—somewhat despairing, meaningless and even desperate—are not more alienated from the polity than are people who are more hopeful and more satisfied with their lot. *In sum, we hypothesize that socio-cultural alienation and political alienation will not generally be found to be significantly associated with each other.*

To this point, we have been talking about social alienation as an integrated whole; as an interrelated set of dimensions which generally hold together and evidence a pervasive attitudinal negativity toward the whole of society. This conception of the nature of social alienation, however, is by no means a consensual view. Indeed, there is a fundamental debate in the sociological literature on the interrelatedness or integration of different dimensions of social negativity, on whether despair, meaninglessness and isolation generally tend to be found together as a summative negative *Weltanschauung,* or whether these are better interpreted as independent variables that are generally unrelated to each other (except, perhaps, in extreme cases). The empirical evidence on this point appears to be about equally divided and hence ambiguous.

In general, the second conception of social alienation seems more useful. To function successfully in a society, most individuals will be estranged, if they are estranged at all, from specific aspects of, but not from the whole of, a society or culture. Moreover, even when the entire society is the referent, people *can* feel isolation without despair or meaningless without social distance.

This point seems especially true of student alienation. From participant-observation of active political alienation among college students in strikes, marches, demonstrations and the like, it would seem that most real social alienation is of this second, more limited form. Operationally, we would predict that standard measures of social alienation would not hold together among college populations and that various dimensions of attitudinal negativity toward society will tend to be independent. But consistent with our view that social alienation is not generally related to political alienation, we would predict that the independent dimensions of social alienation will also tend to be essentially unrelated to student political estrangement.

What is to be said of more specific orientations to social life? The political culture school has hypothesized that a variety of social orientations are associated with political attitudes, including: interpersonal mistrust;[11] individualism versus group identity; satisfaction with interpersonal relationships;[12] the value of cooperative vs. competitive interpersonal style;[13] and the degree of social responsibility or obligation individuals feel.[14] No doubt some of these variables do impact on some political attitudes but, from our general stance that political alienation is basically a function of more explicitly political perceptions and attitudes, we would not expect even these somewhat more specific social orientations to be strongly associated with the attitude of political alienation. They are much more likely to affect the behavioral style in which politically alienated individuals play out their alienation.

In this discussion, then, three hypotheses on the relationship between socio-cultural and political alienation have been advanced. First, operational measures of social alienation (even where these do tend to associate strongly with each other, evidencing a deep sense of social isolation, meaninglessness and despair) are not now significantly associated with political alienation. Second, these operational measures of social alienation and cultural alienation do not presently hold together in student populations, and the individual dimensions of social and cultural alienation are not significantly associated with political alienation in such populations. Finally, more specific orientations to society, like individualism, preference for social cooperation, interpersonal satisfactions, etc., also tend not to be significantly associated with the attitude of political alienation. We hold that socio-cultural and political alienation are different and generally unrelated phenomena in contemporary America.

Each of these hypotheses was tested in a separate study in order that each might be examined in an appropriate socio-political context. These studies are reported in sequence.

SOCIAL AND POLITICAL ALIENATION
IN AN URBAN COMMUNITY

The idea that the attitude of political alienation is part of an individual's general attitudinal negativity toward society has been applied primarily to adult urban populations. Both Srole and Nettler, whose alienation scales combine items referring to politics with items relating to society and culture, were theorizing about and studying adult populations.[15] So too were McDill and Ridley, whose studies utilized the Srole scale, and who concluded that political alienation was the reflection of an "atomic perspective"[16] or general "negative Weltanschauung."[17] Olsen also used the Srole scale, thereby assuming a relationship between social negativity and political alienation in a study of urban adults.[18]

Accordingly, it was decided to seek an adult urban population where we could expect to find at least some individuals expressing a deep and pervasive set of despairing orientations to society in order to test our hypothesis that no significant relationship would obtain between social and political alienation.*

The context of research

We selected a community called East Torresdale, located in the northeast section of Philadelphia. This is an almost exclusively white, lower-middle-

---

*This study was conducted by David C. Schwartz and William Nelsen.

class neighborhood which has been fighting a running battle with social change for some years.

East Torresdale is rather a middle place in our society. Its people have known some, but limited, social mobility, mostly up from blue-collar to white-collar jobs. It is not a new development where young married couples buy a house expecting to move on shortly, but rather a kind of middle-aged neighborhood of high school graduates earning between $8,000 and $12,000 a year.

Middle places can be uneasy, and lower-middle-class communities in America have been especially uneasy of late. Perhaps this is because middle Americans are somewhat fearful of slipping back economically and resentful of the fact that they haven't gotten further. They seem to resent, too, the possibility that others may be having an easier time of climbing the American status ladder than they did. Accordingly, it is perhaps not surprising that the people of East Torresdale have tended to vigorously oppose the construction of low-income housing in their community, especially public housing, on grounds which are explicitly concerned with maintaining the character of their neighborhood and which are latently concerned with excluding blacks. Even the possibility that a small, private-owned apartment house for elderly deaf persons would be constructed in their area was viewed as a threat from "outside" and met by virulent opposition from the neighborhood people.

On the other hand, East Torresdale is quite a modern community; it is neither a pocket of Appalachia-like retreatism nor a violence-happy, vigilante stronghold. It has an active community organization and in recent years residents have engaged in a variety of political actions on behalf of their goals. In most respects, then, East Torresdale seems representative of the area of Philadelphia of which it is a part and quite comparable to many white lower-middle-class neighborhoods in large cities across the country: a good place, we think, to study social and political alienation.

Sample and measures

Questionnaires were distributed to two samples of East Torresdalians in the spring of 1969. First, 32 members of the East Torresdale Civic Association agreed to respond to our questionnaire (out of a total of 55 members at a well-attended meeting of the Association). Secondly, a sample of 66 dwelling units in East Torresdale was selected on a "random-block, random-house" basis, and completed questionnaires were obtained in 44 of these units. Our total sample of 76 persons, representing a response rate of 62.8 percent, has these means: 43 years of age; just over 12 years in school; annual income of $8,000 to $12,000; self-perception as being of the lower-middle class.

The questionnaire permitted measurements to be made on the following variables:

1. *Political alienation from municipal government*: an index composed of these three items of the "agree strongly-disagree strongly" type:[19]

    a. I generally think of myself as a part of Philadelphia government and politics.

    b. When I think about Philadelphia government and politics, I generally feel like an outsider.

    c. Many people feel they used to be a part of Philadelphia government and politics, but no longer. I feel the same way.

2. *Social alienation*: as operationally defined by the five-item Srole measure.[20]

    a. There's little use writing to public officials—local, state or national —because often they aren't really interested in the problems of the average man.

    b. Nowadays a person has to live pretty much for today and let tomorrow take care of itself.

    c. In spite of what some people say, the lot of the average man is getting worse, not better.

    d. It's hardly fair to bring children into the world with the way things look for the future.

    e. These days a person doesn't really know whom he can count on.

Unless otherwise noted, the analysis of data proceeded by correlational method (Pearson's r).

Findings

As hypothesized for this community, the Srole-scale items do intercorrelate at relatively high levels (Table 2.1), indicating the existence of a cohesive network of negative orientations to life in American society among these status-threatened people.

TABLE 2.1

INTERCORRELATION[21] OF SROLE-SCALE ITEMS IN EAST TORRESDALE

	a	*b*	*c*	*d*	*e*
a	—				
b	0.53	—			
c	0.61	0.40	—		
d	0.48	0.46	0.70	—	
e	0.58	0.45	0.70	0.69	—

Sample $n = 76$; all relationships significant at 0.005 or better.

Here we seem to have a reasonably direct test of our hypothesis that social alienation is essentially unrelated to political alienation, for we are not dealing with people who feel negatively only toward specific aspects of social life or who feel depressed about the present but are optimistic about the future. Rather, these are men and women among whom the social alienation represents a well-knit pattern of negativity—a comprehensive estrangement from both their present American situation and from what they think the future will be like for them. Moreover, the mean level of social alienation in the sample (2.38 out of a possible 3.0) would suggest a rather high degree of such alienation in the sample.

Table 2.2 shows the degree of interrelationship between social and political alienation which obtained in this study. The correlation coefficient between the Srole measure and the political alienation index ($r = 0.13$) does not differ significantly from that which might have occurred by chance, and the two scales share less than two percent of their variance. Also, of the five Srole items, only the item relating to public officials bears a significant relationship to political alienation, which suggests that political alienation tends to be more directly associated with evaluations of the polity than with simple extrapolations from social dissatisfactions.

=========== TABLE 2.2 ===========

THE RELATIONSHIP OF SROLE SCALE AND SROLE ITEMS TO
POLITICAL ALIENATION IN EAST TORRESDALE

Question a	b	c	d	e	Srole Scale
0.24*	−0.00	0.18	0.04	0.07	0.13

*Significant at 0.025.

Conclusion

In this study, then, neither the conventional measure of social alienation nor any nonpolitical dimension of that measure is significantly associated with the attitude of political alienation. Here, one major conventional approach to political alienation, i.e., regarding it as part of or related to social alienation, does not appear to be useful in explaining the political alienation of the very people for whom the approach was designed—American urban adults.

Perhaps, however, it would do better on the college campus where what appear to be more manifest forms of social and cultural alienation (like beads and beards and bralessness) seem to be flourishing alongside manifestations of political alienation (in the form of sit-ins, strikes and protest demonstrations). Our hypotheses, again, were to the contrary: that measures of social and cultural alienation would *not* hold together among college students and that the independent dimensions of social and cultural alienation would *not* be significantly associated with student political estrangement.

SOCIAL, CULTURAL, AND POLITICAL ALIENATION IN A STUDENT COMMUNITY

Investigation of these hypotheses took place at the same time that we were studying East Torresdale (in the spring of 1969) and in the same city, Philadelphia, at the University of Pennsylvania.*

The context of the research

Penn would appear to be a highly appropriate setting in which to study social and political alienation, for there is plenty of both and a wide range of nonalienated orientations to society, culture and polity as well.

Penn is an old school, an Ivy League school, but its students and faculty and problems are modern. Manifestations of social alienation abound. Communal living among students and junior faculty is not uncommon in the housing area north of the university. Drug use, long hair, sandals and acid rock are reasonably widespread in the student community. Politically, passive alienation seems to be the prevalent student style, expressed overtly in the student papers and in the omnipresent graffitti, and more typically in a withdrawn, resentful "we are getting screwed" mentality. The passive alienation is now and then activated by events and by a radical leadership which is experienced, generally skillful, humane and non-violent, into bursts of political activity such as the sit-in reported in Chapter 6.

Sample and measures

Measures of social, cultural and political alienation were obtained on a questionnaire distributed to and self-administered by a stratified random sample of undergraduates at the University of Pennsylvania. Questionnaires were distributed to 200 students—100 freshmen and 100 seniors—enrolled in the College of Arts and Sciences, the engineering schools, the College for Women and the Business School. Distribution reflected the proportion that students in these schools constituted of the total undergraduate student body, so that 88 arts and science majors, 52 coeds, 45 business

---

*This study was conducted by David C. Schwartz and Don J. Vogt.

students and 15 engineering students were sampled. The response rate equalled 56 percent, creating a total sample size of 113. The distribution of responses paralleled the original distribution so that, for example, 26 percent of the students to whom we distributed questionnaires were women, and women constituted 25.89 percent of those returning the questionnaires.

These questionnaires permitted measurements on social, cultural and political alienation. Examples of our indexes follow.

1. *Social alienation:* Again, we employed the Srole measure.
   a. It's hardly fair to bring children into the world the way things look for the future.
   b. These days a person really doesn't know whom he can count on.
   c. Nowadays, a person has to live pretty much for today and let tomorrow take care of itself.
   d. There's little use in writing to public officials because often they aren't interested in the problems of the average man.
   e. In spite of what some people say, the lot of the average man is getting worse, not better.

2. *A "political Srole scale":* We reasoned that if the Srole social alienation scale did not significantly correlate with political estrangement, and if a Srole scale modified only to include political rather than social referents did bear strong relationship to political estrangement, then the domain-specific character of alienation would be strongly indicated. Accordingly, we created the following five-item scale, closely paraphrasing the Srole scale, but including only political referents:
   a. When I think of the direction things are going in the government, I feel frightened for the kids growing up.
   b. I'm just not sure I can rely on my representatives in government.
   c. One never knows what the government is going to do next.
   d. Most public officials are concerned with the interests of the average man.
   e. Public officials come and go, but the government seems to keep getting worse.

3. *A political alienation scale:* The following five-item measure of individual estrangement from the American national polity was utilized:
   a. When I think about politics and government in America, I consider myself an outsider.
   b. In American politics and government, power is maintained by secrecy and collusion which excludes people like me.
   c. The way things are in government now, people like me are no longer represented.
   d. I tend to identify myself (feel closely associated) with American politics and government.
   e. When I hear or read about the politics and governmental system of the United States, I feel that I am a part of that system.

4. *Cultural alienation:* Gwynne Nettler's well-known scale for measuring general alienation from American culture was also employed. This scale, composed of 17 "yes-no" or "agree-disagree" type items, is reproduced in the methodological appendix. Here we give a few examples of the items in the scale:

    a. Do national spectator sports (football, baseball) interest you?

    b. Do you think children are generally a nuisance to their parents?

    c. Do you like the new model American automobiles?

    d. Most people live lives of quiet desperation.

    e. Life, as most men live it, is meaningless.

    f. Do you like to participate in church activities?

    g. Do you enjoy TV?

    h. Do you think you could just as easily live in another society— past or present?

Findings

If social alienation constituted a single, integrated network of negative orientations to social life among these college students, we should expect significant intercorrelation of the Srole-scale items with each other. If social alienation were strongly related to political alienation, we should expect significant correlations between the Srole items and the political alienation measure. Our hypothesis was that neither of these expectations would be sustained, and, in our data, neither of them is sustained. The Srole items do not tend to intercorrelate with each other more strongly than could have occurred by chance, and, except for the one Srole item that has a political referent, none of the Srole items are strongly related to political alienation (Tables 2.3 and 2.4).

TABLE 2.3

INTERCORRELATION OF SROLE-SCALE ITEMS AT THE
UNIVERSITY OF PENNSYLVANIA

	a_1	b_2	c_3	d_4	e_5
a	—				
b	0.08	—			
c	0.08	0.18**	—		
d	0.05	0.01	0.14	—	
e	0.11	0.24*	−0.03	0.18**	—

$n = 113$

    * = Significant at 0.01 level.
    ** = Significant at 0.05 level.

===== TABLE 2.4 =====

THE RELATIONSHIP OF SROLE-SCALE ITEMS WITH POLITICAL ALIENATION

Srole	a	b	c	d	e
Political Alienation Scale	0.01	0.13	−0.02	0.38*	0.19**
n = 113					

* = Significant at 0.005 level.
** = Significant at 0.05 level.

In sharp contrast to these results, four of the five "Political Srole" items do significantly intercorrelate. Apparently the dimensions of meaninglessness, isolation and despair (which the Srole scale seems to tap) do run together in the political, but not the social, worlds of these college students (see Table 2.5).

These dimensions of political negativity *are* associated with political estrangement. The four-item scale as a whole had a Pearson Product-Moment Correlation Coefficient of 0.45 with our political alienation measure. This finding indicates the domain-specific character of political alienation in this sample.

===== TABLE 2.5 =====

INTERCORRELATION COEFFICIENT OF POLITICAL SROLE-SCALE ITEMS*

	a	b	c	d	e
a	—				
b	0.40	—			
c	0.25	0.22	—		
d	0.34	0.11	0.36	—	
e	0.33	0.25	0.45	0.29	—
n = 113					

* = All but one coefficient significant at 0.005 level or better.
** = Item b was deleted because of its low level of intercorrelation with the other items.

Our analyses of the relationship between cultural alienation and political alienation yield results similar to the comparison of social and political alienation. First, such cultural alienation as exists among these young people seems not to be a single, integrated network of negative orienta-

TABLE 2.6

INTERCORRELATION COEFFICIENTS OF NETTLER-SCALE ITEMS

	1	2	3	4	5	6	7	8	9	10	11	12	13	14	15	16	17
1	—																
2	0.15	—															
3	−0.02	0.07	—														
4	0.24	0.16	−0.07	—													
5	0.15	0.18	0.06	0.05	—												
6	0.06	0.30	−0.03	−0.04	0.30	—											
7	0.08	0.16	0.08	0.19	0.05	0.06	—										
8	−0.08	0.10	0.02	0.17	−0.13	−0.07	0.11	—									
9	−0.01	0.21	0.24	0.17	−0.08	0.02	0.19	0.15	—								
10	0.25	0.23	0.15	0.13	0.24	0.19	0.30	0.10	−0.03	—							
11	−0.01	0.15	0.03	0.01	0.22	0.46	0.09	0.04	−0.15	0.18	—						
12	0.40	0.21	0.04	0.50	−0.08	−0.07	0.30	0.19	0.22	0.31	0.07	—					
13	0.14	0.06	0.01	0.16	−0.11	0.00	0.01	0.11	0.15	0.14	0.03	0.19	—				
14	0.06	0.11	0.13	0.19	0.08	−0.01	0.23	0.26	0.18	0.27	0.16	0.16	0.15	—			
15	−0.12	0.15	0.03	0.12	0.02	0.09	0.16	0.13	0.09	0.14	0.07	0.17	0.13	0.19	—		
16	−0.15	0.10	−0.25	0.15	−0.04	0.11	0.08	−0.01	−0.18	0.01	0.05	0.19	−0.09	0.10	0.03	—	
17	−0.01	0.08	0.24	0.02	0.05	−0.07	0.11	0.07	0.13	0.13	−0.04	−0.04	0.06	0.34	0.29	−0.16	—

tions to cultural objects, as is evidenced by the lack of strong intercorrelations among the items on the Nettler scale. Secondly, the individual Nettler items, which on face validity do seem to tap various components of cultural alienation, do not significantly correlate with political estrangement (Tables 2.6 and 2.7).

=== TABLE 2.7 ===

RELATIONSHIP OF POLITICAL ALIENATION TO NETTLER-SCALE ITEMS*

(1)	0.097	(10)	−0.073
(2)	−0.087	(11)	0.011
(3)	−0.001	(12)	−0.009
(4)	0.107	(13)	0.020
(5)	−0.023	(14)	−0.105
(6)	0.080	(15)	−0.006
(7)	0.155	(16)	0.194
(8)	−0.046	(17)	−0.119
(9)	−0.052		

$n = 113$

*None of these coefficients are significant at the 0.01 level; two of them, numbers 7 and 16, are significant at the 0.05 level.

Thus, cultural alienation and political alienation bore virtually no relationship to each other in this student population. Table 2.6, however, does show at least one set of Nettler items which intercorrelate with some strength—items 1, 4 and 12. These are: (1) Do national spectator sports interest you?; (2) Do you like the new model American automobiles?; (3) Do you enjoy TV? The existence of this set of intercorrelated items allows us to raise the question whether the absence of a relationship between cultural alienation and political alienation is a function of the lack of intercorrelation in the network of cultural alienation? In other words, is it true that alienation from individual cultural objects does not generalize to political alienation but that a more generalized alienation from the American culture would predict political estrangement?

To answer this question, we examined the correlation coefficients of political alienation with each of the three Nettler items and with the three items combined additively in an index. The results of this comparison show that none of the three items individually correlate significantly with political alienation, but that the combined measure does bear a significant relationship to political alienation (Table 2.8). However, it must be noted that political alienation and this three-item measure share less than seven percent of their variance in common, so that the interpretation of this finding must be extremely cautious.

===== TABLE 2.8 =====

THE RELATIONSHIP OF 3 NETTLER ITEMS AND POLITICAL ALIENATION

TV	Cars	Sports	All 3
−0.01	0.11	0.10	0.26*

*Significant at 0.005 level or better.

A corroborative finding on social and political alienation

A second opportunity to examine the relationship between the Srole scale and a measure of political estrangement among University of Pennsylvania students presented itself in the spring of 1969. An experiment on the relationships between alienation and communications behavior, aspects of which are reported in later chapters, was conducted on 79 American undergraduate volunteer subjects. The preexperimental questionnaire included the Srole scale and a four-item measure of estrangement including: (1) In American politics, power is maintained by secrecy and collusion which excludes even the interested citizen; and (2) The way things are going in our society, my friends and I aren't really represented anymore.

As above, the Srole scale failed to intercorrelate significantly, and, again, the only Srole item that bears strong relationship to political alienation is that item which has a political referent (Tables 2.9 and 2.10).

===== TABLE 2.9 =====

INTERCORRELATION OF SROLE-SCALE ITEMS IN SAMPLE
OF EXPERIMENTAL SUBJECTS

	1	2	3	4	5
1	—				
2	0.086	—			
3	0.252*	−0.047	—		
4	0.092	0.183	0.169	—	
5	0.067	0.031	−0.084	0.172	—

$n = 79$

*Significant at 0.005 level or better.

=== TABLE 2.10 ===

THE RELATIONSHIP OF INDIVIDUAL SROLE ITEMS WITH
POLITICAL ALIENATION

1	2	3	4	5
r = 0.139	4 = 0.106	4 = 0.182	4 = 0.345*	4 = 0.172
n = 79				

*Significant at 0.005 or better.

Conclusion

Among these American college students, then, neither social nor cultural alienation appears to be a general, integrated network of negative orientations; and negative orientations to individual aspects of society and culture do not tend to explain (or to generalize to) political alienation. There is some very tentative indication that, if the cultural alienation index were more tightly intercorrelated, evincing a more broad and general cultural alienation, it might be more strongly linked to political alienation.

The evidence from these two studies tends to support the proposition that there is not now a strong relationship between socio-cultural and political alienation because only weak and limited associations obtain between these variables in samples of urban adults and college students. But the quality of the political alienation which was manifested in those samples tended to be relatively passive; that is, conventionally reformist activity in the adult sample, and attitudinal, but not necessarily behavioral, alienation among the students. Might it not be true that socio-cultural alienation does not powerfully affect these kinds of political alienation, but that it does tend to be strongly associated with more active forms of political alienation such as are expressed in confrontations, demonstrations and protests? After all, most demonstrations and protests have the goal of social as well as political change, so might we not expect the active alienated to have different and perhaps more negative orientations to society than do people whose alienation does not result in protest?

We would not generally expect significant correlations between socio-cultural and political alienation, even among the active alienated in America today. To be sure, there *are* individuals who reject both the American society and the polity. Very probably, their number is increasing. These facts, however, are not inconsistent with our proposition, for we are not arguing that socio-cultural and political alienation are mutually exclusive and cannot occur together. What we are saying is that there is no *necessary* relationship between the two types of alienation and that generally today, even active political alienation tends *not* to be caused by socio-cultural estrangement.

SOCIAL ORIENTATION AND POLITICAL
ALIENATION IN CONFRONTATION POLITICS

To test this latter hypothesis and to explore the effect of more specific social orientations on active and passive political alienation, it was decided to obtain data on measures of socio-cultural and political alienation from matched samples of political protest demonstrators and nondemonstrators, immediately prior to an actual and important demonstration.* This approach offers at least two distinct advantages which differentiate it from much recent research on participation in collective behavior (demonstrations, confrontations and riots). First, by matching the participant and nonparticipant samples on the dimensions of age, gender, education, etc., we are able to observe the socio-cultural and psychological determinants of behavior more clearly under more controlled conditions than are possible in most post facto research designs.[22] Second, when attitude measurements are taken after the occurrence of a demonstration or other collective behavior event, we do not know whether the individual's attitudes and perceptions have changed as a result of his participation in (or nonparticipatory learning of) the event so that the attitudes and perceptions he reports may not really be those that motivated his decision to participate in the political event. Even when such *post facto* designs rely on the recall of participants, systematic bias must be suspected.

Methods: The context of research

An opportunity to avoid these observational difficulties was afforded by the famous Vietnam Moratorium demonstration held in Washington, D.C., on October 15, 1969. The time and advance planning required to conduct this demonstration facilitated our securing access to groups of participants and allowed us to make the relevant observations in a timely fashion. The demonstration itself was a particularly interesting and important occasion for social research because this mass rally and march of some 22,000 Americans in Washington, D.C., marked a turning point, the beginning of national mass activity, in the anti-Vietnam War movement. Indeed, according to historians in the Library of Congress,

---

*This study was conducted by David C. Schwartz and Stanley Renshon.

this nationally coordinated event was unique in the history of anti-war protest in America.[23]

But if the October 15 demonstration was unique as an anti-war protest, it was far from unique as an example of the "new politics." Demonstrations, in fact, have become the major, because most successful, tactic of the "new politics." Learned in and from the civil rights movement of the early 1960s, the tactic of demonstration permits groups with relatively little in the way of institutionalized power, money or access to media to secure much of the latter and perhaps some of the former.

Moreover, demonstrations—at least those as large as the October 15 Moratorium—clearly constitute "confrontations." The numbers, dedication and concern of the protesters, who marched in threes, wearing white armbands, behind the widow of Dr. Martin Luther King from the Washington Monument to the White House, directly confronted the national administration with problems of policy, public relations and potential violence. Certainly the demonstration confronted American and world public opinion: virtually every member of the President's cabinet commented on it, supportive demonstrations took place in many American cities as well as in London, Paris, Dublin, Rome and Tokyo. And, for a time at least, any American who read a newspaper or watched a television news broadcast or heard a radio was confronted, too. In a sense, the tactics of demonstration, the peaceful but potentially violent confrontation, came of age in America on October 15, 1969: ceasing on that date to be a regional or an ethnic or a sporadic phenomenon, it emerged as a regularly recurrent, national, institutionalized feature of the American polity.

Sample and measures

Our sample was drawn from basic, required social science classes at Knox College (Ohio) and the University of Pennsylvania. At each school, approximately half of the class chose to participate in the Moratorium. Data on these students ($n = 50$) was obtained on questionnaires administered during the bus ride from the campus to Washington (that is, observations were made after the students had behaviorally committed themselves to participate in the demonstration but before the full-scale participation in it). Identical questionnaires were administered to the students who elected not to participate in the demonstration ($n = 57$) during a meeting of the class, generally on the same day that the buses left for the demonstration (the Friday before the Saturday demonstration). In addition to the obvious similarity of the participant and nonparticipant samples on contextual variables (for example, same college and same spatial location), the samples are strikingly similar in composition on such dimensions as age, gender and year in school.[24] No statistically significant differences between the samples exist on these demographic dimensions.

The questionnaire permitted observations on six different orientations to society and on political alienation. Each of these orientations is operationally defined as an index composed of individual "agree-disagree" responses to the listed statements:

1. *The Srole scale.*

2. A measure of *Interpersonal Estrangement* composed of the direct item: I find the basic things of value are not generally valued by other people, and the projective item, It is almost impossible for people to really understand each other;

3. A measure of *Interpersonal Mistrust,* (a) If you don't watch yourself, people will take advantage of you; (b) Some people say that most people can be trusted, others say you can't be too careful in your dealings with other people. How do you feel?

4. A measure of the individual's *Value on Group Identification,* (a) A person truly finds himself when he joins with others to achieve common goals; (b) Humans don't really fulfill their potential unless they involve themselves deeply in some group.

5. A two-item index of the respondent's *Preference for Interpersonal Cohesion,* (a) It doesn't pay to be too different from your friends; (b) In general, I'd rather agree with people than argue with them.

6. A four-item index of *Social Obligation,* including (a) Not only does everyone have the right of life, liberty and the pursuit of happiness, he also has an equal moral obligation to protect others from having these rights taken away from them; (b) An individual's responsibility for the welfare of others doesn't extend past his intimate circle of friends and relatives.

Political alienation was measured by a three-item index including: (a) The government no longer seems to represent people like me; and (b) In American politics, power is maintained in secret, shutting out even interested citizens.

Findings

Both the demonstrators and the nondemonstrators were relatively alienated from the American polity, although, not surprisingly, the students who marched in Washington tended to be more estranged than their counterparts who stayed at home. (Mean Alienation: Demonstrators, 2.57; Nondemonstrators, 1.87 out of a possible 3.0; t (a difference of means value) $= 7.12$, significant at the 0.001 level). The objects of investigation here are the impacts of various social orientations on the active alienation of the demonstrators and the more passive alienation of the nondemonstrators.

TABLE 2.11

A COMPARISON OF DEMONSTRATORS AND NONDEMONSTRATORS ON SOCIAL ORIENTATIONS

Mean Score on Orientations	Demonstrators	Nondemonstrators	t Value	Level of Significance
Interpersonal Estrangement	2.82	2.75	0.67	not significant
Interpersonal Mistrust	1.50	1.56	0.80	not significant
Value on Group Identification	2.68	2.69	0.05	not significant
Preference for Interpersonal Cohesion	3.03	2.97	−0.48	not significant
Social Obligation	3.14	3.30	1.67	not significant
Srole Items				
(1) "It's hardly fair to bring children . . ."	2.76	2.54	−1.52	not significant
(2) ". . . A person doesn't know whom he can count on."	2.75	2.91	1.43	not significant
(3) "Live for today"	1.84	1.51	−3.71	0.001
(4) "Public officials don't care"	1.82	1.33	−5.6	0.001
(5) "Lot of man worse, not better"	1.83	1.63	−1.80	not significant

(Higher Scores = Disagreement with orientation).

To deal with these matters, two basic kinds of analyses were performed on the data: (1) a difference of means test (t test) was employed to determine whether the social orientations of the demonstrators differed significantly from those of the nondemonstrators; and (2) a correlational analysis was performed in the separate samples to determine whether the social orientations were more closely associated with the attitude of alienation among the demonstrators than among the nondemonstrators.

These analyses yield a consistent and interesting pattern of findings. First, as can be seen in Table 2.11, the social orientations of the demonstrators do not generally differ significantly from those of the nondemonstrators. Of the ten social orientation measures on which we compared the samples, only two differentiate between the actively and passively alienated: the political item of the Srole scale and the item that suggests that one lives for today and lets the future take care of itself. Interestingly, the demonstrators disagreed with these statements significantly more than did the nondemonstrators.

Second, neither the actively alienated demonstrators nor the passively alienated nondemonstrators are characterized by tightly integrated networks of social negativity. The Srole scale did not hold together in either sample (Table 2.12); and the five more specific social orientations also failed to correlate with each other in both samples (Table 2.13).

TABLE 2.12

INTERCORRELATION OF SROLE-SCALE ITEMS AMONG
DEMONSTRATORS AND NONDEMONSTRATORS

| | *Demonstrators* | | | | | | *Nondemonstrators* | | | | |
	1	2	3	4	5		1	2	3	4	5
2	−0.07					2	0.17				
3	0.10	0.16				3	0.07	0.07			
4	0.17	−0.08	−0.06			4	0.23	0.15	0.30*		
5	0.11	0.07	0.12	0.08		5	0.48*	0.28	0.11	0.36*	

*Significant at 0.05 or better.

Although the students who were actively alienated from politics in America do not orient to society very differently from the passively alienated, and although neither sample is particularly alienated from American society, there is some tendency revealed in this data for the social orientations to correlate more strongly with active than with passive political alienation. As shown in Table 2.14, a few of the social orientations studied here do bear significant relationship to the attitude of political alienation in the demonstrator sample, whereas not one of these

TABLE 2.13

THE RELATIONSHIP AMONG SOCIAL ORIENTATIONS AMONG DEMONSTRATORS AND NONDEMONSTRATORS

Demonstrators

	estrangement	mistrust	group ident.	cohesion	obligation
Interpersonal Estrangement					
Interpersonal Mistrust	0.11				
Value on Group Identification	0.02	0.00			
Cohesion	0.26	0.24	0.18		
Obligation	0.12	0.28	—0.37*	0.34*	

Nondemonstrators

	estrangement	mistrust	group ident.	cohesion	obligation
Interpersonal Estrangement					
Interpersonal Mistrust	0.26				
Value on Group Identification	—0.06	0.11			
Cohesion	0.00	—0.06	0.27		
Obligation	0.38*	0.07	—0.35*	—0.01	

*Significant at 0.05 or better.

social orientations correlates significantly with political alienation among the nondemonstrators.

It should be noted that the social orientations on which the demonstrators differed significantly from the nondemonstrators are not the ones which correlate with the attitude of political alienation. The demonstrators are personally more optimistic and future-oriented than the nondemonstrators (tending to believe more than the nondemonstrators did that public officials do care about what they think and that one does have to plan for the future), but their alienation is more socially pessimistic (that is, significantly associated with the belief that the lot of man is

===== TABLE 2.14 =====

THE INTERRELATIONSHIP OF SOCIAL ORIENTATIONS AND POLITICAL ALIENATION AMONG DEMONSTRATORS AND NONDEMONSTRATORS

| | *Political Alienation* | |
	(Demonstrators)	*(Nondemonstrators)*
Interpersonal Estrangement	0.06	0.08
Interpersonal Mistrust	0.30*	0.05
Value on Group Identification	0.12	0.09
Preference for Interpersonal Cohesion	−0.15	−0.18
Social Obligation		
Srole Items:	0.31*	0.00
(1) "Not fair to have children"	0.35*	0.19
(2) "Can't count on people"	−0.10	0.02
(3) "Live for today"	−0.01	0.15
(4) "Public officials don't care"	0.27	0.37*
(5) "Lot of man, worse"	0.35*	0.06

*Significant at 0.05 or better.

getting worse, not better, to the point where it is hardly fair to bring children into the world). Active political alienation among the demonstrators is associated with a generalized sense of social mistrust, but also with a generalized sense of social obligation. Political alienation, among the nondemonstrators, is associated only with the political item of the Srole scale.

Conclusions

In general, such social alienation as is exhibited by these students is not significantly associated with either active or passive political alienation. Not only does the Srole scale fail to intercorrelate in both samples, but most of the independent dimensions of social alienation contained in the Srole scale bear virtually no relationship to the attitude of political alienation in these samples. And the more specific social orientations of interpersonal estrangement, group cohesion or estrangement and group identification are also essentially unrelated to the attitude of political alienation.

In general, these alienated young people—demonstrators and nondemonstrators alike—resemble each other. Both the content and cohesion of their social orientations are similar. Yet a few social orientations do bear significant association with the attitude of political alienation among the actively estranged, while the correlates of political alienation among the passively alienated were exclusively political.

The data seem clearly to indicate a cognitive compartmentalization process, wherein the passively alienated keep their social and political evaluations quite separate, while a somewhat greater perceptual fusion of the social and political arenas characterizes the actively alienated. Apparently, the attitude of political alienation can be adopted on purely political grounds, but the behavioral outplay of this attitude in confrontation politics is more likely when the individual psychologically links these political evaluations with broader orientations to the society. Since engaging in confrontation requires greater risk-taking than passivity or even conventional reformism, it makes sense that an individual is more likely to undertake such risks when he feels that he is seeking to change both the society and the polity, than when only the polity is seen as needing change.

An understanding of the degree to which, and the ways in which, social orientations affect political alienation requires an identification of the factors which have greater direct impact on alienation. We need to know the basic variables through which social and cultural alienation can work to affect political alienation. This task, seeking to identify the variables which account for an individual's adopting the attitude of alienation, is the central concern of the next chapters of the book. Specifically, if political alienation is not significantly associated with rejection of society, perhaps alienation will be found among people who identify with and value societal norms but who occupy social statuses which deprive them of the opportunity of achieving their values. That, at least, has been the predominant scholarly theory of alienation. In the next section, we examine and challenge the validity of that theory.

SOCIAL BACKGROUND FACTORS AND POLITICAL ALIENATION

The predominant strategy of explanation in the study of political alienation (and, apparently of many other political attitudes and behaviors) has been to seek the social background factors that correlate with it.[1] This approach has much to recommend it. Socio-economic status has been found to be significantly associated with many variables of interest in political study, including voting,[2] participation[3] and elite status.[4] Indeed, these relationships seem to occur so regularly that, by now, we have come to expect the political perceptions, values, skills and styles of people who are relatively well off, better educated and higher in social status to differ systematically from those of relatively poorer, less well-educated, lower-status Americans. Similarly, age, gender, ethnicity, race and social connectedness, too, are expected to produce regular differences in political attitudes and behavior. As these social background factors are usually relatively easy to observe,[5] they appear to be an obvious place to begin inquiry.

From the standpoint of more specific theory, too, it is not hard to see why students of political alienation should have expected social background factors to account for alienation. If politics *is* who gets what, where and how, then people who have gotten comparatively less of the available material rewards should value the polity correspondingly. Moreover, lower-status people are not only relatively deprived in the present distribution of values, they are relatively disadvantaged in seeking to improve their lot through politics. In a system where successful political action typically takes resources, such as money, access to media, skills, group support, traditional prestige, which lower-status people usually lack, lower-SES individuals are clearly disadvantaged in the ordinary processes of American politics. Moreover, given that individual efficacy is part of the prevailing American political myth, it might well be assumed that the relative powerlessness of lower social status would be a source of alienation.

Accordingly, most of the research on alienation in the 1950s and early 1960s focused upon social background characteristics and sought to show significant associations between these factors and political alienation (defined, typically, as the Srole scale or Seeman-type inefficacy scales).

Findings in the individual studies on SES and alienation are not all consistent, of course, but education, occupation, income, perceived class and race have all been regularly shown to be significantly related to alienation.[6]

Another "sociological" variable repeatedly found to have significant association with socio-political alienation is "social connectedness"— usually defined as membership or involvement in social organizations. The negative relationship between social connectedness and socio-political alienation has been found whether connectedness is defined as formal or informal participation in organizations.[7] It has been established both in America and elsewhere and seems to hold even when SES is controlled for. This latter finding is important, for it suggests that social connectedness functions at least partly in independence of SES to produce or inhibit alienation.

We hypothesize, however, that neither the level nor the consistency of an individual's socio-economic status nor his social connectedness are now directly related to political alienation. Indeed, we would not generally expect any social background attribute to be directly associated with political alienation at present. The chain of reasoning that prompts these hypotheses is as follows. First, as shown in the last chapter, the traditional definition of alienation as operationalized in the Srole scale is neither the same thing nor is it now even significantly related to political alienation in the sense of estrangement from the political system. Accordingly, there is little reason from the literature alone to expect the factors that helped to explain alienation from societies or cultures to explain political estrangement. Second, the apparent deepening and broadening of alienation in America in recent years —across many social positions—would operate to reduce the impact of social factors. Therefore, even if social variables have been historically related to political alienation, the relationships between social factors and alienation which were discovered in the 1950s and early 1960s should be significantly attenuated by now. Finally, since SES and connectedness must logically function to produce alienation by affecting psychological factors (that is, the perceptions and evaluations of individuals), one could reason that there might well be no direct relationship between social variables and the attitude of political alienation. We hypothesize, then, that any relationship between SES or social connectedness and political alienation is likely to be indirect.

This hypothesis is not intended to denigrate the explanatory utility of social background factors. What is intended is to put these factors into proper (processual) perspective by (1) showing that they do not have strong direct associations with the attitude of alienation, (2) identifying basic factors that do have strong direct associations with alienation, and (3) showing how social background factors do or do not work through psychological intervening variables to influence alienation.

SES, SOCIAL BACKGROUND CHARACTERISTICS AND POLITICAL ALIENATION IN FOUR URBAN COMMUNITIES

To test our hypotheses we sought research settings that would provide as great a range of socio-economic diversity as possible.* Asserting that being rich or poor, white or black, young or old, male or female, socially connected or relatively isolated now make virtually no difference in predicting whether or not a person is alienated from the American polity, we wanted research contexts with large numbers of people in all these categories.

In America today, it is the city that guarantees such diversity and it is the city, too, where political alienation is most clearly to be found. In the 1960s and 1970s, the smoke and shooting and silent fears which are in part the reflections of political alienation abound primarily in our urban centers.

Accordingly, we chose to conduct research in urban communities. Specifically, during 1968 and 1969, we investigated the relationships between social factors and political alienation in a citywide study of Newark, New Jersey, in area probability samples of black and white communities in Philadelphia, Pennsylvania, and in Philadelphia's wealthy white suburbs—the so-called Main Line.

The context of research

Newark. We interviewed an area probability sample of the teenage and adult Newark population, in the summer of 1968—a year after a riot that had left 25 dead, hundreds wounded (including one member of our interview staff who had been shot during the riot and lost his leg), and millions of dollars in property damage. The smoke in the streets had cleared, though the rubble had not, and the fire in the people of Newark remained.

On any list of objective indicators, Newark, a city of 402,000, is the "worst" city in the country. In 1967 Newark had the highest infant mortality rate, highest crime rate, highest incidence of venereal disease, highest number of new cases of tuberculosis reported, the highest tax rate (and

---

*These studies were conducted by David C. Schwartz, Kent Eklund, William Nelsen and Craig Wynn.

one of the lowest tax bases) of any major city in the nation. In the rate of illegitimate births, Newark was second; its unemployment rate was nearly three times the national average, and one Newarkite in eight was on some form of welfare. Not surprisingly, the city was depopulating (it had been losing people since 1930), but, in a wave of Southern immigrancy in the 1960s, Newark had "gone black," moving from 62 percent white to between 52 and 74 percent black (obviously estimates vary)."

Newark's public services reflected the situation. The police commissioner and mayor were indicted on charges of corruption, and, in City Hall, neither the telephone system nor the soda machines could be made to work. The signs on the outside of the taxicabs said "Pride in Newark," but on the inside there was prominently displayed the phone number to call to complain about the cabbie.

The predominant public responses to this situation were fear, futility and anger. In the Italian North Ward, a self-help or vigilante group had taken to calming its fears by armed men patrolling in cars equipped with a centralized communications system, and this group's tough-talking leader was elected to the City Council. At City Hall, and in the press, the talk reflected futility; principally it was about a plan to turn the administration of the public schools over to the state (or to the Ford Foundation or, seemingly, to anyone else who would agree to take it). And everywhere we talked with people, the latent rage burned.

Newark, then, seemed to be the archetype of the alienated polity.

Philadelphia Communities. In Philadelphia, the situation was cooler; not less alienated, perhaps, but cooler; there had been no major race riots since 1964. Here, the tough-talking Italian was the police commissioner, who had boasted that if Philadelphia had a riot, it would be the shortest one in history. The city had adopted an ordinance giving the mayor authority in emergencies to restrict public gatherings to 13 or fewer people. This ordinance was applied on a couple of occasions, as after the death of Martin Luther King, and no riot occurred. In the popular mind, at least among whites, there was a strong causal relationship.

In other respects, Philadelphia in the spring and summer of 1969 resembled every large American city. Its problems were legion: parking; pollution; an insufficient tax base for the expanded services that its people and its bureaucracies demanded; *de facto* racial segregation in schools, with the public opposed to bussing; teenage gang violence but too few policemen; relatively diminishing federal funds, etc.

The problems are common and commonly recognized; but, as elsewhere, the different communities of Philadelphia disagree on how to solve them. Nearly everybody agrees that ghettoes are bad; but "don't build public housing here" is the cry of white working- and middle-class communities. "And don't bus the kids from the ghetto here, either" and "don't give *them* community control of schools" and "don't ask us suburbanites, who earn our living in the central city, to pay for *your* problems" and so on.

The local community has been described as an "ecology of games,"[10] a pleasant-sounding situation; but in the 1960s in city after city, urban conflicts were increasingly being perceived as zero-sum—filling the environment with angry demonstrations and counter-demonstrations and sometimes with violence. Philadelphia was no exception. During and after school riots occurred, whites threatened to stop the buses if desegregration by bussing was attempted, some blacks demanded local control of schools, suburbanites responded "over my dead body" to the school board chairman's suggestion that the city and suburban school districts merge. Violence was hinted at or threatened on all sides. So committee after committee was formed, study after study was commissioned, public hearings begot more of their kind, reports followed reports, documents multiplied and years went by without public decision on most of these matters.

In this situation, any action will displease more people than it satisfies, so no action—at least no easily observable action—tends to be taken. The result of this is either government paralysis or decision-making by non-decision; the result of that is silent, resentful public alienation.

Because of the differences in political orientation as well as in socio-economic conditions between ghetto blacks, lower-middle-class whites and suburban middle-class whites, we chose to conduct our studies of alienation in a set of communities representative of these three groupings. Personal interviews by a black interviewer were conducted on a sample of people from the North and West Philadelphia black ghettoes. A sample of 87 units was drawn on an area probability basis and 69 interviews were completed. Here, there is diversity on social class (between welfarites, working class and lower-middle class) and other social characteristics but, of course, not on race. Our white, lower-middle-class community (East Torresdale) has already been described above. Here, too, there is diversity by class (working, lower-middle and middle class) and by degree of social connectedness but not by race. Finally, a mailed questionnaire study of the wealthiest ward in Philadelphia and the wealthiest suburban area of Philadelphia was conducted. These communities are contiguous (divided only by the city boundary) and they represent the Main Line *milieu*. Their alienation is that of middle- and upper-middle-class white America.

Measures

Newark. In Newark eleven separate social background factors were identified and observed. These were:

1. *SES level:* a three-item index composed of z-scored items on occupational status, education and income.

2. *Status inconsistency*: an index developed by dichotomizing scores on education, occupational status and income into "high" and "low" on each variable and aggregating respondents into "status consistents" (all high or all low) and "status inconsistents" (one high and two low or two high and one low scores).

3. *Age*.

4. *Gender*.

5. *Race*.

6. *Social connectedness*: a score of "activeness" in social organizations.

7. *Political connectedness*: a score of "activeness" in political and civic association.

8. *Connectedness to printed news media*: degree of reading newspapers and news magazines.

9. *Other media connectedness:* degree of attention paid to radio, TV and business or professional journals.

10. *Perceived leaderlessness*: the degree of perception that no leaders existed on issue-specific concerns.

11. *Length of residence in Newark*.

Due to extraordinary problems of access in Newark, it was necessary to restrict our measure of political alienation to the single-item indicator: When I think about the political system in Newark, I feel like an outsider. This measure has shown strong and consistent intercorrelation with other items designed to measure political estrangement in other studies.

Philadelphia Black Community. In the black ghettoes of Philadelphia, observations were made on four social characteristics:

SES: an index of z-scored items on education, income and perceived status; single-item indicators of religion, gender and political party identification. Political alienation was operationalized as a two-item index: (a) When I hear about politics and government in America, I feel that I am a part of it, (b) I feel that my friends and I are still really represented in our government.

East Torresdale. Too, measures of four social variables were available:

1. *SES*: a four-item index of z-scored items on education, income, perceived status, occupational status and status mobility;

2. *Social connectedness*: An indication of the degree of connectedness to community organization; single-item indicators of

3. *Age*; and

4. *Gender*.

Political alienation from the city government was tapped as an index of such items as: (a) I generally think of myself as a part of Philadelphia government and politics; (b) When I think about Philadelphia government and politics, I generally feel like an outsider.

Philadelphia Suburbs. In this sample,[11] observations were made on the respondent's (1) income, (2) age, (3) gender and (4) degree of alienation from national, state and local political systems. The alienation indexes included such items as these for national political alienation: "When I think about the politics in Washington, I feel like an outsider" and "People like me aren't represented in Washington." The items tapping alienation from state and local politics were identical in form, substituting only the state capitol and the locality for "Washington."

Findings

The evidence provided by these studies is consistent and strong: there is virtually no direct, linear relationship between any of these social background characteristics and the attitude of political alienation. In city and suburb, among whites as among blacks and whether the alienation is from the national, state or local polity, social descriptors did not tend to bear significant, direct relationship with political alienation. These results of the separate studies are presented and discussed below, in order.

Newark. Usable interviews were completed with 131 black and 495 white Newarkites, sampled on an area probability basis from more than 50 sampling points all over the city. The full diversity of the urban center was represented here so that, if social factors do presently have a strong or

---

TABLE 3.1

THE RELATIONSHIP OF SOCIAL BACKGROUND CHARACTERISTICS AND
POLITICAL ALIENATION IN NEWARK

Descriptor	*r*
SES level	0.12
Status inconsistency	—0.06
Age	—0.05
Gender	—0.06
Race	0.06
Social connectedness	0.06
Political connectedness	0.10
Connectedness to news media	0.06
Other media connectedness	0.01
Leaderlessness	0.11
Length of residence in Newark	0.07

significant influence on political alienation, that fact should certainly be revealed in this study. But precisely the opposite is revealed; most of the social descriptors have zero correlation with political alienation and no social descriptor shares more than one and one-half percent of its variance (in common) with political alienation. Table 3.1 presents these findings.

These data cast some doubt on a variety of prevalent theories about alienation. The poor, the black, the status-inconsistent, the new immigrant, the socially-isolated, the young are *not* more alienated from politics as has been suggested by intuition, the popular press and previous sociological studies. Political alienation in Newark is more widespread than that: if ever alienation was located exclusively in the "forgotten sectors" of America's urban society, in the lower classes, that time appears to be over.

This same conclusion is warranted by our findings in Philadelphia and its suburbs. In the white community of East Torresdale, for example, our sample of 76 persons showed considerable variation in age, socio-economic status and social connectedness (and the usual variation in gender), but none of these social differences is significantly associated with political alienation. These findings are shown in Tables 3.2 and 3.3.

======== TABLE 3.2 ========

THE RELATIONSHIP OF SES, SOCIAL CONNECTEDNESS AND AGE TO
POLITICAL ALIENATION IN EAST TORRESDALE

Description	r
SES	0.18
Social connectedness	—0.16
Age	zero

$n = 76$. No relationship is statistically significant.

======== TABLE 3.3 ========

DIFFERENCE OF MEANS:[12] POLITICAL ALIENATION
BY GENDER IN EAST TORRESDALE

	Male	Female	F	Significance
Mean alienation	2.5	2.7	0.63	not significant

Similarly, in the suburban sample, the social background variables we studied bore virtually no significant, direct relationship to political alienation from national, state or local government. Specifically, differences in income, age and gender tend to have no significant relationship to the respondents' degree of estrangement, measured on national, state and local dimensions. These findings are reported in Table 3.4.

===== TABLE 3.4 =====

ANALYSES OF VARIANCE: POLITICAL ALIENATION BY INCOME, AGE
AND GENDER IN PHILADELPHIA'S WHITE SUBURBS*

	Low Income	High Income	F	Significance Level
Mean national alienation	0.64	0.51	1.1	not significant
Mean state alienation	0.68	0.42	4.9	0.02
Mean local alienation	0.44	0.30	1.4	not significant
	Male	Female	F	Significance Level
Mean national alienation	.53	.56	0.04	not significant
Mean state alienation	.71	.44	3.7	not significant
Mean local alienation	.41	.31	1.4	not significant
	Young	Old	F	Significance Level
Mean national alienation	0.56	0.54	0.01	not significant
Mean state alienation	0.50	0.50	0.00	not significant
Mean local alienation	insufficient observations			
$n = 60$				

*alienation runs from high to low, so that lower scores = higher alienation.

It will be observed that the only significant association in this table is that between income level and alienation from the state polity; but this relationship is not in the direction posited in the older sociological literature: low status ⟶ high alienation. Here, the higher-status people are more alienated. Since the median income for this sample was in the neighborhood of $16,000 per year, it is clearly the alienation of the relatively wealthy that is being expressed here. Apparently today even where social descriptors do have direct impact on political alienation, they do so in a manner that indicates strong change in the traditional process of alienation.

The relationships that obtained between social descriptors and the attitude of political alienation in our black communities study also follow this pattern of either no relationship or relationships evincing changes in the traditional process of alienation. The correlation coefficient of socio-economic status with political alienation was 0.16, which is not statistically significant. The relationships between alienation and party, religion and gender in this data are interesting and, in some senses, quite different from what the conventional sociological wisdom might lead one to expect. As indicated in Table 3.5, party identification does make a difference in one's alienation but only in the sense that independents tend to be more alienated than Republicans or Democrats. Apparently the overwhelmingly Democratic black people of Philadelphia were not more alienated from the national polity than Republicans, despite the fact of a Republican in the White House, nor were Republicans more alienated than Democrats despite their political marginality in the neighborhood. Similarly, religion made a difference in one's alienation in these black communities only in the sense that atheists tended to be more politically alienated. As between higher-status and lower-status religions, no difference is observed. Finally, black men are more likely to be alienated from the American political system than black women; but we will show, in the last section of this book, that in this community black women are somewhat more likely than black men to react to their alienation in an activist fashion.

TABLE 3.5

ANALYSES OF VARIANCE: POLITICAL ALIENATION BY PARTY, RELIGION AND GENDER IN PHILADELPHIA'S BLACK COMMUNITIES

Party	Republicans	Democrats	Independent		*F*	*Significance Level*
Mean Alienation	1.25	1.59	2.40		2.6	0.03

Gender	*Male*	*Female*			*F*	*Significance Level*
Mean Alienation	2.08	1.58			6.2	0.01

Religion	*Baptist*	*Catholic*	*Methodist*	*Other*	*None*	*F*	*Significance Level*
Mean Alienation	1.63	1.50	1.38	1.60	2.85	8.2	0.001

From these four studies, we conclude that socio-economic status and the other social background characteristics which have tended to dominate

the scholarly literature (and much of the public discussion) on alienation, tend not to be significantly related to political alienation in the urban
setting. This, of course, is not to say that the American political system has
successfully coped with the urban problems of poverty, of racial and sexual
prejudice, of youth's difficulties and aspirations. Rather, what is suggested
is that the problems and perceived powerlessness of most of these social
sectors are such that the old relationships between status deprivation and
political alienation (if they ever existed) have been wiped out. This finding
also should not be taken to mean that basic social background differences
do not have strong influence on an individual's political behavior for, as
we will show in the last section of this book, social variables do exert
important influences on the ways in which people act out their alienated
attitudes. But first it is necessary to understand how those alienated attitudes are acquired or adopted; and social variables do *not* seem to have an
important, direct, linear bearing on this process.

SOCIAL BACKGROUND CHARACTERISTICS AND
POLITICAL ALIENATION IN SELECTED
UNIVERSITY SETTINGS

If the previous findings run counter to the general discussion of
adult political alienation, they are also in flat contravention of the general
discussion of student alienation. Commentators and scholars of student
politics have recently put strong emphasis on social variables as determinants of student alienation and activism. Here, of course, the emphasis
has been on upper- or middle-class status since being able to afford a
college education is a traditional indicator of higher social status.*

This view sees middle-class individuals (for example, students) as more
economically secure and more psychologically confident than lower-class
persons, hence more free to evaluate the polity and more likely to become
alienated.[13] Under this conception, lower-middle-class individuals would
seem less likely than higher-status people to become politically alienated
because they are less free of economic and status problems, more tied to the
status hierarchy and are less likely to probe deeply into the political and
social processes which underly that status hierarchy. Working-class individuals would remain high in self-identification with the polity, in this view.

Another variant of the social factors-to-alienation notion, which has been
applied to the study of student politics, reverses the traditional view of
social connectedness. Traditionally, it was thought that social connectedness
inhibited alienation. A new conception has it that alienation is likely to
grow out of "inauthentic" social involvement.[14] Attitudes of alienation

---

*These studies were conducted by David C. Schwartz, Stanley Renshon, Fred
Swan and Don Vogt.

should be acquired, according to this idea, not only when men are unconnected to the social and political order but when their involvement in groups—largely but not exclusively a middle-class involvement—does not give them real control over the issue-areas in which their groups are operating. Critics of contemporary American society see this feeling of inauthenticity as widespread and therefore would presumably expect individual connectedness and participation to be regularly associated with alienation.

These conceptions change the posited direction of relationships between social factors and alienation but cling to the belief that such a relationship exists. They suggest that if we study the college campus, an important set of relationships between social background factors and political alienation will be observed.

These hypotheses are plausible; certainly the psychodynamic effects of SES that they posit seem reasonable. Our hypothesis again is *per contra*: look now where you will in America, we believe, and relationships between social factors and political alienation will be weak or nonexistent because of the increasing alienation across all sectors of the population. Our studies in the urban communities did seem to bear out this position. In addition we sought a variety of university environments in which to test it.

The social background characteristics that have been hypothesized to relate to student political alienation include most of those that we have inquired about above—class, social connectedness, age, gender, etc.—but also include characteristics that reflect student status (for example, year in school and academic major field of study).[15] Also, the student's social status is likely to derive in part from the social position of his parents.[16] Accordingly, we sought to explore the impact on political alienation of social, academic and parental characteristics.

These relationships were investigated in six university settings. Questionnaires were administered to: (1) random and (2) volunteer student samples of the University of Pennsylvania; stratified random samples of students at (3) Drexel Institute of Technology and (4) Temple University; (5) matched samples of sit-ins and non-sit-ins at Penn and (6) matched samples of anti-war protestors and nonprotestors from Knox College and from Penn.

The contexts of research

We have already given brief descriptions of our samples of students at the University of Pennsylvania and of the anti-war protestors and nonprotesters in Chapter 2. The Penn sit-in context is described in Chapter 6, so here we will note only the formal characteristics of that sample. Thus, it remains for us only to indicate something of the contexts at Drexel and Temple.

Penn, Temple and Drexel are all in Philadelphia, but it would be hard to imagine three more different schools. Penn is a private, liberal arts university of 7,000 undergraduates and 18,000 full-time students; distinctly a middle-class school. Drexel, at the time of our study in spring 1969, was an undergraduate Institute of Technology[17] with many if not most of its 11,000 undergraduates in a work-study or co-op program in which they alternated between periods of academic study and periods of on-the-job training in local business and government. It is very much a vehicle for the social mobility of the urban working-class and lower-middle-class student it attracts, and is primarily an engineering school with strong programs in business administration and home economics. Despite its urban ambience, Drexel does have a variety of traditional college characteristics in terms, for example, of the dress, fraternal living patterns and carnivals of its students. In this sense it is midway between Penn and Temple.

Temple is all urban ambience. It is an enormous school of 40,000 students located in the streets of North Philadelphia's largest black ghetto (Philly's worst slum). Temple is a state-related school, which means it depends on state funds to stay open but gets less of them because it doesn't call itself part of the State University system. On the continuum from "all campus" to "subway" schools, Temple stands at the "subway" extreme. Academically, Temple is a good school and fast improving. Its lower-middle-class student body is also status-aspirant.

These schools have considerable diversity in the social backgrounds of their student bodies.

Our sample at Drexel was drawn at random from a population of 325 entering freshmen in the business administration program ($n = 109$). At Temple, our respondents were 215 students enrolled in the required introductory course in Political Science. In both cases, participation in the study was voluntary; questionnaires were used and administered in class.

Measures

At Penn, we inquired about gender, income and year in school by direct single-item indicators and constructed multi-item indexes of social connectedness and political alienation. *Social connectedness* was defined as the number of memberships and officerships held by respondents in social organizations. *News media connectedness* was operationalized as the frequency with which respondents reported themselves to read newspapers and watch national news on television. The political alienation indexes were reported in Chapter 1.

Our Drexel questionnaire permitted observations on the following 15 variables:

1. *Family social status*—defined as father's occupation status.
2. *Number of siblings.*

3. *Ecology of student's background*—rural, urban or suburban.

4. *Family geographic mobility*—number of moves in the last five years.

5. *Age.*

6. *Gender.*

7. *Student's party identification.*

8. *Nationality.*

9. *Religion.*

10. *Parental political activism*—button-wearing, attending meetings, etc.

11. *Student political connectedness*—belonging to noncampus political organizations.

12. *Student campus political connectedness*—belonging to campus political organizations.

13. *Student political participation*—a three-item index composed of working for political parties or candidates, attending meetings or rallies and contributing money to parties or candidates.

14. *Student campus political participation*—a three-item index comprising voting, discussing politics and attending meetings during the campus election campaign.

15. *Political alienation*—a two-item index composed of: (a) a self-ranked score on identifying (feeling closely associated) with the American political system as a whole; (b) a self-ranked score on "liking" that system—both rated on a seven-point scale.

In contrast to this extensive list, our Temple study included only measures of age, academic major and political alienation; the only social variable on which our protesters and nonprotesters were compared was a four-item index of parental status. The sit-in samples, however, were asked about class, age, gender, religion, year in school, academic major, political party identification and degree of politicization (working for political parties), as well as political alienation. These measures were direct, nonprojective items except for the alienation measure which is described in the Methodological Appendix.

Findings

Across a wide range of university types and considerable diversity in political situations, the findings in these university settings parallel strongly those which emerged from our urban communities: *in the main, no social background attribute bears consistent, significant and direct relationship to the attitude of political alienation.* Student alienation and campus activism tend to have no significant association with any of the social backgrounds from which the alienated come. The findings of the separate studies are discussed in order.

Penn. At Penn, none of the social background characteristics studied help to predict political alienation. Upperclassmen are not significantly more alienated than lower classmen (the university had not socialized them to alienation). Draft-age men in our sample are not significantly more alienated than are co-eds; students from wealthy families do not find themselves more estranged from politics than are their classmates from poorer families. Being socially connected (in the sense of being a member or officer of social organizations) or connected to the mass news media makes no important difference in alienation. These findings are summarized in Tables 3.6 and 3.7.

TABLE 3.6

ANALYSES OF VARIANCE: POLITICAL ALIENATION BY INCOME, GENDER AND YEAR IN SCHOOL AT PENN

	Male	*Female*	*F*	*Significance Level*
Mean alienation	0.50	0.50	0.001	not significant
	Senior	*Freshman*	*F*	*Significance Level*
Mean alienation	0.40	0.36	0.157	not significant
	Low Income	*High Income*	*F*	*Significance Level*
Mean alienation	0.28	0.51	0.81	not significant

$n = 113$.

TABLE 3.7

THE RELATIONSHIP OF SOCIAL CONNECTEDNESS AND MEDIA CONNECTEDNESS TO POLITICAL ALIENATION AT PENN

Social Variable	*r*
Social connectedness	0.06
News media connectedness	−0.11

$n = 79$; neither relationship reaches statistical significance.

Drexel. The long list of social variables studied among our Drexel respondents enables us to answer a variety of interesting questions that have been the object of considerable speculation across the generation gap. For example: Are middle-class students more likely to be politically alienated, or are lower-class students more disaffected? Do only children, perhaps more used to getting their way in authority relationships, become "turned off" by a polity that does not afford immediate gratification? Are the children of politically active parents more alienated? Are students who are active in politics more likely to become estranged from politics than are less-involved students? Does a student's connectedness to the polity inhibit the acquisition of alienated attitudes? Does connectedness to the university polity suffice for this end? Do differences in nationality, religion, age, gender and political party make for differences in political alienation? In short, what is the impact of a student's socio-political background on the degree to which he is estranged from American politics?

Tables 3.8 and 3.9 give the unequivocal answer to these questions found in our data. Social background factors do not bear significant, direct relationship to political alienation. In this sample, not one of the background characteristics intercorrelates with alienation to a greater degree than could have occurred by chance.

===== TABLE 3.8 =====

THE RELATIONSHIP OF SOCIAL BACKGROUND VARIABLES AND
POLITICAL ALIENATION AT DREXEL

1. *SES*	$r = 0.03$
2. *Siblings*	$r = 0.09$
3. *Neighborhood type* (urban, suburban, rural)	$r = -0.07$
4. *Mobility* (number of housing locations)	$r = -0.16$
5. *Parental political activism*	$r = 0.07$
6. *Student political connectedness*	$r = -0.08$
7. *Campus student connectedness*	$r = -0.09$
8. *Student political participation*	$r = -0.12$
9. *Campus student participation*	$r = 0.03$

$n = 109$; no relationships attain statistical significance.

Temple. Our study at Temple was conducted primarily to discover the relationships between alienation and uses of the mass media (findings on which are reported in the section of this book on the consequences of

TABLE 3.9

ANALYSES OF VARIANCE: POLITICAL ALIENATION BY
SOCIAL VARIABLE AT DREXEL*

	Mean Alienation
Gender	
Male	3.85
Female	3.54
F	0.95
Religion	
Protestant	3.65
Catholic	3.79
Jewish	4.0
Other	3.0
None	3.76
F	0.236
Nationality	
West European	3.87
East European	3.50
American identification	3.88
Other	3.0
F	1.6
Location of parents' home	
Rural	3.0
Suburban	4.1
Small city	4.0
Large city	4.5
F	0.605
Parents' politicization	
High	3.92
Low	3.77
Don't know	3.58
F	0.24
Father's political party	
Republican	4.13
Democrat	3.52
None	3.85
Don't know	3.50
F	1.47
Father's political party	
Republican	3.85
Democrat	3.62
None	3.81
Don't know	4.0
F	0.27

$n = 109$

*Significance level = not significant for all variables.

alienation), but the questionnaire did include items on academic major and age. These variables are of interest because the literature on student politics would lead one to expect that students in the social sciences and humanities should be more alienated than students in the natural sciences, engineering, business and other "more technical" fields. Also, if older students are more alienated than younger ones, we may conclude that something in the university experience (or maturation or generational effects) influences political alienation. At Temple, a student's academic field was not significantly associated with the degree of his alienation from politics ($r = -0.10$, not significant), but age did bear a modest relationship to alienation (-0.24, significant at 0.025) such that older students were more alienated. This latter finding is contrary to our prediction, but Temple is the only context in which this result obtained.

Penn Sit-In. In the Penn sit-in study, social status and year in school do not distinguish between campus activists and nonactivists; and in neither sample are conventional socio-political variables associated with the attitude of political alienation. But socio-economic status did distinguish between students who protested in Washington at the Vietnam Moratorium and their classmates who chose not to participate in that demonstration. The protesters were of somewhat higher social status (and this difference achieved modest statistical significance). Tables 3.10, 3.11 and 3.12 summarize these findings.

TABLE 3.10

DIFFERENCE OF MEANS ON SES AND YEAR IN SCHOOL BETWEEN SIT-INS AND NON-SIT-INS AT PENN

	Sit-ins *(n = 48)*	*Non-Sit-ins* *(n = 46)*	*Significance Level*
SES	2.39	2.14	Not significant
Year in school	2.37	2.26	Not significant

TABLE 3.12

DIFFERENCE OF MEANS ON PARENTAL SES BETWEEN ANTI-VIETNAM WAR PROTESTERS AND NONPROTESTERS

Parental status (high to low)	*Protesters*	*Matched Sample of non-protesters*
	2.22	2.55
	F	*Significance Level*
	2.14	0.05

TABLE 3.11

ANALYSES OF VARIANCE: POLITICAL ALIENATION BY SOCIAL VARIABLES AMONG SIT-INS AND NON-SIT-INS AT PENN

	Sit-Ins				F	Significance Level	Non-Sit-Ins				F	Significance Level
Gender: Mean alienation	Male 20.4	Female 17.5			0.77	not significant	Male 24.78	Female 21.54			1.08	not significant
Party identification: Mean alienation	Republican 20.0	Democrat 30.0	Independent 18.0	Other 20.0	0.97	not significant	Republican 23.33	Democrat 21.86	Independent 26.25	Other 10.00	2.37	not significant
Party membership: Mean alienation	Yes 21.1	No 18.8			.383	not significant	Yes 27.0	No 23.05			1.58	not significant
Worked for political party: Mean alienation	Yes 20.4	No 17.28			0.844	not significant	Yes 25.0	No 23.21			0.44	not significant
Father's politicization: Mean alienation	High 23.57	Low 18.23			2.67	not significant	High 27.64	Low 21.42			5.7	not significant

Of the fifty relationships between social variables and political alienation summarized in the twelve tables in this chapter, only five were significant and at least three of these five represent findings which do not comport with conventional notions of the relationships between these variables. Among students, as among our urban and suburban respondents, there appears to be no consistent, significant and direct relationship between social background characteristics and political alienation.

Is this equally true of their professors?

Work Satisfaction, Career Orientations and Political Alienations Among Political Scientists and Sociologists

Before leaving the arena of societal factors to seek the causes of political alienation in the polity, and in the individual's psychological reactions to the polity, it seems important at least to touch upon the problem of work and its relationship to alienation.* The traditional conception of this relationship is clear: dissatisfaction with the character and environment of work should lead to political alienation. So it is in Marx's theory, where alienation from work is seen as a fundamental cause of the class consciousness which drives his processes of alienation and revolution.[18] And the history of the politicization of labor's demands for enfranchisement and the right of collective bargaining, along with the mobilization of labor for political action in labor parties and in independent political action organizations, lend further credence to this view.

But this conventional viewpoint does not rest on historical evidence alone. In America, work is still a predominant indicium of personal identity, at least for males. "How do you do" is now a formal salutation; but "What do you do?" is a carefully monitored query, basic to the identity of the responder and to the identification or labeling process of the inquirer. Most of us are asked this question frequently and, for the man whose own honest response makes him uncomfortable, whose work identity is not valued by himself or others, alienated action may provide an escape, a new identity, a means of reforming the status hierarchy. Alienated attitudes allow these changes to be enjoyed vicariously and can serve to distantiate the individual from the organized society whose hierarchy devalues him. At a less basic level, for one whose status is accepted but whose job environment is affronting, he, too, can fix responsibility on the polity, for its laws permit the affronting conditions to exist, and it is a convenient whipping post presented daily in the media. One's resentment can always be cloaked as merely the political concern

---

*This study was conducted by David C. Schwartz and Conrad Winn.

of the interested citizen or, even better, as the sophisticated cynicism of one who is "in the know."[19]

A modern variant of this hypothesized relationship between work dissatisfactions and political alienation, sees the relationship as operative today more for intellectuals than for the proletariat. As organized labor and its preferred bargaining practices have been incorporated as legitimate and powerful forces in the ordinary processes of American society and government, labor is seen as increasingly *status quo* or mildly reformist in orientation but definitely nonalienated and nonrevolutionary.[20] In Jules Pfeiffer's parody of this view: "If you want a revolution, forget about the workers, man! They drink beer, ride around in Ramblers and are fat from wealth. Workers of the mind are the only ones who'll bring revolution."[21]

C. Wright Mills and S. M. Lipset agree.[22] In their conception, not only have the intellectuals remained as a special locus of alienation, but they have served to expand the pool of potential alienateds. "Intellectuals who are resentful of their society often stimulate rebellious, . . . apprentice intellectuals"—students.[23] "[F]aculty discontent influences the attitudes and behavior of students[24] [so much that] the faculty within which students are enrolled seems more predictive of [students'] political stance, than class origins."[25]

According to Lipset, the social resentment or alienation which professors pass on to their students derives, in large part, from work-connected dissatisfactions. "[Campus] tensions . . . arise from aggrieved faculty members whose conditions of work and sense of a lack of proper intellectual style create resentment against both the university and the larger society and polity."[26] In particular, professors at large state universities are likely to be politically alienated, due *inter alia* to status insecurities, competitiveness with colleagues and the clear impact of politics—in the form of state legislatures—on the work environment.[27] Social science professors especially are likely to be leftist alienateds but will be restrained by the value-neutral ethos of much of their research.[28]

As the reader will have suspected, given our earlier statements, we believe that this approach is not now particularly useful in explaining political alienation. To be sure, alienated professors will have some impact on students and on each other, but political alienation is, we believe, far more likely to derive from a professor's reaction to politics than to his work environment.

We can derive this notion from the psycho-political models of political science. First, the cognitive compartmentalization between job and politics that allowed a generation of scholars to conclude that politics is just not very salient[29] to most people is still likely to be functioning. Second, even for academics whose job situation is dependent upon state legislatures, American politics is overwhelmingly recognized as national politics, as the political scientists of the 1950s and the early 1960s have taught us. Also, the status of intellectuals is rising in America by almost any measure, and the growth of academic consultancy to government, especially in the social sciences, has been perceived as increasing acceptance of intellectuals in public life, hence status insecurities are unlikely to be directed against government. Job conditions, too, have been improving over the past generation. We are teaching less and researching, consulting, conferencing and vacationing more. And most of that research, consulting, conferencing and even some of the vacationing is government-funded. No doubt some academics are alienated—there are after all matters concerning war,[30] poverty, civil rights, etc., to be considered—but it seems exceedingly doubtful whether much of that alienation derives from work dissatisfaction.

Sample and measures

To test the hypothesis that job and career dissatisfactions do not bear significant relationship to political alienation, a national survey of academic sociologists and political scientists was conducted in the spring of 1969. A listing of full-time, academically affiliated teaching or research personnel in the two disciplines was obtained from the current directories of the American Sociological Association (ASA, $n = 5,000$) and American Political Science Association (APSA, $n = 4,000$). One hundred names for each discipline were selected at random. These individuals received a mailed questionnaire of 59 items, randomly ordered except for demographic items, on a three-page instrument. The response rates were 59 percent for sociologists and 49 percent for political scientists.

The following career-relevant items were asked on that questionnaire:

1. *Academic rank.*

2. *Type of college*—large public (over 8,000 students), large private, etc.

3. *Career satisfaction*—for example, "Do you ever have doubts about your choice of career?"

4. *Status satisfaction*—for example, "Career-wise, how well have you done in comparison to your father?"

5. *Self-ranked competence*—for example, "How would you compare your professional competence to that of your departmental colleagues?"

6. *Recent scholarly productivity*—defined as the number of publications in the two years preceding the survey.

In addition, we inquired about two basic social scientific orientations: (1) Behavioralism versus traditionalism—"In the conflict between those who favor a scientific behavioral approach and those who are traditional, I agree with _____"; (2) The older orientation versus the new non-behaviorism—"Much of the current theory in my discipline is tacitly rooted in conservative political values."

Political alienation was measured as a two-item index composed of: (1) I usually identify myself closely with American politics and government; (2) When I hear about politics in America, I feel a part of it.

Our average respondent was an assistant or associate professor at a large school, who perceived himself to be about as competent or a bit more competent than his colleagues but who still sometimes experienced doubts that he'd made the right career choice. He had published two to three articles in the last two years and was behavioralist in his orientation to social science.

In general, career variables are *unrelated* to political alienation among these social science professors. Whether one's college is small or large, private or public, makes no significant difference to one's alienation from public affairs in America. The status-insecure professor, whether insecure because he is untenured, uncertain of his competence, doubtful whether he made the right career choice or feels that he has not done as well as his father did, is not more politically alienated than his tenured, confident and upwardly status-mobile counterpart. Nor are there any differences on these matters between political scientists and sociologists—apparently, these kinds of career dissatisfactions just don't make for civic estrangement. Among these academics, however, there *is* a slight tendency for the more productive scholars to be more alienated from politics ($r = 0.17$, significant at 0.05) perhaps indicating support for a competitiveness ———> alienation hypothesis, but this accounts for only three percent of the variance in alienation.

Slightly stronger, and more interesting, is the relationship that scholarly orientations do bear to political alienation. Sociologists who dissent from the dominant behavioral paradigm in their field—either in the direction of traditionalism or of neo-nonbehavioralism—tend to be more politically alienated than do "nondeviants." Are these scholarly orientations evidence that work-related variables do affect political alienation, or are they better interpreted themselves as related to political orientations rather than work orientations? Table 3.14 shows the relationship of these scholarly orientations to work and political variables. The only significant correlations are those with political variables, again indicating the weak explanatory power of work-related variables vis-a-vis political orientations in this data.

Conclusion

As we indicated at the outset, we can do no more than touch upon the relationship between work and political alienation here. Although we suspect that the same lack of relationship which was shown in this study would characterize other work populations, we cannot show this to be true. What we can conclude is that: we have studied a population in which there is exhibited some political alienation, some status, career and work dissatisfactions and in which there has regularly been hypothesized a relationship between the two. Our general explanatory stance predicted no such relationship would obtain, and none did obtain. If political alienation, then, tends to be explicable neither in terms of socio-cultural alienation nor in terms of SES or social connectedness or other social background attributes, nor yet in terms of work dissatisfactions, it behooves us to look to the relationship between Americans and their polity for our explanations. This is the subject of the next section of the book.

GENERAL CONCLUSIONS ON THE RELATIONSHIPS BETWEEN SOCIAL VARIABLES AND POLITICAL ALIENATION

For more than a decade, study into the causes of socio-political alienation has inquired predominantly into the direct effects of SES and social background variables on alienation. Until recently, psychological variables had been relatively deemphasized, except for speculative sections at the end of articles on SES where the author guessed about the individual-level variables which might explain his data. The result has been debilitative not only to the explanation of alienation, but to the study of social factors in alienation. To exclude the putative psychological correlates of alienation from research has meant that scholars could not conceive of alienation as a process—for they could show neither how social factors operated to produce alienated attitudes nor how social factors could arouse and channel the alienated behavior which emerges from those alienated attitudes.

The logic of this analysis suggests that we move to identify the basic psychological (or psycho-political) variables that bear strong, direct and causal relationship to political alienation and then to inquire about the relationships that social variables have to these psychological (intervening) variables. We will seek to accomplish these tasks in the next section of this book, where we will show that three fundamental psychological variables account for substantial amounts of the political alienation presently observed in urban and university-America and that social variables operate to affect political alienation, if at all, through these psychological factors. In short, we will show that social variables "produce" political alienation to the extent that they yield certain psychological states, specifically to the degree that an individual's social experiences give rise to perceptions that he is in a fundamental and threatening value conflict with the polity and that the polity cannot be reformed so as to reduce that threat.

More than this, I believe that this formulation is in fact a needed fundamental rephrasing of that which the sociological literature has been

TABLE 3.13

THE RELATIONSHIP OF POLITICAL ALIENATION AND CAREER VARIABLES AMONG A SAMPLE OF SOCIAL SCIENTISTS

	Rank	Type of college	Self-ranked competence	Status satisfaction	Career satisfaction	Recent scholarly productivity	Behavioralism vs. Traditionalism	Behavioralism vs. Neo-non-behavioralism
Sample as a whole (n = 108)	0.09	−0.12	−0.01	−0.04	−0.02	0.17*	0.10	−0.20*
Sociologists (n = 59)	0.12	−0.04	0.03	0.02	0.00	0.17*	0.23*	−0.32**
Political scientists (n = 49)	0.02	−0.23	0.05	0.09	−0.05	0.20*	−0.05	−0.05

*Significant at 0.05.
**Significant at 0.01.

TABLE 3.14

THE RELATIONSHIP OF SCHOLARLY ORIENTATIONS WITH WORK AND POLITICAL VARIABLES AMONG SCHOLARS

	Work-Related Variables					Politics-Related Variables			
	Rank	Type of college	Self-ranked competence	Status satisfaction	Career satisfaction	Ideology	Threat from politicized value conflict	Perceived political inefficacy	Perceived inefficacy of the political system
Behavioralism versus Traditionalism	0.20	0.04	0.06	0.06	0.08	0.18	0.16	−0.20	0.18
Behavioralism versus Neo-non-behavioralism	0.03	0.14	0.01	0.01	−0.09	0.21*	−0.35**	0.08	−0.21*

*Significant at 0.05.
**Significant at 0.01.

driving at all along. The reason that the lower-status individual may have been alienated, as even the discussion in the sociological studies shows, is that this status situation was perceived as a deprivation which was both negatively valued by the individual and which was deemed illegitimate and weakening to the political position he believed himself to be entitled to. When lower status is not seen in this way (because one accepts it as legitimate, or because it is compartmentalized in the social arena and does not intrude into the individual's evaluations of the polity or because all statuses come to carry with them negative evaluations of the polity), then social positions do not relate to political alienation.

III

On the Psycho-Political Process of Alienation

4

THE PROCESS OF
POLITICAL ALIENATION

This chapter is intended as an introduction to the section of this book on the psychological causes of political alienation. Here we present a theory and a body of laboratory-derived data on the psychological processes whereby individuals come to adopt attitudes of political estrangement.

The basic theory is summarized in the introductory section of this chapter. In subsequent sections, we derive the theory from basic psychological premises, state it processually, explain the experimental procedures used to test the theory and present the data on which tentative confirmation of the theory is based.

Toward a theory of political alienation

As was stated in Chapter 1, the principal psychological variable used in the literature on political alienation is the perception of inefficacy. We know that individuals who feel relatively inefficacious—that is, persons who perceive themselves to be unable, by their own behavior, to determine or control desired outcomes—are more likely to withdraw interest, attention and self-identification from the political system.[1]

This formulation, however, seems in need of at least two extensions if it is to be particularly useful in explaining political alienation. First, an individual may feel himself quite incapable of producing or even fostering the values he wishes represented in the institutions, processes and policies of government but not become alienated because the political system already accords with those values. His inefficacy in this situation is simply not salient. A perceived fundamental conflict between an individual's politicized values and the values he perceives to be exhibited by the polity would appear to be a necessary supplement to the perception of inefficacy if alienation is to result. In accord with this, Seeman, who

93

defines alienation as inefficacy, has indicated that the perception of inefficacy produces predicted withdrawal behavior only when efficacy is both valued and thwarted.[2]

Second, an individual may perceive himself to be relatively incapable of bringing about desired outcomes but believe that one or more political reference groups (for example, his union, mate, fate, interest group, benevolent class betters, etc.) will attain his values for him. As these reference groups are seen as operating to resolve the value conflict which made his political inefficacy salient, the individual is less likely to become alienated.

To the notion of political inefficacy (PI), then, the following two variables should be added: (1) a perceived value conflict (VC) between an individual's fundamental politicized values and those seen as represented by the polity; and (2) a perceived systemic inefficacy (SI) such that the political system as a whole is seen to be thwarting and blocking the individual's value satisfaction, and that no self-surrogate exists in the political system that can resolve the value conflict (that is, reform the alienating situation).

We reason that fundamental value conflicts between self and polity are threatening, because (1) perceived cognitive conflict, when it involves salient objects, tends to be threatening;[3] (2) such conflicts also function as a locus for the fixation of free-floating anxiety; and (3) a potential distantation from one's organized society (which is likely to be seen as one resolution of the conflict) may induce a separation anxiety. Such conflicts are denoted herein as situations inducing threat from value conflict (TVC). Notationally, then: $TVC + PI + SI \longrightarrow$ Political Alienation.

This formulation is distinguishable from much previous work on two dimensions. First, by including emotional phenomena like felt-threat, it incorporates affective as well as cognitive or perceptual elements of human psychology, thereby moving toward more comprehensive explanation. Second, it moves toward causal explanation, making explicit a motivation for withdrawal—reduction of threat—whereas the earlier work had left motivation largely unspecified.

Some of the earlier work, however, did seem to make certain motivational assumptions about the functioning of inefficacy in the development of estranged attitudes and withdrawal behavior. These were: (1) the idea that inefficacy was frustrating to the individual and produced estrangement or withdrawal as a displacement of frustration-induced aggression; and (2) the idea that individuals who did not believe they could control their political worlds would naturally be less interested in political information. In the data reported below we compare the impact of threat and anger (as a measure of frustration) on alienation and find threat to be much the more powerful explanatory variable. Further, if our notion of a strong, salient value conflict as necessary for alienation is correct, then, of course, we should expect at least the initial interest in politics of alienated men to rise rather than fall. This prediction is tested and confirmed in the consequences section of the book.

A comprehensive process model for the explanation and prediction of the behavioral consequences of alienated attitudes is stated and tested in Part IV of this book. There, we will show that social background factors, plus personality variables and the group and communication processes which characterize the alienated individual predict to the political behaviors that issue out of alienated attitudes.

Here the question of consequences is touched upon in an introductory manner to indicate that the same variables which produce estrangement, when in different combinations, also produce attitudes favorable to the support of reformist and radical groups and activities.

In particular, we hypothesize that an individual who perceives a salient value conflict between his fundamental political values and those repre-sented by the political system, but who also perceives himself to be politically efficacious to obtain desired changes, is likely to adopt reformist attitudes and engage in reformist behavior (including, perhaps, personal support for reformist groups). He is motivated to political behavior by the desire to reduce the threat from value conflict. He is unlikely to modify his own fundamental values and he perceives no blockage (inefficacy) that might impede the reformist response, therefore we reason that he will tend to move toward a reformist orientation to the system. On the other hand, an individual is likely to support radical or revolutionary groups (and engage in other radical behavior) when he perceives personal and systemic inefficacy under the condition of a threatening value conflict but at the same time places high personal value on political participation, so that he cannot withdraw from political activity or identification without contravening his own values. Seeing no hope to reform the system from within but being motivated to political identification and activist orientations by the threat from value conflict, the individual maintains his participant orientations to politics by shifting allegiance to a radical or revolutionary alternative—that is, to an alienated reformism. Notationally:

TVC alone $\longrightarrow$ Reformist Attitudes

TVC + PI + SI $\longrightarrow$ Political Alienation

TVC + PI + SI + Value on $\longrightarrow$ Radical Attitudes
   Participation   (Alienated Reformism)

A processual model of political alienation

To be maximally useful, these formulations should be explicitly linked to basic principles and processes in individual psychology. Because these formulations refer to change over time in the state of the individual's psychological system relevant to political attitudes, they should be expressed as a process model. This section is devoted to accomplishing these two objectives.

The Stages of Political Alienation. The process of political alienation may be understood as eight linked sub-processes. These are first stated briefly and then explained in detail.

(1) *Maintenance of self-identification with the polity.* In the absence of a strong, threatening value conflict, individuals who have been socialized to identify with a political system will maintain that self-identification. The cognitive set of such individuals will be in balance, so that the perceived relationships between self, politicized values and political system are all positive (mutually supporting).

(2) *Ambivalence.* The initial perception of a threatening conflict between an individual's fundamental politicized values and the polity unbalances the cognitive set. The individual, in this situation, will tend to make some reassessment of the strength with which he holds the political values and the strength of his identification with the polity.

(3) *An approach-approach conflict.* If, on reflection, the threatening value conflict persists, then—above a "tolerance of ambivalence" threshold—individuals will tend to confront an approach-approach conflict where they must choose between two highly prized objects: values and polity.

(4) *A double approach-avoidance conflict.* If the values are truly basic to the individual's identity, if the individual sees himself as personally inefficacious to reform the polity in accordance with his values, if he perceives no self-surrogate who can move the system, then the conflict will be seen as irreconcilable. Under these circumstances, the individual will typically try to maintain his values by withdrawing self-identification from the political system.

(5) *Felt-threat and anger: The concomitants of withdrawal of self-identification.* Feelings of personal inefficacy and systemic unresponsiveness tend to evoke feelings of frustration and anger. Psychological distantiation from one's political system is also likely to evoke felt-threat.

(6) *Alienation from all or part of the polity: Differentiation or generalization.* If the individual can locate responsibility for the value conflict and inefficacy in one element of the polity, he will tend to do so. He differentiates between segments or elements or institutions of the political system and becomes alienated only from part of the polity. If the individual cannot be convinced or convince himself that some differentiable element of the polity is at fault, his alienation is more likely to be directed at the polity as a whole.

(7) *The generalization of alienation.* Even if the individual does

become convinced that only part of the polity is blameworthy, his efforts or his observation of other people's efforts to reform that element may convince him to the contrary that the polity as a whole is at fault. Under this condition, he tends to withdraw his self-identification from the entire political system.

(8) *Active alienation: From withdrawal to radicalization.* Individuals who place high value on involvement in politics will find that withdrawal of self-identification contravenes their own values. Such individuals are more likely than are others to reinvest their self-identification with alienated, radical or revolutionary groups.

The behavior and transition rules of the theory are stated below. If the transition conditions for movement from one specified stage to the next are not met, the psychological system will remain in the specified state (or move to an unspecified state). This theory, of course, does not specify every possible alternative state so other paths and patterns may exist. These states or stages, then, constitute a partial "psycho-political space" and this theory explains only one of the ways that men may become politically alienated.[4] I believe, however, that it is the principal path to political alienation. The data presented in this chapter, and in the rest of the chapters in this part of the book, tend to support this belief.

A cognitive structure which exists in persons who have undergone effective political socialization experiences and who support an existing political system—at least by regarding themselves as citizens or participants therein—may be represented either as: (1) an identity between images of the political system and politicized values (such that typically no distinction is made between the two); (2) a balanced cognitive set of highly positive relationships between images of the self, the polity and politicized values.[5]

Such a cognitive structure may be iconically represented as:

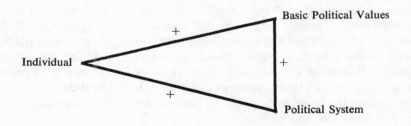

The figure is a balanced triad or set (multiply the 3 signs, + = balance, − = imbalance), connoting that governments are deemed legitimate when they are perceived to facilitate, or to be consonant with, the significant politicized values of the population.

Such a sense of legitimacy and support for government is jeopardized when the political system comes to be viewed as opposed to individuals' basic political values (that is, that the political system is either actively discriminating against those values or that it is unable to create or protect the conditions necessary to enjoying those values). An individual who perceives his government in this way will become ambivalent toward the situation. However, he will continue to value the political system because he has been socialized to do so and because that system emits allegiance-evoking symbols. On the other hand, the stability of his positive valuation of the polity will be shaken because the system is seen as not fulfilling its instrumental function of satisfying felt needs. This ambivalence constitutes stage 2 of the alienation process. This cognitive state can be represented as follows:

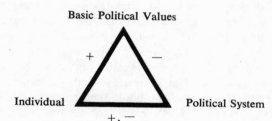

The outcomes of this stage are: (1) the individual's perceptions of the political system and his own politicized values become more separate and therefore potentially productive of conflict and (2) some reevaluation of the polity becomes necessary. Also, we might expect some small diminution in self-identification with the polity.

This ambivalence has motivational implications; above a "tolerance of ambiguity" threshold, some attitude change is to be expected. Three gross directions which this change might take can be identified. First, the individual can "remain where he is," reducing the psycho-political disturbance of ambivalence by modifying some of his less salient political values. Second, he may "move toward the system," modifying his attitudes and/or behavior in the direction of increased political activity in pursuit of desired change. Finally, he may "move away from the system," reducing disturbance by entering a phase of withdrawal of self-identification or passive alienation from politics.

These efforts to reduce the psycho-political disturbances of ambivalence move the individual to the third stage in the alienation process. The three possible resolutions suggest that the structure of the individual's problem in the third stage is akin to the basic psychological spatial conflict forms. These conflict forms are approach-approach conflict, approach-avoidance conflict, avoidance-avoidance conflict and double approach-avoidance conflict. The individual in the third stage faces either an approach-approach or a double approach-avoidance conflict. He values both the political system and his political value set, so the approach-avoidance and avoidance-avoidance forms can be eliminated from consideration.

In approach-approach conflict environments, two points of reinforcement (here, polity and politicized values) are desirable objects. Any movement toward either object tends to place the individual in a position of reinforced stimulation from that object, resulting in a further movement toward the object. In periods of "early political ambivalence," in the absence of effective external stimuli (from revolutionary organizations and/or others), movement is likely to be toward the system.

> Under the circumstances of every-day living, however, it is doubtful whether pure approach-approach conditions ... ever exist. In nearly every case, the choice of one goal generates an avoidance tendency due to the fact that the other goal may have to be relinquished ... such double approach-avoidance conflicts are not readily resolved. By and large, these ... conflicts reduce to a kind of avoidance-avoidance paradigm ... [where conflict must continue unless withdrawal or significant reevaluation is feasible].[6]

The problem will be structured as a double approach-avoidance conflict under the following conditions: (1) the politicized values at stake are so fundamental and/or so many that the individual cannot comfortably modify them;[7] (2) the individual perceives himself to be inefficacious to attain his values through reformist behavior; (3) the individual perceives no other persons or groups who can attain his values for him; (4) the individual continues to place some value on the political system so that the negative evaluation fostered by conditions 1 to 3 above produce significant psycho-political disturbance.

Under these conditions, the individual moves to the fourth stage of the alienation process where some withdrawal of his identification with the polity is likely to be attempted.

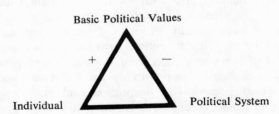

The perceptions of personal and systemic inefficacy posited above produce feelings of frustration and aggression. In addition, the disturbance is associated with significant tension and threat. There are three reasons for this: (1) a perceived negative relationship between one's basic values and one's organized society is threatening; (2) cognitive conflict is itself tensionful; and (3) some free-floating anxiety is likely to become fixed on politics (as the polity becomes an identifiable source of threat, undirected anxiety becomes attached to that source). Free-floating anxiety increases if, as is typical, the individual perceives social and political events which cause others to reevaluate and withdraw from the polity. It also tends to increase if the individual experiences other politically relevant disturbances, such as normlessness and meaninglessness, or observes other persons experiencing them. Thus the individual, in the fourth stage, may well be fixing extraordinary amounts of free-floating anxiety onto the political system.

As the bonds between self and society weaken, latent rage tends to reinforce feelings of frustration, aggression and threat. Such rage results from the too constraining character of general socialization when the conditions to which one has been socialized fail.[8]

Thus the previously participant individual does not merely withdraw from political behavior in an emotionally neutral manner. Rather, there is associated with that withdrawal a mutually reinforcing syndrome of frustration, felt-aggressiveness, rage, threat and tension. The implications of this syndrome for the individual's later political behavior are enormous.

To assess the political behavior that is likely to issue from alienation, we must also know the scope of that alienation. At the end of the fourth stage, the individual has withdrawn his self-identification from either all or part of the polity. But there is a tremendous difference between the behaviors associated with partial withdrawal and the behaviors which accompany a rejection of the polity as a whole. Reformers and even conformists can devalue one or another political institution, but a relatively complete estrangement from polities characterizes the revolutionary.

There are two paths by which partial political alienation takes place. First, the individual may simply have perceived that only some political institutions were incompatible with his basic political values and hence have withdrawn identification only from those subsystems of the polity. Alternatively, he may initially withdraw from the political system as a whole but later be able to differentiate cognitively between the total polity and some part of the system perceived to require and permit reform. If the individual can ascribe responsibility for the value conflict to some separable political personnel or institution and still support what he regards as the fundamental character of the polity, he is likely to maintain substantial self-identification.

If the individual withdraws self-identification (and possibly attention) from part of the polity and finds that this is successful in reducing the threat from value conflict, or at least the salience of that threat, he is likely to remain in that orientation. If the threat continues, perhaps because his basic values are still not realized in the polity, we may expect the individual to adopt attitudes and behaviors oriented toward influencing the political institutions.

If his "threat-coping" or reform efforts permit the individual to perceive himself as politically efficacious, at most only partial alienation will obtain (that is, the psychological system will remain in the state of partial alienation). If, however, the individual's threat-coping behavior is met only by a series of perceived system blockages, then felt-threat will be reinforced and a sense of both personal and systemic inefficacy will be induced. These obstacles to value attainment and threat-reduction also generate frustration. *The order is important:* salient political value conflicts yield threat, and a failure to reduce threat generates threat-reinforcement, perceived political inefficacy and frustration. When the individual perceives that all of the political institutions he deems relevant to attaining his values are closed to himself and his self-surrogates, the threat and frustration generalize to the system as a whole (sub-process 7) and total withdrawal is attempted.

Any national political system is sufficiently complex that differentiation can go on for some time before the perceptions which produce the generalization come into being. This may explain why alienation subprocesses sometimes take place over long periods of time. Note that the reformer continues to work within the system before withdrawing, so that the pool of politically alienated persons is made up not only of those who opt out early (sub-process 4) but also of a subset of ex-reformers who are relatively familiar with the persons and processes of the system. If these ex-reformers become radicalized, they tend to be strategically crucial in revolutionary planning and infiltration.

When do men adapt to their alienation by radicalizing? A comprehensive explanation of this phenomenon is beyond the scope of this chapter and is therefore left to the consequences section of the book. Here we hypothesize that individuals who are highly politicized, that is, who place a high value on political participation, will radicalize rather than withdraw because withdrawal would contravene their own values. Under the conditions that produce withdrawal in other individuals (that is, threat from value conflict + perceived political inefficacy), highly politicized men will start or support revolutionary organizations in order to attain their values, to reduce threat and to play out their frustrations.

In sum, we theorize that salient value conflicts, in the absence of perceived political inefficacy, produce reformist attitudes; that such conflicts in the presence of perceived inefficacy produce political withdrawal; and that politicized value conflicts and perceived inefficacy, in persons placing high value on participation, produce radicalized-rebellious attitudes. The alienation-relevant political attitudes which an individual adopts are a function of his location in the process of alienation.

Methods and measures

Laboratory experimentation was chosen as the first mode by which to test these hypotheses in order to obtain necessary control over the sequential introduction of stimuli. To test the processual model, it was necessary to observe the same individuals through the whole sequence of stages. This could not be done through panel interview techniques without an unfeasibly large sample, as neither our theory nor the previous work specify the "potential alienateds" precisely enough, in advance, for efficient sampling. Relevant verbal material was largely unavailable. Accordingly, neither the relatively direct observation of individuals becoming alienated nor the less direct observation of such persons via content analysis was feasible. The experiment described here is designed to provide one appropriate context in which to observe whether operation of the process, as modelled, does obtain. In this section, the logic and procedures of research are stated and then explained in detail.

The basic experimental design was a multiple "test-experimental treatment-retest" design. Student subjects were randomly assigned to one of four experimental groups: (1) VC—a sample in which a value conflict between subjects (hereinafter S) and the polity was induced; (2) VC. PI—a sample in which both the value conflict and a perception that S was inefficacious to attain his values was experimentally induced; (3) VC. PI, SI—a sample in which all three of the relevant perceptions were experimentally induced; and (4) Control—a sample wherein S received politically relevant materials of equivalent length to the experimental treatments but which did not manipulate any of the three independent variables. Measures of the independent variables and the dependent variable, alienation, were recorded before any experimental treatment was accomplished. Then, S was given the experimental treatment, a set of documents designed to induce the relevant perceptions. A second recordation of TVC, PI, SI estrangement, attraction to reformist activity and support for radical groups was then made. Thereafter, S received up to four more sets of documents, reinforcing the experimental treatment, after each of which all of the relevant variables were measured. Each aspect of this experiment is explained below.

Measures: Reliability and Validity. The experimental protocols included a series of direct (nondisguised), single-item indicators of the relevant variables. These were:

Estrangement. To what extent do you identify with (feel closely associated with) the American political system *at this time?* (Rate on a scale from 1 to 7, 7 meaning most positive identification).

Value conflict. Do you think that the major institutions of the American political system agree with your values about politics? Yes . . . . No . . . . This was a filter question for the following item.

Threat from value conflict. If not, how threatened do you feel by this apparent discrepancy? (Rank on a scale from 1 to 7, 7 meaning most threatened).

Political inefficacy. Please rate, on a scale from 1 to 7, how effective you feel you can be, *at this time,* in influencing American politics. (7 meaning most effective).

Systemic inefficacy. Please rate, on the same scale, how effective you feel that American politics is, *at this time,* in reflecting the needs and wishes of the American people.

At the time of this experiment, these items were selected on the basis of their face-validity (hence the direct, nondisguised character of the indicators). Subsequently, however, these same items have been employed in other studies in conjunction with several other face-valid items as part of a set of scales of TVC, PI, SI and political alienation. From the high degree of intercorrelation that these items achieve with other index items, we conclude that these measures have attained an acceptable level of index validity. These intercorrelations are presented in the methods appendix. (See listings for Chapters 1, 5, 6 and 7.)

In addition to TVC, PI, SI and estrangement, we were interested in measuring S's support for groups perceived by S to be radical, S's attraction to reformist activities and the degree to which S valued political participation. Support for radical groups was tapped by the following indicator, offered as face-valid: "To what extent do you identify with or are attracted to what you would consider radical groups, *at this time.* (Rate on a scale from 1 to 7, 7 meaning most positive identification or attraction)." Attraction to reformist activity was measured by a three-item index, which was comprised of S's self-ranked attraction to political picketing, mass meetings, rallies, political strikes and sit-ins. This index had an inter-item correlation coefficient significant at 0.001 (indicating acceptable internal validity) and a reliability coefficient of 0.88. S's value for political participation was tapped by an index of his memberships in political organizations, attendance at political functions, campaign activity, financial contribution, display of political buttons and/or stickers, and voting. This index had inter-item intercorrelation coefficients significant at 0.0005 and a reliability coefficient of 0.91.

Experimental Groupings and Form. As three independent variables are posited to drive the alienation process (value conflict, personal political inefficacy and system inefficacy), at least eight experimental groupings were possible: (1) VC alone; (2) PI alone; (3) SI alone; (4) VC, PI; (5) VC, SI; (6) PI, SI; (7) VC, PI, SI; and (8) control. Constraints of time and resources necessitated choosing only four groups: (1) VC; (2) VC, PI; (3) VC, PI, SI; and (4) control. The VC and control groups were necessary to test the hypothesis that VC alone is a necessary but insufficient condition for alienation. The VC, PI, SI group was needed to test the hypothesis that VC, PI and SI is a sufficient condition to produce alienation. The VC, PI sample, rather than the VC, SI group, was selected because we recognized that PI has been of greater interest in alienation research than SI.

The logic of excluding the possible samples of PI alone, SI alone and PI, SI was that our theory states that VC is necessary for the alienation process to produce any attitude change. Also, by combining all experimental samples in a secondary analysis, we could still observe any instances of PI alone, SI alone and PI, SI and note their consequences.

The experiment was a modified simulation in which subjects were given a hypothetical political situation they were instructed to suppose to exist. S played no artificial or hypothetical role but was instructed to react as he himself honestly felt at any given point in the experiment, so that the simulation aspect of the experiment refers to the political context. The form of this study might be called an experiment in a simulated environment.

Introduction and Reinforcement of Stimuli. VC was induced in a realistic hypothetical situation in which

> a recent bill ... would effect a revision of the federal electorate. The new federal electorate ... would be made up solely of persons who have passed a rigorous political information test ... (requiring sophisticated knowledge of both American government and political issues) ... This bill includes provision for a change in the Electoral College so that rural areas will be over-represented ... to ensure that urban areas do not dominate them.

The hypothetical situation was justified on elitist philosophical grounds which tended to be in conflict with S's values for equalitarianism, fairness, concern for the underprivileged, etc.

PI was induced by having S take and fail a rigorous, multiple choice, political information test said to be similar to the one contemplated in the simulated environment so that S was prospectively disenfranchised. This test asked S *inter alia:*

> Who is the present United States Ambassador to South Vietnam?
> Who is the Senate Majority Whip?
> Where do federal bills for raising revenue originate?
> Who is the present National Democratic Party Chairman?
> What is the "cross-filing" system in primaries?

On debriefing, it was clear that S felt the exam was fair, that he should have had the required knowledge. Also, PI was induced by telling S that "you have been told not even to bother writing or calling your Congressman, since they consider these letters ... the sour grapes of the disenfranchised."

SI was induced by indicating strong political support for the elitist bill. Such statements as:

"[The bill] has generated strong support from all major institutions in the American political system"; "President ... has also given his support"; "The bill has won the strong endorsement of both the Republican and Democratic congressional leaders"; "Both the Democratic and Republican National Committees have issued statements in favor of the ... legislation ..."; "Most State Governors have either come out in favor of the bill or remained silent, calling it: a proper domain of the Congress, not of state governments."

The control sample received a document of comparable length to the experimental treatments which dealt with the relatively neutral political issue of uniform registration law proposals. This document had been successfully pre-tested for equivalent interest with the experimental treatments, and the pre-test had also shown that the document was successful in not affecting TVC, PI or SI.

At the end of the experimental treatment (and each subsequent reinforcement), S was given an opportunity to leave the political situation and turn his attention to a promised, but nonexistent, "social situation." Thus S did not have to remain in the experiment in order to cooperate with the experimenter. This, and the fact that no time constraints were put on S, was designed to reduce the "demand characteristics" of the experimental situation.

TVC, PI and SI were then selectively reinforced in up to four additional documents. TVC was reinforced by discussing the immediacy, likelihood of passing and undemocratic consequences of the bill:

"Congress ... has taken measures to remain in session until the bill is voted on"; "Congress has assured the President that the bill will be put to a vote before the election, so that his program ... will have the benefit of a restricted electorate ..."; PI was reinforced by the inclusion of a second information test, taken and failed by S, and also by excluding S from reported local political activity: "There have been a few abortive protest efforts, but you have not been contacted ..."; "Unlike previous election years, you have received no campaign literature ... nor have you been contacted by ... campaign workers." SI was reinforced by reporting the failure of institutions and groups who might be self-surrogates for S to ameliorate the situation: "Opposition party candidates now also support the bill ..."; "(opposition to the bill) is so splintered and poorly organized that ... there is little chance for effective opposition"; "(third parties) have been (unable) to agree on a suitable candidate ..."; "The Supreme Court ... has chosen to remain silent rather than to assume powers ... it does not possess"; "has recently operated on a highly restrictive interpretation of judicial self-restraint."

Sociology of the Experiment and External Validity. As indicated, there were no time constraints put on S in an effort to minimize extraneous conditions of tension. S tended to complete the experiment in approximately two and one-half hours. S did not have to remain in the political situation, and his projected behavioral responses to the situation were all asked in open-ended questions, so that the attitudinal responses reported below are probably not a function of experimenter-induced set. S was required to devote to the political experiment only that amount of attention, energy and interest he desired. By implication, the degree of participation in the political experiment can be construed as consistent with S's "normal" (that is, nonexperimental, "real world") political participation.

Debriefing revealed high degrees of involvement in the political situation and that S tended to perceive that situation as realistic. Again, these factors operate to increase external validity (that is, the relevance of experimental findings to "real political behavior.")

Subjects were paid American student volunteers from the University of Pennsylvania and Temple University, each receiving six dollars for his participation in the experiment. Access to the student community predisposed us to that subject population, and the desire to have a subject population for whom similarity of salient politicized values might be obtained without extensive sampling predisposed us to restrict participation to American students. The subsequent sample interview studies of alienation in area probability samples of urban communities and selected university campuses which are reported in the chapters which follow strongly suggest the external validity of the findings reported below for American populations.

Findings. The results of this experiment tend to confirm both the validity of the hypotheses and the utility of the process model preferred above. The relationships posited to exist among the variables, and the time sequence in which these are postulated to become operative, both seem to obtain in our data. These findings are discursively presented in this section. All predicted relationships obtain at t-score or chi-square values equivalent to the 0.05 level of significance or better.

Initially, the theory posits that the introduction of stimuli inducing value conflict should result in S's ambivalent evaluation of the political system. We should expect, then, an initial decline from pre-experimental levels of attractiveness of the system to S's in the experimental sample, but not a significant decline which would signal alienation. This is precisely the situation which obtained. The mean decline of system attractiveness for the experimental samples was a fraction of a scale point (on a seven-point scale). The Control group evinced less decline in the attractiveness of the political system, as predicted, and the difference between Experimental and Control groups, again as predicted, does not achieve statistical significance (see Table 4.1).

======================== TABLE 4.1 ========================

CHANGE IN INDIVIDUAL ATTRACTION TO THE POLITICAL SYSTEM
AS A RESULT OF THE INTRODUCTION OF VALUE CONFLICT STIMULI

Group	C[2]	n	*t-score*	*Significance level*
Control	—0.63	12		
			0.94	not significant
Experimental[1]	—0.83	39		

[1] All experimental groups combined.
[2] = mean change from pre-experimental measurement to first post-stimulation measurement.

Interestingly, for our hypothesis that TVC is a major functional drive in the alienation process, even this ambivalent, insignificant decline in systemic attractiveness was associated with a significant increase in TVC in the experimental samples. Control showed an insignificant increase in TVC; the difference between Experimental and Control samples is significant at the 0.05 level (see Table 4.2).

======================== TABLE 4.2 ========================

CHANGE IN TVC AS A RESULT OF THE
INTRODUCTION OF VALUE CONFLICT STIMULI

Group	C[2]	n	*t-score*	*Significance level*
Control	0.46	12		
			1.87	0.05
Experimental[1]	1.51	39		

[1] All experimental groups collapsed.
[2] = mean change from pre-experimental measurement to first post-stimulation measurement.

After at least some ambivalence results in stage 2 of the process, the theory states that an approach-approach conflict is generated when VC is reinforced (stage 3). If this is so, we should expect another significant increase in TVC after R (initial reinforcement). Again, such a significant increase did occur in our experimental samples but not in the Control group (Table 4.3).

TABLE 4.3

INCREASE IN TVC AFTER INITIAL REINFORCEMENT

	Move	X^3	n	t-score	Significance level
	0^1	2.5	12		
Control				1.11	not significant
	1^2	2.9	12		
	0^1	4.1	39		
Exp.[1]				1.77	.05
	1^2	5.9	37^5		

[1] 0 = introduction of stimuli.
[2] 1 = first reinforcement.
[3] X = mean level of TVC on a seven-point scale.
[4] All experimental groups combined.
[5] N is different in move 2 because two subjects elected
to terminate experiment after move 0.

Stage 4 is, perhaps, the crucial stage in the processual theory of political alienation. There, we posit that significant estrangement from the political system will result from the simultaneous existence of TVC, perceived personal inefficacy (PI) and perceived systemic inefficacy of PS (SI).

We tested this hypothesis both statically and dynamically. Statically, if the hypothesis obtains, we should expect: (1) least alienation (that is, highest identification with the political system) in the control sample; (2) a statistically significant difference in the increase of alienation between the Control group and the VC and VC, PI samples; (3) no significant differ-

TABLE 4.4

DIFFERENCE IN ALIENATION AMONG EXPERIMENTAL
GROUPS AFTER FINAL REINFORCEMENT

TABLE 4.4

Group	X^1	n	t-score	Significance level
TVC	3.1	15		
			1.91	0.025
Control	4.6	12		

[1] X = mean level of identification with political system on a seven-point scale.

ence between the VC and the VC, PI samples; and (4) a significant increase in alienation between VC and VC, PI samples, on the one hand, and the VC, PI, SI sample on the other. As reported in Tables 4.4 to 4.8, all of these conditions were satisfied in our data.

TABLE 4.5				
Group	X^1	n	t-score	Significance level
TVC, PI	2.9	12		
			2.37	0.01
Control	4.6	12		

^{1}X = mean level of identification with political system on a seven-point scale.

TABLE 4.6				
Group	X^1	n	t-score	Significance level
TVC	3.1	15		
			0.93	not significant
TVC, PI	2.9	12		

^{1}X = mean level of identification with political system on a seven-point scale.

TABLE 4.7				
Group	X^1	n	t-score	Significance level
TVC	3.1	15		
			2.13	0.025
TVC, PI, SI	1.5	12		

^{1}X = mean level of identification with political system on a seven-point scale.

TABLE 4.8				
Group	X^1	n	t-score	Significance level
TVC, PI	2.9	12		
			1.94	0.025
TVC, PI, SI	1.5	12		

^{1}X = mean level of identification with political system on a seven-point scale.

TABLE 4.9

EXPERIMENTAL CONDITIONS ASSOCIATED WITH CHANGES IN SUBJECT'S IDENTIFICATION WITH THE POLITICAL SYSTEM

Experimental conditions	Cases of Increase in Identification	Cases of Decrease in Identification	Cases of No Change in Identification	Within Cell Variance Accounted for (% of n in Predicted Direction)	Between Cell Variance Accounted for (% of All Decreases Accounted for)
Increase in TVC	7	5	3	33	13
Increase in PI	2	2	1	40	5
Increase in SI	2	4	4	60	10.5
Increase in TVC and PI	3	0	1	0	0
Increase in TVC and SI	2	7	3	58	18
Increase in PI and SI	2	4	2	50	10.5
Increase in TVC, PI and SI	1	16	2	84*	42*

* = The chi-square value of this finding is significant at the 0.001 level or better.

Alternatively the hypothesis can be tested by observing the frequency with which decreases in identification with the political system are associated with postulated changes in TVC, PI, SI and combinations of these. Here the evidence seems particularly striking. Alone, TVC, PI and SI are at best moderately associated with decreases in identification (see Table 4.9 where only 33 percent, 40 percent and 60 percent of the changes in identification are in the predicted direction). The combinations of TVC + PI, TVC + SI or PI + SI correlate no better (Table 4.9). *Under the condition TVC, PI, SI, however, 16 of 19 changes are in the predicted, downward direction; 84 percent of the variance in the cell is accounted for.* These cases constitute 42 percent of all downward change in identification with the political system. Thus, out of seven possible combinations, a single cell—the confluence of TVC, PI and SI—accounts for 42 percent of the between cell variance (Table 4.9).

TVC, PI and SI seems to account rather well, then, for decreases in individual identification with the political system.

But are all such downward changes in system identification to be classified as alienation? If a highly allegiant person becomes slightly less so, is this alienation? If an individual who starts out with low self-identification with the system diminishes his identification still further, is this what we mean by alienation? Or is the core of the alienation concept the movement from positive to negative identification with the polity? These three types of downward change in identification—from more positive to less positive, from positive to negative and from negative to still more negative—seemed to us to be sufficiently different as to be worthy of separate investigation. The data summarized in Table 4.10 bears this out. *The TVC, PI, SI condition accounts for 80 percent of all positive to negative changes in identification.* Apparently, TVC alone, PI alone, SI alone and the various pairwise combinations of these are enough to effect limited downward identification changes from highly positive to less positive self-linkage with the polity. But they are insufficient to drive the alienation process from positive to negative identification with the polity; for that result the combination of TVC, PI and SI is required. After the line between positive and negative identification has been crossed, then the single variables and paired combinations can again account for limited downward shifts from negative to more negative political identification.

Concomitant with political withdrawal, according to the theory, S should manifest both felt-threat and anger (stage 5). Across our data, both TVC and general felt-threat are significantly correlated with alienation (see Table 4.11). As threat arises much more rapidly than anger, and assumes consistently higher levels than does anger, it is suggested again that threat is the major operative drive in early political alienation. Anger, which is often a derivative measure for felt-frustration, has secondary importance in attitudinal withdrawal (Table 4.12).

=============================== TABLE 4.10 ===============================

EXPERIMENTAL CONDITIONS ASSOCIATED WITH THREE TYPES
OF DIMINUTION IN SUBJECT'S IDENTIFICATION WITH
THE POLITICAL SYSTEM

Experimental Condition	Cases in Which Subjects Moved from Positive to Less Positive Identification[1]	Cases in Which Subjects Moved from Positive to Negative Identification[2]	From Negative to More Negative Ident.[3]
Increase in TVC	1	0	4
Increase in PI	1	0	1
Increase in SI	1	1	2
Increase in TVC and PI	0	0	0
Increase in TVC and SI	2	1	4
Increase in PI and SI	2	1	1
Increase in TVC, PI and SI	2	12*	2

[1]A diminution in identification from a score of 7 to 6 or 5 and/or from 6 to 5.
[2]A diminution in identification from a score of 7, 6 or 5 to a score of 3 or 2 to 1.
[3]A diminution in identification from 3 to 2 or 1 and/or from 2 to 1.
* = 80 percent of all positive to negative changes. The chi-square value of this finding is significant at the 0.001 level or better.

The theory further posits that the process whereby withdrawal takes place involves the perceptual differentiation of certain salient political institutions from the political system as a whole (stage 6). The responses of S in the experimental sample show the early mean decline in the attractiveness of the Presidency and Congress to be significantly greater than that of the American system as a whole. No such difference is observable in the Control group as indicated in Table 4.13.

However, by T_r (last completed reinforcement) that difference had gone to zero, indicating the operation of our stage 7, the generalization of alienation to the system. Again, of course, no generalization of alienation was to be expected in the Control sample and none resulted (see Table 4.13).

====== TABLE 4.11 ======

CORRELATION OF TVC AND GENERAL THREAT WITH SUBJECT'S
IDENTIFICATION WITH THE POLITICAL SYSTEM

	Control	*Experimental Samples*	*Significance Level*
TVC	0.06 $n = 49$	−0.59 $n = 220$	0.05
General threat	−0.01 $n = 49$	−0.51 $n = 220$	0.05

====== TABLE 4.12 ======

A COMPARISON OF MEAN LEVELS OF THREAT AND ANGER,
ACROSS TIME, BY EXPERIMENTAL GROUPS

Experi-mental Group	*Mean Increase*						*Mean Level*					
	in anger			*in threat*			*anger*			*threat*		
	T0	T1	Tf	T0	T1	Tf	T0	T1	Tf	T0	T1	Tf
TVC	0.4	0.3	0.8	1.0	0.8	1.3	4.3	4.6	5.2	5.1	5.8	6.2
TVC, PI	0.5	0.5	0.7	1.4	0.8	1.0	4.1	4.5	5.1	4.6	5.3	6.1
TVC, PI, SI	0.7	0.5	0.9	1.8	1.0	2.0	4.7	5.2	6.0	5.1	5.9	6.8
All exp. groups collapsed	0.6	0.4	0.8	1.4	0.8	1.8	4.4	5.7	5.4	4.9	5.6	6.4
Control	0.1	0.0	0.2	0.2	0.1	1.3	3.8	3.8	4.0	4.1	4.1	4.2

[1]T0 = on pre-experimental measurement.
[2]T1 = as measured after introduction of stimuli.
[3]Tf = as measured after final reinforcement of stimuli.

Table 4.14 shows that, as hypothesized, subjects who have salient value conflicts with the political system tend to hold reformist attitudes (here, attraction to reformist participation). This is indicated in the significant difference between the control and TVC samples on support for reformist activity. Also as hypothesized, attraction to reformist activity does not diminish when personal political inefficacy is added to TVC but only when both PI and SI are added.

Finally (stage 8), we anticipated that those scoring above the mean on the pre-experimental "politicization" index would tend to radicalize; that is,

=========== TABLE 4.13 ===========

CHANGING IDENTIFICATION PATTERNS: DIFFERENTIATION
TO GENERALIZATION OF ALIENATION

Experimental Group:

Political Referent	Mean Decline in Identification	'Score of PI-PS*	Decline by Final Reinforcement	'Score of PI-PS*
Presidency	1.84	1.73 (p = 0.05)	0.87	0.87 (p = not significant)
Congress	2.06	2.39 (p = 0.01)	0.63	0.62 (p = not significant)
System as a Whole	1.03	—	0.76	—

*Political Institution minus the Political System.

Control Group:

Political Referent	Mean Decline in Identification	'Score of PI-PS*	Decline by Final Reinforcement	'Score of PI-PS*
Presidency	**	—	**	—
Congress	0.13	t = 0.21 (p = not significant)	0.29	t = 0.38 (p = not significant)
System as a Whole	0.32	—	0.34	—

*Political Institution minus the Political System.
**Increase in the attractiveness of the Presidency.

they would find political groups which they regarded as radical to be at-tractive to them. This was expected because the highly politicized would find the behavior of political withdrawal to be in conflict with the value of participation. As anticipated, the highly politicized in the experimental sample were significantly more likely to radicalize than their less politicized counterparts. This relationship was neither expected nor observed in the Control sample (see Tables 4.15, 4.16 and 4.17).

TABLE 4.14

ATTRACTION TO REFORMIST ACTIVITY
BY EXPERIMENTAL GROUPS

	Control	*TVC*	*TVC, PI*	*TVC, PI, SI*
Control	34[1]			
TVC	[2]$\triangle = 29$ p = 0.05	= 63[1] p = 0.01		
TVC, PI	= 90 p = 0.001	= 61 p = 0.01	124[1] —	
TVC, PI, SI	= 19 p = 0.05	= 10 p = not signifi- cant	= 71 p = 0.01	53[1] —

[1]Gross scale point changes in attractiveness of reformist activity from pre-experiment to final reinforcement.
$\triangle$ = raw difference in gross changes between groups.
[2]p = significance level of $\triangle$.

TABLE 4.15

RAW SCORES OF ATTRACTION TO RADICAL GROUPS
BY EXPERIMENTAL SAMPLES

Sample		Mean Radical Attraction at Final Reinforcement	Radical Attraction Mean Change During the Experiment
Experimental sample, High politication	(= 10)	6.1	3.3
Experimental sample, Low politication	(= 34)	4.2	0.9
Control sample, High politi- cation	(= 6)	3.8	0.7
Control sample, Low politi- cation	(= 9)	3.7	0.5

TABLE 4.16

THE VALUE OF T AND SIGNIFICANCE LEVEL OF COMPARISONS BETWEEN
EXPERIMENTAL SAMPLES ON ATTRACTION TO RADICAL GROUPS
DEFINED AS MEAN FINAL ATTRACTION SCORE

	Experimental High	Experimental Low	Control High	Control Low
Experimental, High politication	—			
Experimental, Low politication	$+ = 2.63$ Significant 0.01	—		
Control, High politication	$+ = 2.87$ Significant 0.005	$+ = 0.49$ n.s.	—	
Control, Low politication	$+ = 2.97$ Significant 0.005	$+ = 0.73$ n.s.	0.21 n.s.	—

TABLE 4.17

THE VALUE OF T AND SIGNIFICANCE LEVEL OF COMPARISONS BETWEEN
EXPERIMENTAL SAMPLES ON ATTRACTION TO RADICAL GROUPS
DEFINED AS MEAN CHANGES IN ATTRACTION SCORE

	Experimental High	Experimental Low	Control High	Control Low
Experimental, High politication	—			
Experimental, Low politication	$+ = 1.83$ Significant at 0.025	—		
Control, High politication	$+ = 1.84$ Significant at 0.025	$+ = 0.88$ n.s.	—	
Control, Low politication	$+ = 2.07$ Significant at 0.025	$+ = 0.63$ n.s.	$+ = 0.36$ n.s.	—

Conclusions

Thus the general process model of political alienation posited above seems confirmed. Subjects moved from allegiance to ambivalence, from ambivalence to threatening value conflicts, from conflicts to reformist attitudes directed toward differentiated institutions of the polity. When that threat-coping reformism failed, subjects perceived personal and then systemic inefficacy and moved, from that combined position of TVC, PI and SI, to the generalized withdrawal mode of alienation. Subjects under those conditions who placed high value on political participation tended to radicalize rather than withdraw. Accordingly, we find the acquisition of politically alienated attitudes to be appropriately represented as a multi-stage process model and conclude that politicized fear and futility (TVC, PI and SI) constitute basic explanatory variables in the process of political alienation.

5

PSYCHO-POLITICAL CORRELATES OF POLITICAL ALIENATION IN FOUR URBAN COMMUNITIES

This chapter represents an effort to test our psychological theory of political alienation in a series of American urban and suburban communities. Specifically, we seek to determine whether or not TVC, PI and SI bear strong and direct relationships to the attitude of political alienation from national, state and local political systems. To the extent that this theory helps to explain alienation from local and state as well as national polities, its utility will obviously be increased.

Moreover, it is by now an old story that what one gains in simplification and control in the laboratory, one loses in relevance to the "real world." In order to determine whether the theory which best accounted for student alienation in the simulation setting could help to explain individual alienation from real political systems, we decided to conduct a series of sample interview surveys. This affords an opportunity to test the multi-method or convergent validity of the theory.

Two substantive problems are addressed in this chapter: (1) the extent to which TVC, PI and SI explain alienation from urban as well as national and state political systems; and (2) the interactions between individual orientations to the different levels of government. These problems derive from gaps in the existing literature.

Despite burgeoning scholarly interest both in urban politics and in political alienation, there have been relatively few systematic efforts to integrate these interests, to explain individual estrangement from urban political systems.[1] Most research has been centered upon estrangement from the national society,[2] polity or culture.[3] Yet, in our era of strife-ridden cities, the need for a theory of urban political alienation seems clear. Alienation is, after all, associated with a great number of attitudes and behaviors which are at least as relevant to urban as to national politics; for example, riot-ing,[1] reformism,[5] nonvoting, protest voting,[6] negative attitudes toward metropolitan area reorganization[7] and school integration.[8] Therefore, in the studies reported below, we give special attention to alienation from urban politics.

It is by no means clear that a theory that works well in explaining indi-vidual orientations to one level of government will also help to explain orientations to a different level. Although Americans, like most of the world's population, are members of multiple political systems—being simul-taneously citizens of national, state and a variety of local governments—recent research has shown that the political orientations and behavior of individual citizens can and do differ markedly among these different levels.[9] We know, too, that orientations to one governmental level tend to have significant impact upon orientations and behavior at other levels.[10] If one finds the national level of government to be most salient, as most Americans appear to do, one is significantly more likely to be more participant in, and more trusting of, the national polity, than one is of state and local political systems.

From these facts, it is clear that a comprehensive understanding of political alienation requires some charting of the various possible inter-actions among individual's orientations to the different levels of government. Such a charting would minimally require answers to the following questions: (1) Do people who regard the nation as the most important political en-tity tend to be alienated from local or state politics? (2) Conversely, does the fact that a given level of government is less salient to an individual mean that he is unlikely to be estranged from that level because he is less likely to pay attention to it? (3) If an individual is alienated from one level of government, is he more likely or less likely to be alienated from other levels?

Our hypotheses are: (1) that alienation, from all levels of government, can be explained similarly—that TVC, PI and SI will bear strong and direct relationships to political alienation from urban, national and state systems; and (2) that the differential salience which an individual accords to the different levels of government will not affect the degree to which TVC, PI and SI relate to political alienation from these levels of govern-ment.

Samples

These hypotheses were tested in four urban community studies in New-ark and Philadelphia. As the reader will recall, our samples are described in Chapters 2 and 3.

Measures and findings

Newark. As has been indicated above, severe problems of access in Newark imposed stringent space restrictions on the alienation-relevant items that could be included in our interview schedule, such that several of our variables had to be tapped via face-valid single-item indicators. This means of measurement, of course, entails relative limitations. The items used in this study, however, have also been used in conjunction with other face-valid indicators of the same variables in other studies (two of which are reported in this chapter) and have achieved high correlations with these items. These correlations suggest that the items employed here have acceptable validity as measures of the variables they purport to tap.[11]

Specifically TVC was measured by the projective item: (W)hen I think about the future of kids in Newark, I get very scared (TVC = expected negatively valued outcomes). PI was tapped as a two-item index: (a) Sometimes politics and government in Newark are too complicated for people like me to understand; and (b) Voting is the only way people like me can ever do anything about what goes on in Newark. This index had an inter-item correlation coefficient significant at 0.005, indicating acceptable internal validity. Our measure of SI was: The politicians and the administrators in Newark don't really care about people like me. This standard item was taken as an indicator of perceived systematic inefficacy because the referents emphasize personnel of the system rather than the respondent and his behavior. Finally, political alienation was observed via the direct question: When I think about the political system in Newark, I feel like an outsider.

The relationship of these three variables to alienation is as predicted. Each of the three variables is significantly related to political alienation ($p = 0.005$), and the confluence of TVC, PI and SI accounts for substantially more of the observed variance in alienation than does TVC alone, PI alone, SI alone or any pairing of these (Tables 5.1 and 5.2).

TABLE 5.1

THE RELATIONSHIPS AMONG POLITICAL ALIENATION,
TVC, PI AND SI

	TVC	*PI*	*SI*
Newark sample as a whole	0.48	0.32	0.54
White sub-sample	0.45	0.32	0.58
Black sub-sample	0.57	0.30	0.35

TABLE 5.2

MULTIPLE CORRELATION COEFFICIENTS SQUARED (R²) OF ALIENATION WITH ALL COMBINATIONS OF TVC, PI AND SI

	TVC	*PI*	*SI*	*TVC, PI*	*TVC, SI*	*PI, SI*	*TVC, PI, SI*
Newark sample as a whole	0.23	0.10	0.29	0.28	0.36	0.35	0.40
White sub-sample	0.21	0.11	0.34	0.28	0.37	0.39	0.42
Black sub-sample	0.32	0.09	0.12	0.34	0.39	0.28	0.40

It will be noted that the confluence of TVC, PI and SI accounts for more than 40 percent of the observed variance in alienation for the Newark sample as a whole, and for both black and white sub-samples.

Although TVC + PI + SI leads to political estrangement from the urban polity both for whites and blacks, the psychological process of alienation is not identical across racial samples. This can be observed in the regression analyses (Table 5.3), where the independent contribution of TVC, PI and SI to alienation is determined by controlling, in turn, for each of the other two independent variables.

TABLE 5.3

STANDARDIZED REGRESSION COEFFICIENTS (BETA WEIGHTS) OF TVC, PI AND SI ON ALIENATION

	Beta Weight of TVC Controlling for PI & SI	*Beta Weight of PI Controlling for TVC & SI*	*Beta Weight of SI Controlling for TVC & PI*
White sub-sample	0.10	0.11	0.46
Black sub-sample	0.42	0.08	0.07

Table 5.3 shows a substantial difference between whites and blacks in the relative importance of the independent variables in producing alienation. While all three of the independent variables are significantly related to alienation in both samples, threat from value conflict contributes most to alienation among black Newarkites whereas the perception of the urban polity as closed to self and self-surrogates contributes most to alienation among whites in Newark. One might hypothesize that this difference is

attributable to the more immediate and pressing nature of threatening value conflicts in the black community, whereas whites find the perceived unresponsiveness of the polity to be more salient.

The preceding studies (the experiment in Chapter 4 and the Newark survey) tend to indicate that threat and inefficacy are significantly associated with political alienation from both national and urban systems. We would be more convinced of this, however, if it were shown to be true in one sample; if the same people's orientations to all of the levels of American government were observed at the same time—so that the process of alienation to each level, and the interactions among these processes, could be observed simultaneously. To be maximally useful, moreover, these observations should be taken on a sample of people among whom we might expect maximum variation in orientations to the different levels of government. Jennings and Niemi have shown that this is likely to occur among high SES, highly educated Americans.[12] Accordingly, our most detailed exploration of the relationships among TVC, PI, SI and alienation from every level of government was accomplished in our sample of upper SES, highly educated, suburban Philadelphians. Again, our hypotheses were that threat, PI and SI would be significantly associated with alienation from every level of government and that the patterns of salience that the individual accords to the different levels of government would not interfere with these relationships.

Measures and findings in suburban communities

Measures. The following measures were employed:

1. *Alienation from national, state and local politics.* A three-item index contained these "agree-disagree" type items:
   (a) When I think about the politics in _____ (Washington, Harrisburg, my town), I feel like an outsider.
   (b) When I think about the government in _____ (Washington, Harrisburg, my town), I don't feel as if it's my government.
   (c) People like me aren't represented in _____ (Washington, Harrisburg, my town).

2. *Perceived inefficacy in national, state and local politics.* A two-item index:
   (a) It is really impossible for one man to make his voice heard in _____ (Washington, Harrisburg, my town).
   (b) Only large groups like big business and labor unions . . . can get what they want in _____ (Washington, Harrisburg, my town).

3. *Perceived system inefficacy at national, state and local levels.* A single-item indicator, asked about each level: "There is at least one group in _____ (Washington, Harrisburg, my town) which seems to speak for my interests.

TABLE 5.4

PRODUCT-MOMENT CORRELATION COEFFICIENTS AND R^2 OF THREAT, INEFFICACY AND ALIENATION FROM MULTIPLE LEVELS OF GOVERNMENT

	Threat	PI	SI	R^2 of Threat PI, SI	Alienation from National Polity	Alienation from State Polity	Alienation from Local Polity
Alienation from national polity	0.50*	0.30*	0.11	0.26	—		
Alienation from state polity	0.42*	0.29*	0.21	0.21	0.64*	—	
Alienation from local polity	0.56*	0.33*	0.39*	0.34	0.49*	0.67*	—

$n = 60$.
*$p = 0.025$.

4. *Threat from perceived inefficacy*[13] *at national, state and local levels.*
A single-item indicator, asked about each level: When I think of how basically helpless I am to affect the decisions in _____ (Washington, Harrisburg, my town), I get scared.

In addition to the threat, inefficacy and alienation measures, two other individual orientations to the different levels of government were tapped: (1) an indicator of the level of government deemed most salient to the respondent; (2) an index which identified the level of government with which respondents were most satisfied.

The survey, conducted in the winter of 1969, met with a disappointing response rate of 30 percent ($n = 60$), which is not atypical for surveys of this type but which is sufficiently low that the findings reported below should be regarded as highly tentative in character.

Our data (Table 5.4) indicates a broad similarity in the process of political alienation from all levels of government in the United States. Threat and inefficacy are rather consistently related to estrangement and the confluence of perceived threat, personal political inefficacy and systemic inefficacy accounts for substantial amounts of the variance in alienation from all levels. These data also suggest that an individual's orientations to one level of government affect his orientations to other levels and that the single best predictor of alienation from any level of government is alienation from the other levels of government. From this, it is clear that some "diffusion of alienation" process does take place, although we cannot infer its directionality from these data.

=== TABLE 5.5 ===

ANALYSIS OF VARIANCE: SALIENCE AND ALIENATION BY LEVEL OF
GOVERNMENT

	Mean National Alienation	*Mean State Alienation*	*Mean Local Alienation*	*F*	*Significance*
Level of government deemed most salient	—	—	—	—	—
National ($n = 7$)	0.86	0.57	0.14	0.67	ns
State ($n = 43$)	0.49	0.42	0.30	0.36	ns
Local ($n = 24$)	0.63	0.67	0.50	0.43	ns

Alienation orientations to different levels of government, then, obviously do have important impacts on each other. But, as hypothesized, interactions between alienation and other political concerns—salience and satisfactions—did not occur in our data. Whether an individual held the nation, state or locality to be the most salient polity made no significant difference in his alienation from any level of government (Table 5.5). Similarly, levels of an individual's satisfaction with a given level of government had no appreciable impact on his alienation either from that level or from any other (Table 5.6).

TABLE 5.6

GOVERNMENTAL SATISFACTION AND ALIENATION BY LEVEL OF GOVERNMENT

Level of Government Satisfaction	*Alienation (Mean Level)*	*t = value*	*Significance*
National satisfaction			
High	1.24		
		−0.38	ns
Low	1.45		
State satisfaction			
High	1.20		
		−0.26	ns
Low	1.30		
Local satisfaction			
High	2.18		
		−0.18	ns
Low	2.00		

Conclusion

In our Newark study, the TVC, PI, SI ——→ Alienation model worked rather well to explain alienation from an urban polity. Here we have tested the model with reference to all three levels of government and, again, substantial amounts of the variance in alienation are accounted for by threat and inefficacy. We also find that alienation tends to diffuse across the different levels of government and that both alienation and its diffusion seem unaffected by an individual's perceived salience and satisfaction patterns. These findings—and their convergence from both laboratory and field study—permit the tentative conclusion that our model describes a basic process of alienation for Americans of widely different backgrounds. In the studies which follow, we explore the validity and utility of the model in two particularly important arenas of alienated politics—the black community and the lower-middle-class white neighborhood.

Although TVC, PI and SI appear to be generally related to political alienation, there are clear and important differences between TVC, PI and SI in the degree of their impact on alienation among different populations. This is especially true as between PI and SI. In Newark, for example, PI was consistently weaker in association with alienation than was SI and even weaker among alienated blacks than among estranged whites. The differential impacts of PI and SI might be explained by the degree to which individuals expect or aspire to influence the polity *personally,* as opposed to having their political impact primarily through collective action. We reason that people who orient to the political system in individualistic or personalized fashion are more likely to become alienated as a result of PI than are individuals who expect to have little personal influence on public affairs. Similarly, individuals who expect their representatives or other reference groups to handle political matters will be more estranged when the system seems immovable. This formulation may, indeed, also account for the racial differences observed above. If whites orient to politics more as individuals than as whites (perhaps because being white is not generally a salient feature of their identity except in communities beset by racial strife) and if black people orient to politics more collectively (in part because of increasing racial consciousness), then among whites we should expect PI to be more predictive of alienation than is SI, but among blacks SI should be more highly associated with political alienation than is PI.

This hypothesis can be explored by comparing the relationships which obtained between PI, SI and political alienation in the black communities of North and West Philadelphia with those occurring in the white community of East Torresdale. Of course, our principal purpose for the conduct of these studies (and of reporting them here) is as a test of the TVC, PI, SI ⟶ Alienation hypothesis.

Black and white Philadelphia communities: Examples of Measures

In the black communities, political alienation from the national polity was studied using a two-item index: (1) When I hear about politics and government in America, I feel that I am a part of it; and (2) I feel that my friends and I are still really represented in our government. TVC: When I think about the way our government is running things, I'm often frightened. PI: There is just about nothing that I can do to get the laws and policies I favor adopted in America. SI: Today, in American politics, leaders seem unable or unwilling to do what I most want to see done.

In East Torresdale, alienation from the urban polity was the referent. All of our measures were multi-item indexes:

Political alienation. I generally think of myself as a part of Philadelphia government and politics.

TVC. City officials and people in this neighborhood have little or no contact with each other (a major issue in the area).

SI. I don't believe my views are being well represented in City Hall, through my elected representatives.

The relationships which were obtained in these studies are summarized in Table 5.7.

=================== TABLE 5.7 ===================

THE RELATIONSHIPS AMONG TVC, PI, SI AND POLITICAL ALIENATION
IN PHILADELPHIA'S BLACK AND WHITE COMMUNITIES

	TVC	*PI*	*SI*
Black community ($n = 69$)	0.33*	0.05	0.44*
White community ($n = 76$)	0.27*	0.41*	0.14

*Relationship significant at 0.01 level of significance.

These findings suggest that black and white Philadelphians do orient to politics differently; that while the general hypothesis that TVC + PI + SI leads to political alienation seems to be true, it is also true that racial differences operate to influence the importance and the pattern that these causal variables assume in the alienation processes.[14] These differences, however, should not be stressed at the expense of the underlying similarity. The basic point we are making is that in representative urban communities politicized fear and futility drive men from their polity.

Social variables, TVC, PI and SI in urban communities

We have seen in Chapter 3 that social background variables do not generally have significant, direct associations with the attitude of political alienation. Here we have shown that TVC, PI and SI do tend to have impact on that attitude in a strong and consistent manner. Accordingly, several questions arise. Do social background variables operate in the alienation process by affecting TVC, PI and SI? Are the poor, the undereducated, the socially isolated more threatened by the American polity? Do they see themselves as less efficacious in the polity? Do they tend to perceive the polity as more unresponsive than do wealthier, better educated, better connected Americans?

These questions were explored in each of the urban communities studied here. The results of these explorations are presented in Table 5.8.

The role of social background variables in the process by which alienated attitudes are acquired, as indicated in this data, is exceedingly limited.

TABLE 5.8

PEARSON PRODUCT-MOMENT CORRELATION COEFFICIENT OF SOCIAL VARIABLES WITH TVC, PI AND SI

*Newark***	TVC	PI	SI
SES	—0.02	0.31	0.06
Social connectedness	0.04	0.16	0.01
General media connectedness	0.08	0.09	0.04
News media connectedness	0.07	0.19	0.00
Political connectedness	0.02	0.07	0.05
Leaderlessness	0.03	0.13	0.13

Black Philadelphia Communities			
SES	0.00	0.14	—0.02

White Philadelphia Communities			
SES	0.04	0.21*	0.04
Social connectedness	0.15	0.21*	0.29*

Philadelphia Suburbs	*National Threat*	*National PI*	*National SI*
Education	—0.11	0.07	0.16
Income	0.24*	0.09	0.16

	State Threat	*State PI*	*State SI*
Education	—0.22*	0.17	0.21*
Income	0.08	0.16	0.14

	Local Threat	*Local PI*	*Local SI*
Education	—0.26*	0.14	0.28*
Income	—0.36*	0.15	0.15

*Significant at 0.05 or better.

**In Newark, due to the large *n*, a coefficient as low as .088 would be statistically significant (0.05). The reader will note, however, that only SES and PI share any appreciable amount of their variance.

In the black community, SES had no significant impact at all on any of the three variables that drive the alienation process; in Philadelphia's "white town," upper-status people see themselves as somewhat more efficacious than lower-status people but these variables share only about 4 percent of their variance in common. The story is similar in Newark and in Philadelphia's suburbs.

There are a few significant associations between social variables and TVC, PI and SI. Low SES people in Newark did feel themselves to be somewhat less efficacious, but upper-status people in the Philadelphia suburbs were both more threatened and higher in SI. Perhaps this is why social status is not more powerfully related to alienation; it cuts both ways such that lower status yields PI but not TVC or SI, and higher status is associated with the latter but not the former.

At any rate, there *are* a few significant associations reported in Table 5.8. SES clearly has some indirect impacts on the adoption of alienated attitudes. But what seems impressive about these data is not that the influence of SES on alienation can be charted through the mediation of TVC, PI and SI it is that that influence is presently quite weak and inconsistent.

There are some class differences here but these relatively few and weak differences should not be allowed to obscure the essential commonality of the alienation process: the operation of politicized fear and futility. Under these conditions, some men and women withdraw from the polity thereby weakening it, while others radicalize and challenge it. In the next chapter, we explore the alienation process among people now more prone to radicalize than to retreat—American college students.

6

ON THE CAUSES AND EXPRESSION
OF POLITICAL ALIENATION AMONG
AMERICAN UNIVERSITY STUDENTS

That the present and recent past have been times of trouble for American universities, that many university students are politically alienated and that the agonies of the academy are, in part, the result of that alienation—these contemporary facts of life need little documentation here. The 1960s witnessed a long string of University disorders and shutdowns, mass arrests of students, administrative and faculty resignations, non-negotiable demands which meant round-the-clock negotiations and the flowering of committee after committee, which seemed to be the inevitable response of campus bureaucrats and revolutionaries alike. In the last couple of years campus disruptions have been fewer and less dramatic, but student political alienation and activism remain higher and more significant than they were before the disorders began.

As with many phenomena that arouse intense scholarly interest, student behavior has been the subject of much recent speculation and of a fast-growing body of research. Accordingly, there are now a great number of putative explanations for student activism.[1] These range from psychiatric speculations ("The kids are sick," "No! The kids are the healthiest members of society."),[2] through considerations of family and peer socialization, to the impact of social class,[3] the size and character of the university,[4] the relationship between the school and the state and even the level of development of the society.[5]

Thus, the importance, timeliness and complexity of understanding student political behavior seem clear. In this chapter we attempt a modest contribution to knowledge about student political behavior by asking and providing some tentative answers to two questions. First, is political alienation among American university students driven by the same psychological processes that characterize American adults? Second, does that alienation and the variables associated with it discriminate between

130

student activists and nonactivists? In answering these questions we shall have reference to some of the family and class variables alluded to above. By treating both with alienation, which has not been well studied among college youth, and with some family, class and school variables which *have* been previously researched, we hope to advance our understanding of student political behavior in a cumulative manner.

Psychological variables in student political alienation

We tested our basic hypothesis, that individuals who perceive themselves to be in fundamental irreconcilable and threatening value conflicts with the political system tend to become alienated from the polity, in samples of American undergraduates at the University of Pennsylvania, Temple University, Drexel Institute of Technology and Atlantic County Community College.* As described in previous chapters, these four schools represent a wide diversity of college types. Accordingly, if the TVC + PI + SI ⟶ Alienation notion describes the process of political alienation on all of these vastly different campuses, the generality of the proposition would seem to be strongly indicated.

Specifically, our samples were: (1) a stratified random sample of Penn undergraduates conducted in the spring of 1969 ($n = 113$); (2) a random sample of the Penn community conducted one year later ($n = 205$); (3) a volunteer sample at Temple, drawn from a large required social science course ($n = 215$); (4) a random sample of freshman business administration majors at Drexel ($n = 109$); and (5) a volunteer sample of first-year students at Atlantic County Community College ($n = 45$).

The measures employed in each of these studies were quite comparable to each other; they were basically similar, too, to those used in our urban community studies. In all of these studies the referent was alienation from the national polity. As the reader is by now familiar with the type of measures employed in our studies, and the specific indexes utilized here are fully reported in the Methods Appendix to this book, we turn directly to a consideration of the findings which emerged in our studies of student political alienation.

Table 6.1 shows the relationships between TVC, PI, SI and political alienation for each of the samples. Each of these variables bears significant, consistent and positive relationship to alienation. The confluence of TVC, PI and SI accounts for substantial proportions of the variance in alienation in each sample (the R^2 ranges from 0.30 in the Drexel sample to 0.72 in the Atlantic County College group, with a mean approximating 0.40).

Across these vastly different places, among students from highly diverse backgrounds and of exceedingly different interests, the process of political

---

*The studies reported here were conducted by David C. Schwartz, Don J. Vogt, Steven Goldberg and Stanley Renshon.

===== TABLE 6.1 =====

PEARSON PRODUCT-MOMENT CORRELATION COEFFICIENTS AND R^2 OF TVC,
PI AND SI WITH POLITICAL ALIENATION IN FIVE STUDIES OF
AMERICAN COLLEGE STUDENTS*

	TVC	*PI*	*SI*
Penn 1969 ($n = 113$)	r = 0.48	r = 0.40	r = 0.57
Penn 1970 ($n = 205$)	0.54	0.45	0.51
Temple ($n = 215$)	0.20	0.27	0.38
Drexel ($n = 109$)	0.23	0.16*	0.44
Atlantic County Community College ($n = 45$)	0.71	0.76	0.67

*All relationships are significant at 0.005 or better, except the starred entry.

alienation seems remarkably similar. The variables that account for the political alienation of college students on the campuses of large, prestigious universities seem also to explain the estrangement of students in smaller, lesser known institutions. Middle-class students who withdraw approval and identification from our political system appear to do so for much the same reasons that their less advantaged counterparts do; arts and social science students do not seem to become alienated in a manner which is very different from that characterizing the disaffected business student.

The idea that students at smaller colleges engage in local disturbances or reform activities as imitative behavior, learned from events at Berkeley or Wisconsin or Columbia, *may* have *some* validity as an identification of the mechanism by which deep-seated dissatisfactions become protest behavior. *But the process by which those attitudes of dissatisfaction are acquired is more general and nonimitative.* In sum, these findings provide considerable support for the hypothesis that the alienation process is one in which people—here, young people—find themselves scared and troubled because the things they value, or hold dear for others, are not similarly cherished by their organized society, and neither they nor others seem capable of changing that fretful situation.

Most of the current scholarly and public interest in student politics has focused less on the processes whereby students adopt attitudes of alienation than on dramatic protest behaviors (which, in our view, are the consequences or expression of alienated attitudes). Thus, to complement the existing literature, it seems useful to study the process of alienation in protest politics to show that dramatic protests are, in fact, the consequences of alienation. We do this in two protest-politics research settings: a campus sit-in and a national anti-war demonstration.

THE ALIENATION-BASIS OF PROTEST POLITICS

In the spring of 1969, the University of Pennsylvania had a week-long sit-in and sleep-in at the administration building. In many respects, the Penn sit-in resembled its more publicized counterparts at other universities. There was a demonstration protesting the taking and use of ghetto land for university-affiliated purposes; then a march; then a large group of students sat-in at the administration building. A variety of splinter groups formed, both within the sit-in and outside on the campus, and emergency meetings were called by new committees of uncertain status. The mimeographed sheet and rumor supplemented the campus newspaper as an information and misinformation source. Some faculty joined the sit-in; many spoke to the large continuous assemblies which the "community of sit-ins" established. Armbands became fashionable. Campus-wide meetings were held, as were emergency gatherings of the trustees. Black and white groups in the sit-in differed. The president of the university was called a puppet as the tone of rhetoric radicalized; the atmosphere of a simultaneous revolutionary cell meeting, town meeting and pajama party prevailed. Kids came and went; some alumni changed their wills. The trustees promised to seek $10 million for ghetto development corporations, and the sit-in ended.

In other respects, the Penn sit-in differed substantially from confrontation politics on other campuses. Buildings were not "occupied," and classes and university business continued. Demands were not stated in non-negotiable terms and in fact negotiation was constant. A self-congratulatory atmosphere concerning the "responsible" behavior of the students was present, and civility, though sometimes clearly forced, was mostly maintained. Little or no violence occurred. The students called it a great learning experience and called for a continuation of the "sit-in spirit."

Participation of Penn students in the sit-in varied from a low of about 200 to a high of approximately 1,200, out of a total student body of 18,031, of which 6.983 were full-time undergraduates. In order to explore some of the underlying reasons for student protest behavior, and particularly to determine whether our alienation notions helped to distinguish between sit-ins and non-sit-ins, we distributed questionnaires to a random sample of sit-ins and to a comparable sample of non-sit-ins employing the following procedures:*

On the fourth night of the sit-in, between 2 A.M. and 6 A.M., we randomly distributed 100 survey instruments among the sit-ins. Of these, 70 completed questionnaires were returned, but 15 of the persons who responded did not psychologically identify themselves with the sit-in (apparently the sit-in attracted at least some spectators out on late dates) and

---

*These studies were conducted by David C. Schwartz, Fred Swan and Stanley Renshon.

another six respondents were not University of Pennsylvania students, so that we reduced our sample of student protestors to 49 in number. We employed a two-stage sampling of non-sit-ins: match-pairing with sit-ins on the dimensions of gender, year in school and major field of study, followed by randomization procedures for selection.

Hypotheses

Our basic hypothesis was that the sit-ins would be more alienated from the American political system and would tend to perceive a greater linkage between that political system and their university than would non-sit-ins. If that were so, then it would seem that the student protest behavior could be interpreted as macro-political action, at least in its meaning for the students, as well as an expression of such dissatisfaction with aspects of the university as we might find.

Secondly, if student protesters felt more inefficacious in the ordinary institutions of American public life but as efficacious or more efficacious as other people in campus political action, then the choice of sitting in at the university instead of, say, the City Council would be explicable.

Finally, we were also interested in determining the degree to which the hypotheses and findings of other researchers would apply to the sit-in at Penn. Would our student activists come from wealthier,[6] political participant,[7] and equalitarian families?[8] Would they see their parents as somewhat hypocritical;[9] be liberal in their political ideology;[10] find their political activities more satisfying and less tensionful than courses and other aspects of college life? More, are these young people reformers or revolutionaries? In sum, we sought to investigate some characteristics of the student protester's backgrounds, college experiences and evaluations of these experiences. We were interested in these factors because, to the extent that we found protest behavior associated not only with political alienation but also with personal experiences and evaluations of college life, we could interpret the roots of student activism as a complex of macro-political, micro-political and personal motivations.

Measures

The hypotheses required an attempt to measure some 15 variables. These variables, and examples of the questionnaire items are as follows:

1. *Threat from value conflict (TVC)*. The index contained two "agree-disagree" type items: (a) Do you feel generally threatened by the policies or structures of American government? (b) When I think about public affairs in America, I feel threatened.

2. *System inefficacy (SI)*. A four-item index included: (a) Do you think that desirable change is possible within our present political system?

(b) Do you think the Nixon administration *can* solve or begin to solve the problems of the black community?

3. *Political inefficacy (PI).* This single-item indicator was comparable to items used in previous studies and was offered here on its face-validity: Do you personally feel that you can be effective in changing (the) policies or structures (of American government) via the ordinary institutions of American government?

4. *Political alienation.* A single-item indicator which was comparable to that used in almost all of our studies and achieved high inter-item correlations in previous studies: When I think about public affairs in America, I feel like an outsider.

5. *Threat from value conflict with the university.* Do you feel generally threatened by the policies or structures of this university?

6. *Political inefficacy in the university.* Do you personally feel that you can be effective in changing (university) policies or structures via the ordinary institutions and processes of this university?

7. *University linkage with political system.* To be interested in school is to be interested in politics because today politics controls education.

8. *Family SES.* A two-item index of income and occupation.

9. *Student political participation.* A three-item index of previous political party activity and planned party activity.

10. *Parental political participation.* A four-item index of parent's previous political party activities.

11. *Comparison of anxiety about personal relationships vs. political relationships.* A two-item index, composed of: (a) Political activity is less tensionful than the classes and school work at college; (b) I get into more unpleasant conflicts with my parents or teachers or friends than I do with political opponents.

12-15. *Direct Single-Item Indicators of Liberalism vs. Conservatism: Perceived hypocrisy of Parents; Satisfaction with Courses vs. Politics; and Stated Belief in Need to Destroy Society* (Revolutionism).

Findings

The findings presented in Table 6.2 tend to support our basic hypothesis that student protest behavior ought to be interpreted, at least in part, as macro-political in its actor-meaning for the students. The sit-ins *are* significantly more alienated from the American polity than are the non-protesters and *do* perceive a greater degree of linkage between the university and the political system significantly than do the non-sit-ins. The student activists are also substantially more participant in the national polity and tend significantly to be more liberal in their ideological orientation to national affairs than their non-activist counterparts.

=========================== TABLE 6.2 ===========================

DIFFERENCES BETWEEN STUDENT PROTESTERS AND NON-SIT-INS ON ALIENATION AND POLITICAL, PARENTAL AND UNIVERSITY-RELEVANT VARIABLES

	Mean for Sit-ins	*Mean for Non-sit-ins*	*Significant Level of Difference in Means*
Political alienation*	1.88	2.39	0.225
TVC*	2.25	2.67	not significant
PI	2.13	2.02	not significant
SI	1.57	1.36	0.025
TVC from university*	2.32	2.76	0.05
PI from university	2.20	1.88	not significant
University-political link*	2.14	2.54	0.01
Family SES	2.39	2.15	not significant
Student political participation*	1.94	2.09	0.0005
Parental political participation*	1.53	1.61	not significant
More anxiety about personal relationships than politic of relationships*	2.32	2.37	not significant
Liberalism*	1.59	2.30	0.01
Perceived hypocrisy of parents	2.06	1.54	0.05
Politics is more satisfying than class work*	2.16	3.06	0.01
Revolutionism: stated belief in need to destroy society*	2.32	2.37	0.025
Student participation in family*	1.45	1.40	not significant

*Scores on starred variables run from high to low, so that lower scores = higher variable magnitude (for example; sit-ins were more alienated than non-sit-ins).

The micro-political sphere, the university, also is shown to have its impact on student activism. The sit-ins feel significantly more threatened by the structures and policies of the university than do non-sit-ins. Lest professors blame politicians for their woes, we should add that the student protesters find their political activities to be more satisfying than college course work whereas non-sit-ins find them about equally satisfying.

In light of widely reported hypotheses on the relationships between personal characteristics and student activism, it is perhaps surprising to note how few personal factors seemed to motivate our Penn sit-ins. Our protesters did not come from either richer or poorer social backgrounds than the non-sit-ins; it made no difference to the predisposition to sit-in whether one's parents were politically active or not; and whether or not one's family was equalitarian, permitting one to join family political discussions, seems not to be a significant factor inuring towards campus activism. Our sit-ins were not any more anxious about personal and campus relationships, compared to political relationships, than were the non-sit-ins. If some students are "fleeing in terror from the dance-hall to the political club," to use a well-known phrase, they were not fleeting to the sit-in for these escapist purposes. The general absence of personal factors which differentiate between student activists and non-protesters in this study does not, of course, show that other personal factors might not be important in the study of student behavior; but it does certainly call into question that school of thought that considers students' political behavior to be merely the result of growing pains, more personal than political in origin.

If students are upset with American politics why do they choose to sit-in on the campus? In the Penn situation, why did they not oppose the land-taking at the administrative level in hearings at the relevant municipal agency, or at City Council which has oversight responsibility for that agency, or in the courts? Why do students play out their macro-political disaffection in the micro-political arena of the university? Part of the answer has already been given in the finding of the perceived link between school and polity. We also hypothesized that the protesters would feel more effective on the campus than they do in the polity and more effective on the campus but less effective outside it than non-sit-ins, but neither of these hypotheses is supported in this data. In fact, however, as this is being written, university-affiliated people, including students, are beginning to use the more ordinary channels of political action to solve some of the problems of the university-community conflict. In this vital sense, the sit-in was a politicizing experience. One of the least understood consequences of campus disorder is the development of attitudes and resources which make further disorders unnecessary.

In this connection, we asked the question "Do you think our present political system must be destroyed and replaced with another one?" Perhaps no aspect of student protest so disturbs non-protesters than this matter of potential revolution. Table 6.2 shows that sit-ins do tend to answer our query more affirmatively than do non-sit-ins *but also that the mean value for both sit-ins inclines toward the negative response* (where 1= agree; 2 = don't know; and 3 = disagree). Given the heavy participation of student activists in political party activities, this finding suggests that this student protest behavior is more appropriately interpreted as reformist rather than revolutionary in orientation.

Conclusion

The student protesters whom we studied are alienated from the polity that is or should be "theirs"; they see the university as linked to that polity and as threatening to them in its own right. They have tried through political party activity to effect change, but they now believe themselves to be ineffective to change either the political system or the university by ordinary means; hence their use of more extraordinary means of protest. That the non-sit-ins do not feel significantly more effective in changing the political and university systems than do the sit-ins, suggests that increases in value conflict or in the perceived link between school and society is likely to increase the number of protesters. If this analysis has broader validity, then, unless these feelings of political fear and futility can be changed, no surcease from campus strife can be predicted; for powerlessness frustrates and absolute powerlessness frustrates absolutely.

A study of anti-war protesters

Although the college campus has been the seedbed and safe haven of student political alienation, the streets have increasingly become its stage. This development is understandable in light of our earlier findings. If students demonstrate at universities in part because they perceive the campus and its issues as part of the polity from which they are alienated, they are at least equally likely to see public places—the streets and monuments that symbolize American politics[11]—as appropriate loci of protest. When, moreover, students learn that confrontation politics works on the campus, that it tends to simplify and get response from the complex decision-making apparatus of the academy, we would predict, from learning theory, that similar protest behaviors would be employed in the more complex, time-consuming and slow responding arena of national politics.

This analysis views the mass protest demonstration, the peaceful but potentially violent confrontation, as the continuation of campus protest by similar means. If this is so, several hypotheses can be derived: First, the protest demonstration by students is basically a response to political alienation. Second, the attitude of alienation which gives rise to protest demonstrations should be explicable precisely as we have already explained both active and passive student alienation—as a function of politicized fear and futility. This hypothesis is a crucial one because if both active and passive alienation have a common base, then those individuals who are politically withdrawn, non-participant and seemingly apathetic constitute a potential mass base for anti-system behavior.[12] In contemporary America, where a substantial portion of the population may be described as basically non-participant, the possible consequences are enormous.

If student participants in off-campus protest politics are similar to our campus sit-ins, we would hypothesize that: (1) at present, they are more appropriately characterized as reformers than as revolutionaries; (2) they are seeking primarily to change laws (or policies) but not basically denying the legitimacy of public officials to make law or that individuals have some moral, political obligations to abide by those laws; (3) in sum, the alienation of student protesters is driven by attitudes concerning the quality of public officials which are more cynical than sinister.

Methods and measures

To investigate these hypotheses, printed survey instruments were adminis-tered to matched samples of college students: one group was composed of participants in the Vietnam Moratorium demonstration in Washington on October 15, 1969, and the other was a control group of students from the same classes at the same schools who elected not to participate in the demonstration. Our description of this important demonstration and our method of studying it is presented in Chapter 2. Here perhaps we need only repeat that the samples were effectively matched on such basic demo-graphic dimensions as age, gender and place of living; the interviews were administered to the participants on the buses going to Washington (that is, after behaviorally committing themselves to participate in the col-lective behavior event but before full-scale engagement in it—so that we are not tapping the motivations of participants after those motivations might be changed by the event); and the observations on the non-demon-strators were made in class, generally on the same day that the participants left for Washington (again, before their learning about the actual event could change their attitudes).

The instrument permitted observations on the relevant variables: aliena-tion, TVC, PI, SI, reformism, revolutionism, political cynicism and belief in political obligation. These variables were operationally defined as follows.

1. *Political alienation.* A three-item index of "agree-disagree" ques-tions, included: The government no longer represents people like me; In American politics power is maintained in secret, shutting out even interested citizens.

2. *Threat-anger from value conflict* (TVC). A two-item index was composed of: When I think about the way our government is running things, I'm often frightened; When I think of the difference between what I want and what the government is doing, I get angry.

3. *Perception of systemic inefficacy* (SI). There is at least one political group that effectively represents my views; There don't seem to be any groups in American politics that can accomplish what I think needs doing.

4. *Perception of personal, political inefficacy* (PI). Three face-valid items were employed as indicators of PI:
   (a) I don't think public officials care much about what people like me think.
   (b) I feel that I can be effective in getting the policies I favor adopted by the government.
   (c) People like me don't have much say in how the government runs things.

The intercorrelation of these items, however, is not sufficiently high to accept them as an index. Therefore, each item was separately employed in the analyses of the data and we report the standard item (c) in the text of this chapter and the others in footnotes.

5. *Political cynicism.* Politicians spend most of their time getting re-elected or re-appointed; Money is the most important factor influencing public policies.

6. *Radical reformism.* A three-item index was indicative of the respondent's support for (even extra-legal) demonstrations and marches as a tactic: It is the direct form of political action (like marches and sit-ins, etc.) that brings results; It will probably be necessary to break some laws in order to bring about . . . the ideals that people like me hold.

7. *Revolutionism or acceptance of violence as a tactic.* A four-item index indicated the respondent's acceptance of violence as a tactic to achieve his political goals: The chance that direct political action . . . may result in violence is a chance we just have to take; It seems as if only violent incidents really produce the kinds of change that I would like to see happen.

8. *Political obligation.* A two-item index tapped the degree to which the respondent believed he should accept authority as legitimate because the authorities were selected democratically: A person should . . . cooperate with democratically elected leaders, even though they were not the ones he personally preferred; Conformity to . . . policies that you don't agree with is wrong, even if they were arrived at democratically.

Findings

If our analysis of student protest behavior is correct, we should expect to find the demonstrators significantly more alienated, more reformist and more cynical about politics than are the non-demonstrators but to find no significant difference between the samples on their acceptance of political obligation or their acceptance of violence. In addition, TVC, PI and SI should be significantly associated with the attitude of political alienation in both samples. All of these hypotheses are confirmed in this data.

Table 6.3 shows the difference of means between the demonstrators and nondemonstrators on alienation, reformism, political cynicism, acceptance of political obligation and revolutionism or acceptance of violence as a tactic. As posited, the demonstrators are significantly more alienated, reformist and cynical than the nondemonstrators but exhibit no significant difference from the nondemonstrators on political obligation or revolutionism. Indeed, the demonstrators are insignificantly higher in political obligation and lower in revolutionism than the passively alienated nondemonstrators.

TABLE 6.3

A COMPARISON OF DEMONSTRATORS AND NONDEMONSTRATORS ON BASIC POLITICAL ORIENTATIONS

	Mean *Demonstrators* *(n = 50)*	*Nondemonstrators* *(n = 57)*	*t-score*	*Significance*
Alienation (high to low)	1.82	2.57	−7.12	0.001
Reformism (high to low)	2.21	2.97	−4.08	0.001
Cynicism (high to low)	2.02	2.38	−2.95	0.01
Political obligation (high to low)	2.31	2.33	−0.24	not significant
Revolutionism (high to low)	2.66	2.65	0.15	not significant

It should be noted, however, that both political alienation and reformism are significantly associated with revolutionary attitudes (Table 6.4); here, as elsewhere, there is much evidence that reformers can radicalize, and that the passively alienated are potential recruits for violent movements.

TABLE 6.4

CORRELATION OF THE RELATIONSHIPS OF POLITICAL ALIENATION AND REFORMISM WITH REVOLUTIONISM IN SAMPLES OF DEMONSTRATORS AND NONDEMONSTRATORS

	Demonstrators *(n = 50)*	*Nondemonstrators* *(n = 57)*
Political alienation	0.32	0.47
Reformism	0.33	0.33

All relationships significant at 0.05 or better.

To test our hyopthesis that TVC, PI and SI are significantly associated with both passive and active alienation, a correlational analysis was performed within each sample. The results of this analysis are presented in Table 6.5.

=== TABLE 6.5 ===

THE RELATIONSHIP OF TVC, PI, SI WITH POLITICAL ALIENATION IN DEMONSTRATORS AND NONDEMONSTRATOR SAMPLES

	Demonstrators *(n = 50)*	*Nondemonstrators* *(n = 57)*
TVC	0.35*	0.64*
PI$_3$[15]	0.40*	0.50*
SI	0.02	0.32*

*Significant at .05 or better.

As predicted, these variables tend to be significantly associated with the attitudes of political alienation in both samples, indicating basic similarity in the psychological process of both passive and active alienation. There is, however, one interesting exception: the perception of systemic inefficacy (SI) is essentially unrelated to political alienation among the demonstrators. In light of the recurrent, regular association of SI with political alienation shown in our earlier studies and exhibited here in the nondemonstrator sample, this aberrant finding is surprising. Might it be that SI is generally important in producing alienation but dysfunctional to those individuals who are determined to play out their alienation in active protest behavior? After all, if the demonstrators really believed that the system was unmovable, why should they bother to demonstrate? If the demonstrators perceived that the groups involved in the demonstration did not really represent their views or if they saw those groups as unlikely to achieve anything, why should they participate with those groups in the protest? The perception of systemic inefficacy (SI) might have helped originally to bring about the attitude of alienation but might have been repressed or reversed in order to rationalize active protest behavior. This topic, the processes whereby different political behaviors issue out of alienation, is the subject of the next section.

Here we conclude that, in general, TVC + PI + SI does lead to political alienation, to active as well as passive alienation in student populations.

Social variables and TVC, PI and SI in student populations

We have seen that, among urban adults, social background variables have quite weak and indirect impacts on political alienation and on TVC, PI and SI. In Chapter 3, we observed that social background factors have weak association with political alienation among college students, and here we have found TVC, PI and SI to be strongly and consistently related to student political alienation. Accordingly, we are led to inquire about the interrelationships between social variables and TVC, PI and SI among students. Data were generated on these interrelationships at Penn, Drexel, at the sit-in and the anti-war demonstration. (Table 6.6).

=========== TABLE 6.6 ===========

THE RELATIONSHIP BETWEEN SOCIAL BACKGROUND VARIABLES AND TVC, PI AND SI IN STUDENT POPULATIONS

	TVC	*PI*	*SI*
Penn ($n = 205$)			
Father's occupation	−0.20*	−0.13*	−0.15*
Income	0.05	0.07	0.09
Perceived class	0.01	−0.03	0.05
Penn Sit-In			
Sit-ins ($n = 50$) SES	0.28*	−0.15	−0.27*
Non sit-ins ($n = 50$) SES	0.10	0.00	0.15

*Significant at 0.05 or better

Vietnam Moratorium			
Demonstrators ($n = 50$) SES	−0.31*	−0.03	0.15
Nondemonstrators ($n = 57$)	−0.06	−0.22*	−0.05
Drexel ($n = 109$) SES	−0.05	−0.08	−0.00
Political connectedness	0.23*	−0.08	−0.03
Campus political connectedness	−0.07	−0.17*	−0.01
Student political participation	−0.15	−0.26*	−0.15
Campus political participation	−0.12	−0.15	−0.21*
Siblings	−0.24*	0.09	0.06
Neighborhood type (that is, urban, suburban, rural)	−0.09	0.07	0.05
Mobility	−0.02	−0.10	−0.12
Parental political activism	0.08	−0.20*	0.14

* = Significant at 0.05 or better

The relationships exhibited in Table 6.6 suggest again that social class is a weak and inconsistent predictor not only of alienation but of the psychological evaluations of the polity which are basic correlates of alienation.

At Drexel, SES had no impacts at all on TVC, PI or SI; at Penn income and perceived class had no impacts, but the father's occupational status did have some influence (Low status $\longrightarrow$ high threat, high PI). In the Penn sit-in, social status was more linked to TVC, PI and SI among the demonstrators than the nondemonstrators but this was not the case in the anti-war demonstration. Moreover, low status was associated with low SI in the Penn sit-in and with low PI among the nondemonstrators in the Vietnam Moratorium study. Mostly, SES bears nonsignificant association with TVC, PI and SI in these data.

At Drexel we investigated a broader range of social background, not merely SES, variables. There, the students who were politically connected tended to be more threatened by value conflicts with the polity than were students who had not joined macro-political organizations indicating, as hypothesized, that TVC acts as a "politicizer." Drexel students who remained unconnected to the polity, did tend to regard themselves as more inefficacious in that polity and students from politically active families also tended to perceive themselves to be more effective in politics. Finally, we found that "only children" and children with few siblings tend to higher TVC than those from larger families, suggesting the need for more refined, detailed research into the relationship of family dynamics to political socialization and political alienation.

Thus, there are *some* statistically significant relationships between background factors and political evaluations in our data, but the fact remains that these relationships are quite weak. In no case do social background factors have even 10 percent of their variance in common with the political evaluations which inure toward alienation. Although more intensive examination of family, peer and school socialization processes is obviously called for, we conclude that the broad outline of the relationship between social factors and political attitudes which lead to alienation is clear: alienation and its psychological preconditions (TVC, PI and SI) bear generally weak and indirect relationships to social background variables.

7

POLITICAL ALIENATION
AMONG POLITICAL SCIENTISTS
AND SOCIOLOGISTS

Our interest in student alienation led us to be interested in faculty alienation, for professors have been described as important socialization agents
in producing student alienation and protest behaviors.[1] We hypothesized
that the TVC, PI, SI ⟶ Alienation formulation would be confirmed among professors as among students.

To explore the basis of professorial alienation, a national survey of
academic sociologists and political scientists was conducted in the spring
of 1969.* Social scientists were selected because of their presumed greater
alienation as compared to academics in general.[2] The comparison between
professional students of the polity and scholars of the broader social system
seems inherently interesting. Recent studies have indicated greater dissent
from U.S. foreign policies among sociologists than among political scientists.[3] Does this policy-reformism manifest itself in great alienation? Then,
too, the dominant paradigms in the two disciplines differ. Does the emphasis on social stratification produce more political disaffection among
sociologists than characterizes political scientists with their more pluralist
paradigm?

Sample and measures

From our description of this study in previous chapters, it will be recalled
that questionnaires were mailed to, and self-administered by, a random
sample of academic political scientists and sociologists whose names were
taken from the current biographical directories of the American Sociological and American Political Science Associations. Of the nearly 5,000 full-
time, academically affiliated sociologists and almost 4,000 such political

---

*A study conducted by David S. Schwartz and Conrad Winn.

scientists, 100 individuals from each directory[1] were chosen at random. The response rate was 59 percent for sociologists and 49 percent for political scientists, so that the total sample size for this study was 108. Of these, 35 persons resided in the northeast, 30 in the midwest, 29 in the far west and 14 in the south, which approximately paralleled the geographic distribution of the two populations.

The questionnaire was a three-page, 59-item instrument which permitted observations on a wide range of variables including: TVC, PI and SI and political alienation; ideology; and a variety of orientations to political, social and scholarly issues. The operational definitions of these variables are presented in the discussion of each group of variables presented below.

Psychological correlates of political alienation

As in the other studies in this section, political alienation and its putative psychological correlates, TVC, PI and SI, were measured as indices composed of "agree-disagree" type items. Alienation was a two-item index: (1) I usually identify myself closely with American politics and government; (2) When I hear about politics in America, I feel a part of it.

TVC was operationalized as a three-item measure, with significant internal validity (intercorrelation), comprised of: (1) When I think of the difference between what I want for the world and what American politics are doing in the world, I often feel scared; (2) Unlike some of the gloom and doom prophets, I don't feel afraid about the future of American politics; (3) The basic things I value for people are not generally shared in American public life (and this is frightening).

Political inefficacy was tapped by these two items: (1) I feel that I can be effective in getting the policies and laws I favor adopted in American politics; (2) I probably could never have any effective influence on public policy.

Our SI items, designed to measure the degree to which the individual perceived the existence of a self-surrogate in the polity, did not significantly intercorrelate, so we used the following seemingly face-valid indicator: There is at least one group in America that effectively represents my views.

Bivariate correlation and multiple regression analyses were performed on these data (Table 7.1). For the sample as a whole, the confluence of TVC, PI and SI accounts for 38 percent of the variance in political alienation—an amount quite similar to the degree of explanatory power observed in our studies of urban alienation and of university students.

The pattern of similarities and differences between sociologists and political scientists which emerges in Table 7.1 appears consistently in our data. These academic social scientists do follow some of the same paths to political alienation but, given the great similarities in role and lifestyle, the differences between them seem especially significant.

TABLE 7.1

PEARSON PRODUCT - MOMENT CORRELATION COEFFICIENTS AND MULTIPLE
REGRESSION (R^2) OF TVC, PI AND SI WITH POLITICAL
ALIENATION AMONG ACADEMIC SOCIAL SCIENTISTS

		TVC	PI	SI	R^2 of TVC PI, SI with Alienation
Sample as a whole	$n = 108$	0.51[1]	0.44[1]	0.24[1]	0.38
Sociologists	$n = 59$	0.26[2]	0.26[2]	0.24[2]	0.21
Political scientists	$n = 49$	0.35[1]	0.20[2]	0.03[3]	0.18

In Table 7.1, for example, we observe that political alienation seems to be driven far more by the existence of threatening value conflict among political scientists than among sociologists. Accordingly, we might expect political scientists to differ appreciably from sociologists in the associational patterns between political values and political alienation. Our analyses bear this out.

Political values and political alienation

In the study of American politics, region[5] and party identification[6] have been traditionally stressed as major determinants or indicators of political values, while the importance of ideological stance[7] has been relatively de-emphasized. However, if our previous analysis of the changing character of American political attitudes is correct, we would expect region and party to have relatively little direct impact on alienation today. Further, it now seems reasonable to expect that the increasingly ideological character of our politics would be revealed in a significant relationship between a person's self-ranked position on the ideological spectrum and the degree to which he is alienated. These impressions seem to be supported in our data.

Here, ideology was measured in two ways: (1) a seven-point "semantic differential" scale from right to left; and (2) a qualitative description in which the respondent associated himself with "conservatism," "liberalism," "socialism," etc.

Political scientists were far more ideologically consistent than sociologists; the correlation coefficients on these two items were 0.78 for the political scientists and 0.38 for the sociologists. Accordingly, it seemed more useful to keep these items separate in our analyses than to combine them in an index.

In this study, ideological stance does bear substantial relationship to political alienation. For the whole sample, the semantic differential measure correlates with alienation at 0.38, and the coefficient between the qualitative indicator of ideology and alienation was 0.26. For political scientists the respective correlation coefficients are 0.49 and 0.48, while sociologists show a 0.28 intercorrelation between the semantic differential measure of ideology and alienation, and an insignificant 0.04 for the qualitative indicator.

As hypothesized, neither party nor region accounts for political alienation among these academics (Tables 7.2 and 7.3).

TABLE 7.2

REGION AND POLITICAL ALIENATION AMONG ACADEMIC SOCIAL SCIENTISTS

	Mean Alienation	*SD*	*Significance Level*
Northeast	1.79	0.30	not significant
Midwest	1.88	0.22	not significant
South	1.75	0.38	not significant
Far west	1.69	0.25	not significant

$R = 1.38.$

TABLE 7.3

PARTY IDENTIFICATION AND POLITICAL ALIENATION AMONG ACADEMIC SOCIAL SCIENTISTS

	Republican	*Democrat*	*Independent*
Mean Alienation Score	1.83	1.73	1.84

$F = 1.13$; not significant.

In this study, opposition to the Vietnam War was more strongly associated with alienation among sociologists than among political scientists, by 0.41 to 0.28. The relationship between the intellectual basis for opposition to the war and alienation differed still more sharply across the disciplines. In both groups, people who disagreed with U.S. Vietnam policy tended to do so on ideological or moral grounds, but sociologists in this category were not significantly more alienated than those who opposed the war on pragmatic bases (zero correlation), whereas political scientists who opposed the war on ideological or moral grounds were significantly more likely to be alienated (0.27, significant at 0.05).

Another ideologically relevant difference between political scientists and sociologists has to do with ethnocentrism. We asked our respondents to agree or disagree with the statement "One trouble with Americans is that they are just not patriotic enough." This indicator bore a 0.48 intercorrelation with ideology among political scientists but was not significantly related to ideology among sociologists. As might be expected, political scientists who disagreed with this statement tended to be alienated (0.37), but sociologists were not (0.18, statistically insignificant).

Ideology, personal values and political alienation

Among political scientists, we found a rather tightly intercorrelated network of ideology, religiosity and communications patterns. Political scientists who ranked themselves on the left of the American political spectrum, tended also to be unreligious (0.47) and to select most of their friends from among university staff or other intellectuals (0.51). These latter variables significantly intercorrelated with political alienation (0.31; 0.38). None of these relationships obtained among sociologists.

Among sociologists, however, scholarly values tended to intercorrelate with ideology. Sociologists who believe that "much current sociological theory is rooted in conservative values" and that "academics ought not to withdraw from the public policy dialogue" tend significantly to be on the left of the ideological spectrum (0.21; 0.40) and to be politically alienated (0.34; 0.42). None of these relationships is discernible among political scientists.

Perhaps the most important difference in the impact and functioning of ideology among these two sets of scholars has to do with the interrelationship between ideology and TVC, PI and SI. Ideology and TVC, PI, SI are significantly associated with alienation. If ideology and TVC, PI, SI are themselves highly intercorrelated, then, considering both sets of factors probably adds little increment in explanatory power; if they are essentially unrelated, then we can account for substantially more of the alienation because TVC, PI, SI and ideology function independently to explain alienation. Table 7.4 shows the relationship between ideological stance, measured on the semantic differential, and TVC, PI and SI. It will be observed that these two sets of factors share very little of their variance. Hence, we infer that TVC, PI, SI and ideology function essentially in an independent more than in an interactive manner to produce alienation. It is interesting to note again, however, the marked contrast between the two disciplines.

TABLE 7.4

THE RELATIONSHIP OF IDEOLOGY TO TVC, PI AND SI
AMONG ACADEMIC SOCIAL SCIENTISTS

	TVC	*PI*	*SI*
Sample as a whole	r = 0.25*	0.12	0.11
Political scientists	r = 0.18	0.18	0.08
Sociologists	r = 0.33*	0.05	0.13

*Significant at 0.005 or better.

Conclusion

Fear and futility, then, seem to explain substantial amounts of American political alienation. In cities and suburbs, on college campuses, among whites as well as blacks, amidst protesters and their professors, whether we consider alienation from the national, state or city political system—the process by which Americans come to withdraw their sense of self-identification and belongingness from the polity appears similar. TVC + PI + SI ⟶ Alienation.

It would appear, too, that this alienation is waxing both in degree and spread. If ever political disaffection in America was isolated in social classes or in small numbers of manifest misfits who could not adjust to our broad social and cultural arrangements, that time is no more.

What can be expected out of this alienation? What are the consequences when men and women—frightened and futile—take their identification from each other by withdrawing it from their organized society? These questions are the subject of the next section of this book.

IV

On the Consequences of
Political Alienation

8

THE CONSEQUENCES OF ALIENATION: A THEORY OF ALIENATED POLITICAL BEHAVIOR

Thus far, we have been trying to explain why and how people adopt the attitude of alienation, finding the principal causes in other attitudes and psychological elements. Here we seek to move beyond attitudes to behavior; to show *that* the attitude of alienation is a basic predictor of important political behaviors and to show *how* the attitude of alienation, in confluence with other variables, predicts to such behaviors. The studies reported in this section of the book are devoted to these tasks. This introductory chapter states a theory of individual political behavior which the studies below were designed to test and to apply.

The fact that an attitude is found to be significantly associated with a given behavior constitutes only the beginning of an explanation of that behavior. To be intellectually satisfying, a theory of individual political behavior should address itself to at least four additional problems in the linkage between political attitudes and behavior. First, since individuals may hold a given attitude toward the polity and yet engage in virtually no overt political behavior, we want to know the conditions under which the attitude is likely to be acted upon. Second, because individuals may behave in politics quite differently from what their attitudes would lead us to expect, we need to know the conditions under which behaviors are likely to be consonant with or different from expressed attitudes. Third, a theory of individual political behavior would have to account for the phenomenon in which different people hold a given attitude in common but behave very differently toward the attitude object. Alienation, for example, is associated both with very active forms of politics like revolution and with what appears to be highly passive politics like nonvoting and general nonparticipation. *Finally, and most importantly, a theory of individual political behavior should also explain how attitudes function to "produce" behavior: that is, it should model the attitude-to-behavior process.*

153

Recent theory and research suggests that these problems might be re-solved and our explanation of political behavior thereby substantially im-proved if, in addition to conventional attitude research, we concentrated on the behavioral orientations (that is, attitudes toward specific behaviors and classes of behavior) that are linked to attitudes in the individual's psychic set. It is argued that attitudes toward behavior, including the disposition to act on one's attitudes and the direction such behavior would take, are much more likely to explain political behavior than are attitudinal prefer-ences alone. If we know, for example, not only that an individual has a posi-tive attitude toward X but that he regards Y as the appropriate means of seeking X (or otherwise behaving toward X), we are significantly aided in predicting his subsequent behavior because we now know which situational variables are likely to affect his behavior—namely, those involving behavior Y. If the individual is then confronted with a concrete situation involving X, we would predict that his behavior will vary with the degree to which he can act in Y manner. We would hypothesize also that, as between two or more situations in which he can express attitude X, he will tend to act in those situations where Y behavior seems most appropriate or, at least, where Y can be adopted in the concrete situation. Thus, to choose a simple example, if Mr. Jones has a positive attitude toward reform of the electoral college and his behavioral orientation is toward personal, face-to-face politics (rather than impersonal activities), we might predict that he is more likely to attend meetings or see his congressman about it than to write him a letter or sign a petition.

It would appear that the four problems in linking attitudes to behavior which were discussed above *are* ameliorated by identifying the behavioral orientation which an individual associates with his attitudes. First, it be-comes easier to solve the problem of discovering the conditions under which some overt behavior, relevant to a given attitude, is to be expected. We would predict that overt behavior will be exhibited in situations involving the attitude to the extent that the situation is perceived to permit a pre-ferred behavior to be adopted. For example, we would not expect overt behavior to take place in situations where individuals who desire to seek specific social changes *by group action* are confronted by some apparent injustice *when they are alone*.

Similarly, the probability that a man will behave inconsistently with his expressed attitudes should also vary with the degree to which his preferred behavior can be adopted in the concrete situation. An example of this would be the individual who has a positive attitude toward racial integra-tion but who participates in discriminatory social organizations because his behavioral orientation is toward reform rather than toward withdrawal. Also, the behavior of two people who hold an attitude in common but who behave very differently toward the attitude object is easily explicable if the two men have different behavioral orientations. Finally, the notion of behavioral orientations helps to explain the attitude-to-behavior linkage by operating as a crucial intervening variable. The individual's attitude of alienation, in confluence with personality factors, predicts to the basic behavioral orientations he is likely to adopt. The orientation, in turn, is then activated or aroused by media, group and situational variables to "produce" behavior.

The behavioral orientation, then, is a motivational element. It is an instrument for the achievement of basic values (of which attitudes are an expression). Together, attitudes toward political objects and attitudes toward political behavior (behavioral orientations) constitute political predispositions. When the predisposed individual is aroused by specific situational stimuli, we can say that the predisposition is activated into behavior. Concrete political behaviors, then, may be explained as responses to stimuli

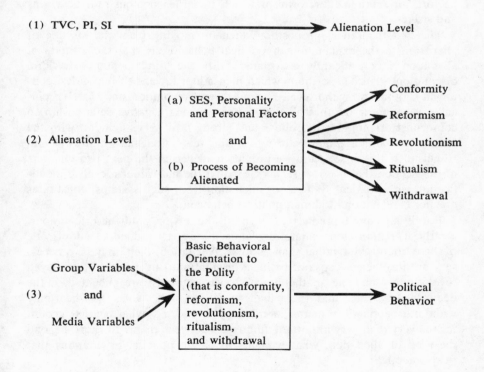

(1) TVC, PI, SI ⟶ Alienation Level

(2) Alienation Level

(a) SES, Personality and Personal Factors

and

(b) Process of Becoming Alienated

→ Conformity
→ Reformism
→ Revolutionism
→ Ritualism
→ Withdrawal

(3) Group Variables and Media Variables

*

Basic Behavioral Orientation to the Polity (that is conformity, reformism, revolutionism, ritualism, and withdrawal)

⟶ Political Behavior

*Arouse and channel

FIGURE 8.1

from the political system which activate the individual's predispositions into behavior.

Schematically, one simple version of this model can be represented as shown in Figure 8.1.

What we are asserting, then, is not merely that alienation is correlated with concrete behaviors, however interesting these behaviors may be, but that alienation predicts powerfully to the fundamental behavioral orientations that men adopt toward the polity; orientations like reformism, revolutionism, conformity, ritualism and retreatism which underly the concrete political behaviors in which men engage. We are aiming, then, at a level of explanation more general than that of the recent research on alienation. We regard it as more theoretically useful to know, for example, not merely that alienation is significantly involved in a sit-in or a demonstration or a political strike but also that alienation helps account for the basic behavioral orientation of reformism which underlies demonstrations, sit-ins and strikes.

The first theoretical proposition, then, in moving from the attitude of alienation to the explanation of political behavior, is that the attitude of alienation is significantly associated with the fundamental behavioral orientations or predispositions which men adopt toward their polities: conformity, ritualism, withdrawal, reformism and revolutionism. More specifically we hypothesize that alienation bears strong negative relationship to conformist orientations to politics and strong positive association with the change-relevant orientations of reformism, revolutionism, withdrawal and ritualism. If this is so, (and we provide evidence in the next two chapters of this section that it is), it seems clear that the individual's level of identification with political systems, or alienation from such systems, constitutes a major explanation of human political behavior.

But if alienation predicts to each of the major political orientations, clearly alienation alone cannot explain why a given individual adopts one of these orientations rather than another. Alienation, then, may be a necessary but insufficient cause of political orientation. But if both the wildeyed revolutionary and the apathetic, withdrawn, retreatist are alienated, if the dedicated reformer and the ritualistic citizen, who votes half-heartedly without expecting it to matter, are equally disaffected, what factors account for the very real, very important differences between them? In short, beyond the level of alienation, what explains the basic political orientations that people adopt?

Initially, the process by which an individual becomes alienated influences the behavioral orientations which issue from his alienation. Thus, alienation is not a Markovian process, in which only the present state of the system influences the next state; how one arrives at a given level of alienation also has its impact. We hypothesize, for example, that individuals who become alienated as part of a group will differ significantly in the behavioral orientations they adopt from people who become alienated "on their own." Evidence supporting this proposition is provided in the next chapter.

Second, the variables that together produce alienation—TVC, PI and SI—also have independent effects on the selection of basic orientations to the polity. For example, the logic of our model of alienation has it that TVC is a politicizing agent that leads to reformism when PI and SI are absent, and to alienated attitudes when PI and SI are present. In individuals who are not yet alienated, TVC alone, PI alone and SI alone do affect reformism (and the other basic political action orientations), but, among the alienated, apparently the summative process of becoming alienated reduces the independent impact of TVC, PI and SI. Here, again, the process of alienation influences the selection of a basic orientation to politics. Contrast, for example, Mr. Jones who is characterized by a highly threatening politicized value conflict and then comes to regard himself and the polity as inefficacious with Mr. Smith who acquires the perceptions of PI and SI first and only then becomes aware of a threatening political value conflict. Mr. Jones is at first likely to adopt a reformist orientation, seeking to reduce the TVC, but later to find that the added PI and SI, which move him in the direction of alienated attitudes, also move him, at least in the short run, toward a less active mode of political orientation (perhaps withdrawal or ritualistic reformism). Mr. Smith, *ceteris paribus,* would probably have first adopted a fairly conventional or passive orientation to politics because he perceived himself to be inefficacious and the polity immovable and because, in the absence of TVC, he felt nothing to goad him to political activity. For him, the addition of TVC may well destabilize this orientation and make him at least potentially available for more active alienated behavior.

What else accounts for the differences in fundamental political predispositions? The basic political orientations which we are seeking to explain are, of course, the political counterparts of what Merton calls "individual adaptions to anomie" or "forms of deviant behavior." Accordingly, after we have considered the level and process of alienation as predictors to these orientations, it seems most useful to look for additional explanatory power where Merton suggests it is to be found—in the social structure which creates certain strains toward these orientations and in those personality structures most likely to be influenced by those strains.

The burden of the evidence in our research indicates that social stratification variables tend to have only sharply limited and generally indirect impact on the attitude of political alienation and on the psychological variables that predispose toward alienation. Today, at least, the acquisition of the attitude of alienation is not very importantly affected by social class determinants. But, as we indicated in our discussions of confrontation politics, there is an enormous difference between the acquisition or learning of an attitude and the learning of standards that govern its outplay. Upper-

and upper-middle-class individuals are likely to play out their alienation in active reformist or even revolutionary behavior because they have the resources and the relative economic and psychological invulnerability to do so, and because they have generally internalized norms of citizen duty and participation which make activism an appropriate option. On the other hand, nonparticipation, passive resistance and withdrawal are the classical responses to alienation (and oppression) of the poor, the weak, the less educated. Men *are* more likely to suffer evils, while evils are sufferable, then to right them, as the founding fathers said, but, clearly, some men are more disposed to do so than are others, and the fact is that the poor always have not only more evils to suffer but less physical and psychological resources to right the insufferable ones. As we will show in the next two chapters, SES is an important variable intervening between alienation and the selection of a basic behavioral orientation to politics.

The personality or psychological factors which we hypothesize would predict to the adoption of a given political orientation flow from the foregoing analysis. Clearly a comprehensive consideration of the relationships between personality and political orientations lies beyond the purview of this book. Therefore, we consider here only a few personal factors which seem rather directly related to the individual's resources and readiness to engage in activist rather than passive behaviors.

Practically all descriptions of people engaged in active politics stress the sheer physical energy exhibited by participants and required by the political process. Accordingly, we hypothesize that, given alienation, people who perceive themselves to be high in energy level will adopt active political orientations, while low-energy types would select more passive responses to their alienation. Energy level would appear to be a crucial resource predicting to the behavioral orientations men are willing (and able) to adopt.

A second personal factor that we hypothesize will predict to behavioral orientations is the ability to be comfortable with one's own anger. The value conflicts which help to produce alienation can, of course, be enraging. In a polity where the prevailing myth is one of individual participation, individual efficacy and governmental responsiveness, the perceptions of PI and SI are likely to produce frustration-driven anger. Alienation is typically associated, then, with anger, and anger should predict to active forms of alienated behavior. But Americans, at least in certain social sectors, are taught to repress their anger, to internalize it, hide it, channel it, to be wary of it. Anger causes individuals who have learned these reactions to their own anger to be uncomfortable, even frightened. We hypothesize that people who are frightened by their own anger, tend to be more passive in their politics than are people who are more comfortable with political rage.

Still another set of personal factors that should help to explain the basic political orientations which an individual adopts is his sense of invulnerability to reprisals. People who feel that their economic or social position is so well established that it will not be endangered by likely repercussions from political conflict are, we think, more likely to adopt more active behavioral orientations. To test this, we included measures of perceived economic invulnerability and fear of government reprisals in our studies.

The last psychological factors included in our studies are "need for conformity" and "desire for reintegration with the polity." We expect passive orientations to be adopted by alienated people who also are characterized by high levels of need for conformity or desire for reintegration with the polity.

In essence, we are saying that the nonalienated individual tends to regard the political system as functional for, or instrumental to, his basic values and, therefore, tends to prefer political behaviors that are valued in or at least accepted by the norms of that political system. Thus, there is some tendency for nonalienated people to conform (or to adopt reformist or other behavior orientations because of the SES and personality factors identified above).[1] However, when an individual perceives the political system as inconsistent with his fundamental politicized values and incapable of being made consistent with those values, he becomes alienated from the polity, withdrawing his self-identification from it. For the alienated man, the reason or rationale for conforming, the link between his values and conformist behavior, is attenuated or weakened and he is likely to select a new nonconformist behavior mode.

Political alienation is typically associated with basic behavioral orientations to politics other than conformity; alienated people are far less likely to be conformists than are the nonalienated. The specific political behavior orientation which a given alienated person is likely to select is dependent upon his social status, his personality and his political attitudes. Alienated people who are upper-class, energetic and secure of their psychological, economic and political well-being tend to prefer active modes of expressing their alienation and to be reformist or revolutionary in their orientations. Those who are of lower SES, less angry, less energetic and less invulnerable to repercussions in the economy, polity or psyche tend to adopt more passive orientations to the polity, to withdraw or to become ritualists.

Of course, the fact that an individual initially reacts to his alienation by adopting a passive behavioral orientation means neither that he is satisfied with the polity (as the theorists of the silent majority argue), nor that he will stay passive (as is assumed by theorists who contend that passive population sectors are basically good for stable government). Withdrawal is often followed by radicalization. In politics, as in social life, the individual who is quiet because conflicted or withdrawn because he is frightened by his own anger can explode. Revolutionary and reformist groups can and regularly do activate the passively alienated, often by legitimizing the outplay of rage and by providing a target or scapegoat for its expression.

This raises the whole question of predicting behavior from political predispositions.

The activation of predispositions

How does an individual's basic political orientation explain his political behavior? If we know, for example, that Mr. Jones orients to the political system as a reformer, what else do we need to know if we are to predict his political behavior? We know that if Mr. Jones acts politically at all, it is likely that he will act as a reformer, but will he act at all and where or in what contexts will he act?

The basic processes associated with explaining behavior from predispositions would seem to be arousal (or activation) and channelling. Generally, we may assume that the probability that Mr. Jones will engage in overt behavior is determined partly by the strength of his predispositions and partly by the strength of the political stimuli. The behaviors he adopts and the arenas or contexts in which he behaves are likely to be those suggested and rewarded by the individuals and groups whose stimulation activates his political predispositions.

As the social psychologists have taught us, the presence of others (reference groups or audiences) stimulates or arouses behavior. The behaviors that are facilitated by these factors tend to be those which are dominant, tend to be those to which the individual is already predisposed.

This is really nothing very new to the study of political behavior. We have known for some time now that people who vote regularly or who are otherwise active in politics tend to be those who are most exposed to the stimuli of the media, political groups, friends interested in politics, etc., and that people tend to vote as their friends or other reference groups do.

For the politically alienated man then: (1) the stronger and more salient his value conflict, the stronger is his predisposition to act politically; (2) the greater the stimuli from media and reference groups, the more likely he is to express his alienated behavioral predispositions; and (3) the more satisfying his relationship to these reference groups, the more reinforced he is likely to be in his alienated attitudes and behaviors. Alienated political behavior is likely to be explained as a combined function of these three variables: (1) the strength of the predisposition to behave (relative to the behavior threshold); (2) the strength of the stimuli (relative to threshold); and (3) the reinforcing or facilitating, rather than inhibiting, character of the stimuli (which affects number 2 above).

After we have charted the individual's transition from the attitude of alienation to the adoption of the basic behavioral predisposition in the next two chapters of this section, we attempt, some basic charting of the processes whereby these predispositions are aroused and channeled toward political behavior. In the third data chapter of the section, we explore the hypothesis that alienation is associated with a behavioral tendency to seek additional political stimulation, in particular, to read more about revolutionary and radical reform efforts. To the extent that this hypothesis is confirmed, the alienated individual is moved toward behavior because his communications behavior provides him both with additional political stimulation to activate his predispositions and with new reference groups who can channel the resulting behavior. In a sense, the alienated person places himself in a new political and personal communications structure which may reinforce his alienation and which may insulate him from hearing the ordinary appeals of the political system.

The fourth data chapter in this section, "From Political Alienation to Revolutionary Support," shows that the process by which the alienated individual comes to give his allegiance to a new reference group is fundamentally related to the same variables which are operative in the alienation process, that people come to support a revolutionary or radical reform group when their attitudes of alienation from the polity are reinforced and also when the reference group is seen as involving low TVC, PI and SI.

If such reference groups are seen as efficacious, they tend to be perceived as satisfying alternatives to the institutions of the polity—again, a possible insulation against the ordinary political system. In the last chapter of this section, we show how this process has operated in a black ghetto to isolate the politically active population from the political parties.

9

ALIENATION AND THE ADOPTION OF BASIC POLITICAL ORIENTATIONS IN A UNIVERSITY COMMUNITY

In the preceding theoretical chapter, we advanced three central hypotheses about the ways in which individuals adopt basic behavioral orientations to the political system. These are: (1) that there exists a set of fundamental orientations to the polity—conformity, ritualism, reformism, revolutionism and withdrawal—that are more or less independent of each other; (2) that the attitude of political alienation is significantly associated with each of these orientations; and (3) that, given a high level of alienation, differences in the process of alienation and in the individual's socio-economic and personality structure will predict which of these orientations he is likely to adopt. This chapter is a report of an effort to test these hypotheses in the winter of 1970 at the University of Pennsylvania.

Measures

As part of a continuing effort to monitor political processes in several selected university communities, a questionnaire was mailed to a random sample of 500 students and faculty at the University of Pennsylvania in January 1970. Responses were received from 205 people or from 40 percent of the sample.

The questionnaire permitted observations on each of the variables indicated in the preceding chapter as having an impact on the adoption of basic orientations to the polity. Multi-item indexes were constructed for: (1) the five behavioral orientations; (2) the attitude of alienation; (3) TVC, PI and SI; (4) SES; and (5) seven personality factors (energy, anger, psychological comfort with one's own anger, perception of economic and political invulnerability, need for conformity and desire to be reintegrated with the polity). In addition, indexes were constructed to measure two other behavioral orientations, protest voting and support for

162

demagogues, and a single-item indicator was used to inquire whether the individual became alienated as part of a group or on his own.

A full description of each of these measures is contained in the methodological appendix. Here we will report only one of the items used to measure each of these 20 variables in order to give the reader some idea of our measures.

Variable	*Item*
1. Conformity	I use (or plan to use) only the regular, ordinary channels of political activity in this country: voting, lobbying, writing letters to Congressman, testifying before legislative and administrative agencies, working through the courts.
2. Ritualism	There are some public policies that I still advocate because I used to believe that they would work, even though now I am not very convinced that they would work.
3. Reformism	I'd like to help bring about major changes in American politics—a peaceful revolution in our attitudes, priorities, policies and institutions.
4. Revolutionism	I would support a social movement in this country that would bring about an end to slums, poverty, pollution and prejudice in public life—even if considerable violence were necessary to carry out that program.
5. Withdrawal	I don't feel a part of this political system, so I don't (or won't) vote.
6. Attitude of political alienation	In American politics, power is maintained in secret, shutting out even interested citizens.
7. TVC	When I think about the difference between what I want for people and what American politics is doing to people, I feel scared.

8. PI

There is just about nothing that I can do to get the laws and policies I favor adopted in America.

9. SI

Today, in American politics, leaders seem unable or unwilling to do what I most want to see done.

10. SES

As employed in the analysis reported below, income alone is used as an indication of SES due to the lack of variation in education and the weakness of our perceived class measure.

11. Perception of energy

I think of myself as being low in energy. I'm often physically listless or tired or run down.

12. Anger

When I think about the negative impacts of United States policies at home or abroad, my response is to get mad.

13. Psychological comfort with own anger

When I think about mean and unfair things, like the murders of John Kennedy, Robert Kennedy and Martin Luther King, my own anger makes me scared.

14. Perception of economic invulnerability

I'm certain that I'll do all right financially no matter what political stands I may take.

15. Perception of political invulnerability

I don't like to sign petitions because you never know how government officials might use it against you later.

16. Need for conformity

I like to go along with people in their views on politics.

17. Desire to be reintegrated with the polity

I keep hoping that things will change in America soon so that I can feel a part of our public life again.

18. Protest voting

When I think about myself as performing the act of voting, I think of it as a protest.

19. Support for demagogues

If a demagogue or extremist could get America to give real racial justice, end poverty and pollution and bring us peace—I'd support a demagogue.

20. Process of alienation — group versus individual

I became alienated because I got friendly with some people who were alienated.

Findings

To test the hypotheses that the behavioral orientations were independent of each other, were significantly associated with alienation and were predicted to by SES and personality factors when alienation is high, correlational analyses, analyses of variance and regression analyses were performed on the data. In general these analyses tend to confirm each of the hypotheses. That the basic behavioral orientations are more or less independent of each other, for example, can be observed in Table 9.1.

TABLE 9.1

THE RELATIONSHIPS AMONG CONFORMITY, RITUALISM, REFORMISM, REVOLUTIONISM AND WITHDRAWAL AT THE UNIVERSITY OF PENNSYLVANIA

	Conformity	*Ritualism*	*Reformism*	*Revolution*	*Withdrawal*
Conformity (High scores = low conformity)	—				
Ritualism (High scores = low ritualism)	0.04	—			
Reformism (High scores = low reformism)	−0.29*	0.18	—		
Revolutionism (High scores = low revolutionism)	−0.45*	0.01	0.05	—	
Withdrawal (High scores = high withdrawal)	0.26*	0.04	0.05	0.10	—

$n = 205$
* = Significant at 0.01.

The only significant correlations in Table 9.1 are those between conformity on one hand, and reformism, revolutionism and withdrawal on the other (all negative relationships); all of the other orientations bear virtually no relationship at all to each other. We interpret this to mean that, as suggested in our theory statement, the potentially system-changing behavioral orientations of reformism, revolutionism and withdrawal constitute fundamentally different ways in which men can orient themselves to the political system.

Table 9.2 shows the basic interrelationships between the attitude of political alienation and the fundamental behavioral orientations to the polity that obtained in our data. As hypothesized, political alienation bears a strong negative relationship to conformist tendencies and significant positive relationships to the orientations of reformism, revolutionism and withdrawal. The hypothesized relationship between alienation and ritualism, however, is not supported in this data.

====== TABLE 9.2 ======

THE RELATIONSHIP OF POLITICAL ALIENATION TO BASIC BEHAVIORAL ORIENTATIONS TO THE POLITY

	Conformity	Reformism	Revolutionism	With-drawal	Ritualism
Alienation	0.62*	0.25*	0.47*	0.29*	0.05
$n = 205$					

*Significant at 0.005.

It seems, then, that alienation does constitute an important predictor of at least some basic political predispositions. Alienated people do tend to be nonconformist in their orientations toward political activity, to be reformers or revolutionaries or to withdraw from political participation and involvement.

But which of these orientations are they likely to adopt? What factors other than alienation level account for the individual's selection of an active or a passive political tendency? We argued, above, that three sets of factors would operate to condition the individual's response to alienation: the process by which he became alienated, his SES and other demographic characteristics and his personality.

Initially, we believe that individuals who become alienated as part of a group will tend to differ in their reactions to alienation from people who become alienated alone. We reason that this should be so for two reasons. First, group processes (group pressures, "protection of the group," etc.)

should generate greater homogeneity of response. Second, if the group is a satisfying "surrogate community," it can insulate the individual from the polity by reducing his need to interact directly with other social agencies or groups, thereby affecting his orientations to the politically organized society. To test this hypothesis, the mean scores on each of the five basic predispositions of those who became alienated because of group affiliations were compared with those of respondents who became alienated without such affiliations. The results of this "difference of means test" can be seen in Table 9.3.

=========== TABLE 9.3 ===========

DIFFERENCE OF MEANS ON THE BASIC BEHAVIORAL ORIENTATIONS BETWEEN INDIVIDUALS WHO BECAME ALIENATED IN GROUPS AND THOSE WHO BECAME ALIENATED ON THEIR OWN

Behavioral Orientation	*Mean Alienation of "Group Alienated"*	*Mean "on their own"*	*Level of Significance*
Conformity (High to Low)	2.71	2.50	0.07
Ritualism (High to Low)	1.66	2.08	not significant
Reformism (High to Low)	1.00	1.08	not significant
Revolutionism (High to Low)	1.73	2.26	0.005
Withdrawal (High to Low)	1.42	1.08	0.002

It will be observed that becoming alienated as part of a group of friends tends significantly to produce withdrawal and revolutionism as orientations to politics. Apparently, the operations of groups in the alienation process yield a preference for extreme solutions, solutions which tend to isolate the individual from the ordinary processes of politics.

Our second hypothesis concerning the impact of the alienation process on people's political orientations, was that among nonalienated people, TVC, PI and SI have independent effects on the orientations toward politics; while for the alienated, the summative process of "going alienated" would reduce these impacts. Basically, this would mean: (1) that TVC should be significantly associated with *active* orientations among the non-alienated; (2) that PI and SI should have significant association with *passive* orientations among the nonalienated; but (3) that among the alienated these different effects should cancel each other out.

This hypothesis was tested by dividing the respondent population, at the mean, into "high alienated" and "low alienated" and observing the differences in the correlations between TVC, PI, SI and the behavioral orientations in the two samples. Table 9.4 illustrates the results of this analytic operation.

TABLE 9.4

THE RELATIONSHIP OF TVC, PI, SI AND THE BEHAVIORAL
ORIENTATIONS AMONG HIGH AND LOW ALIENATEDS

	Conformity	Ritualism	Reformism	Revolt	Withdrawal
	Low Alienation Condition				
TVC	−0.50*	0.18	0.23*	0.05	0.06
PI	0.00	0.15	−0.01	0.20**	0.18
SI	−0.35*	0.28*	0.18	−0.13	0.04
	High Alienation Condition				
TVC	−0.36*	0.13	−0.08	0.16	−0.12
PI	−0.07	0.12	−0.07	0.13	−0.16
SI	−0.28*	−0.11	0.00	0.25*	−0.10

* = Significant at 0.01.
** = Significant at 0.025.

This data tends to support the hypothesis that TVC, PI and SI have significant impacts on the probability of adopting a given behavior orientation. Table 9.4 reveals that TVC is significantly associated with the active orientation of reformism among nonalienated individuals (0.23), and its impact on reformism *is* reduced to insignificance among the alienated (0.08). Similarly, SI is significantly associated with the passive orientation of ritualism in the nonalienated sample (0.28), and its independent impact on that behavioral orientation is not only reduced to insignificance, but actually has the direction of impact reversed (−0.11)— in the alienated group. Finally, the variable PI *is* significantly correlated with revolutionism among the nonalienated (0.20), but its independent effect on that orientation weakened to insignificance among the alienated (0.13).

Having shown that both the level and process of alienation predict to the behavioral orientation that people adopt toward politics, it is necessary to consider the social structural and personality variables which are the context in which alienation takes place. Do the rich react differently to alienation than the poor? Are men more active or more passive in their alienation than women?

To answer these questions, analyses of variance were performed on the data, allowing us to observe the impact of the demographic variables on the behavioral orientations, while holding alienation at a constant (high) level. Some interesting answers to the questions are reflected in the data summarized in Table 9.5.

TABLE 9.5

DIFFERENCE OF MEANS: THE IMPACT OF SES AND GENDER ON THE BASIC BEHAVIORAL ORIENTATIONS, CONTROLLING FOR ALIENATION

	High SES	Low SES	Signifi-cance Level	Male	Female	Signifi-cance Level
Mean Conformity Score (High to Low)	2.52	1.69	0.001	1.68	2.46	0.001
Mean Ritualism Score (High to Low)	2.70	1.21	0.001	1.00	1.10	0.044
Mean Reformism Score (High to Low)	1.09	1.41	0.001	1.33	1.28	0.001
Mean Revolution-ism Score (High to Low)	2.29	2.82	0.001	2.73	2.15	0.001
Mean Withdrawal Score (Low to High)	1.15	1.01	0.004	1.02	1.16	0.004

In this university community, SES does have a clear impact on the outplay of alienation in that higher-status respondents are significantly more likely to react openly to their alienation than are people from lower socio-economic backgrounds. Upper-SES types, for example, are significantly less conformist and less ritualistic in their orientation to politics than are the lower SES respondents. But SES does *not* distinguish between active and passive orientations; upper-class alienation is associated with both withdrawal and activism (reformism and revolutionism). It would appear that high SES acts to free the individual from both the *need to conform* to the participation norms of our polity and from the *need to appear to conform* (which characterizes the ritualist). But SES, alone, does not allow us to distinguish between people likely to withdraw from politics and those more likely to radicalize.

TABLE 9.6

DIFFERENCE OF MEANS: THE IMPACT OF PERSONALITY VARIABLES ON
BASIC BEHAVIORAL ORIENTATIONS, CONTROLLING FOR ALIENATION

Mean Behavioral Orientation	High Energy	Low Energy	Signi-ficance	High Anger	Low Anger	Signi-ficance	Psychological Comfort with Anger High	Low	Signi-ficance
Conformity High to Low	3.00	2.08	0.001	2.42	1.47	0.001	2.30	1.68	0.001
Ritualism High to Low	2.50	2.20	not sig.	2.34	1.94	0.022	2.32	1.94	0.038
Reformism High to Low	1.35	1.97	0.001	1.62	2.58	0.001	1.84	2.20	0.013
Revolutionism High to Low	3.00	2.63	not sig.	2.69	2.55	not sig.	2.70	2.50	not sig.
Withdrawal Low to High	2.50	2.19	not sig.	2.34	1.94	0.022	2.32	1.93	0.038

Mean Behavioral Orientation	Economic Invulnerability High	Low	Significance	Political Invulnerability High	Low	Significance
Conformity	1.66	2.25	0.001	1.90	2.31	0.001
Ritualism	2.08	2.25	not sig.	2.00	2.39	0.021
Reformism	2.37	1.81	0.001	2.18	1.74	0.001
Revolutionism	2.50	2.69	not sig.	2.56	2.72	not sig.
Withdrawal	2.07	2.25	not sig.	2.00	2.39	0.021

Mean Behavioral Orientation	Need Conformity			Negative Evaluation of Alienation		
	High	Low	Significance	High	Low	Significance
Conformity	1.81	2.33	0.001	2.16	2.10	0.012
Ritualism	2.09	2.30	not sig.	2.67	2.15	0.08
Reformism	2.47	1.55	0.001	1.73	1.98	0.001
Revolutionism	2.56	2.70	not sig.	2.83	2.62	not sig.
Withdrawal	2.08	2.30	not sig.	2.66	2.14	0.08

TABLE 9.7

SUMMARY OF SIGNIFICANT ASSOCIATIONS IN TABLE 9.6

Alienated Conformist	Alienated Ritualist	Alienated Reformist	Alienated Withdrawn
Low energy, low anger, low psychological comfort with own anger. Satisfied with alienation, high need conformity and high political and economic invulnerability.	Low in anger. Low in psychological comfort with own anger. Satisfied with alienation. High in political invulnerability.	High in energy, anger, psychological comfort with own anger. Dissatisfied with alienation. High in economic invulnerability. Low in political invulnerability.	High in anger and psychological comfort with own anger. Dissatisfied with alienation. Low in political invulnerability.

Precisely the same is true of gender. Among these alienated university people, women are significantly less likely to be conformists and ritualists than are men, but gender does not distinguish between withdrawal and reformism or revolutionism. The women in our sample are significantly more likely to withdraw from the polity than are men, but they are also far more likely to be reformists in their politics and even to welcome violent change.

These findings may appear surprising because traditional American gender-related role differences call for women to be more docile, accepting, nonpolitical, etc. But it should be remembered that these are the very norms that are increasingly being rejected by today's educated woman. In the next chapter, we will show that alienated black women, well-educated or not, also tend to reject the politics of docility, that they too tend to be less conformist and more radical in their behavior orientations than are alienated black men.

Social location variables, then, do have an impact on the behavioral orientations to politics that people adopt but they are not sufficient to discriminate between active and passive orientations. As social location variables are basically "shorthand" for learning experiences, we are principally interested in them because we believe that people in different social locations will experience the world differently and, consequently, will have different attitudes, behavioral orientations and behavior. Accordingly, we should expect personality factors, as more direct measures of different mind states, to help us discriminate between active and passive orientations to politics.

Again, this hypothesis was tested by a difference of means analysis which permitted observation of the impact of personality on behavioral orientations while holding alienation at a constant high level. The results of these analyses are presented in Table 9.6 and summarized verbally in Table 9.7.

These data suggest that the individual's personality structure has a strong and consistent impact on the basic behavioral orientations he is likely to adopt toward politics. Initially, personality distinguishes between the change-relevant orientations (that is, reformers and retreatists) and status-quo orientations (conformists and ritualists). Conformists and ritualists differ from reformers and retreatists on virtually every dimension studied here. Our alienated conformists and ritualists are neither angry nor psychologically comfortable with such anger as they do feel. They are satisfied with their alienation, feeling invulnerable to political reprisals (perhaps because they plan no activity that would bring reprisals their way). Alienated reformers and retreatists, on the other hand, are both angry and comfortable with their anger; they are dissatisfied with being alienated and feel quite vulnerable to potential repercussions which might derive from their political behavior.

The personality factors can also discriminate more sharply *within* the status-quo and change-relevant categories, that is, personality factors tend to separate conformists from ritualists and reformers from retreatists. Alienated conformists, for example, have all of the psychological characteristics that the ritualists do but also tend to be low in energy, high in need conformity and to perceive themselves as economically and politically invulnerable. Alienated reformers have all of the psychological characteristics of retreatists but they also are high in energy and tend to perceive themselves as economically invulnerable. Both reformers and retreatists feel politically vulnerable, but the reformer is more secure of his economic position than the retreatist. Both the reformer and the retreatist are dissatisfied with their alienation, but the reformer tends to have a higher energy level with which to do something about it.

These findings on energy and economic vulnerability often seem to be known intuitively by reformers and revolutionaries who are trying to activate a passively alienated or withdrawn population. Such individuals and groups typically oppose the use of drugs and alcohol and denigrate religion for draining energy that might be better spent in political activity. Typically, they do provide their members with economic security or try to put down the very notion of economic security as bourgeois or materialistic.

It will be noted that none of the personality measures studied here had significant impact on revolutionism. This may be because our personality measures were too few or too crude, or because revolutionary followership is primarily a function of alienation and group activation of alienation. In our data, at any rate, revolutionism is associated with the level of alienation, with the process of alienation, with SES and with gender but not with the personality factors we studied.

This fact not withstanding, the general process by which the individuals in this sample adopted their basic behavioral orientations to the political system does conform to the model described in the previous chapter. The individual's level of identification with the polity does predict to his substantive orientation to politics in that alienated people tend to become significantly less conformist in their politics than people who remain high in self-identification with the American polity. The process of alienation has its impact, too, as people who become alienated through group affiliations tend either to withdraw from political involvement or to become revolutionary in their orientations. Upper-class individuals and women seem to be somewhat more change-oriented than are lower-SES types and than men are. Finally, alienation has different consequences for different personalities. Persons who react to alienation in an angry, dissatisfied manner but who are psychologically comfortable with their reactions, tend to withdraw or, if they are energetic and economically secure, to become reformers. Less angry, less dissatisfied with alienation, less comfortable with anger are the ritualists and (the less energetic but more economically secure) conformists.

Protest voting and support for demagogues: Intermediate behavioral orientations

The reader will recall that our basic strategy for the explanation of alienated political behavior is: (1) to explain the process by which individuals adopt basic orientations to the polity; and then (2) to show how media, group and situational processes activate and channel these predispositions.

A close variant on this strategy—really an extension of it—would be to determine whether more specific orientations, that is, predispositions to more specific behaviors, could be explained by the same model that seems to work for the more basic orientations. If this were true, it might help our explanations in political study because the factors activating the simpler behavior orientations might be clearer. For example, if an individual had a strong predisposition to vote for colorful but extremist candidates, then the mere appearance of such a candidate might be sufficient to "trigger" the behavior. Predicting behavior from the more general but more gross orientations like reformism would rarely be as simple as this.

Accordingly, to determine if our model of the adoption of basic orientations might also help us to understand more specific behavior orientations, we included measures of our respondent's orientations toward protest voting and toward supporting demagogues. These more specific orientations should be related to some of the more general ones, to alienation and, given alienation, to demographic and personality variables. The data summarized in Tables 9.8 and 9.9 support each of these hypotheses.

=========== TABLE 9.8 ===========

PEARSON-PRODUCT CORRELATION OF PROTEST VOTING AND
SUPPORT FOR DEMAGOGUES WITH ALIENATION AND WITH THE BASIC
BEHAVIORAL ORIENTATIONS TO POLITICS

	Aliena-tion	Conform-ity	Ritual-ism	Reform-ism	Revolu-tionism	With-drawal
Protest Voting	−0.49*	−0.42*	0.06	0.07	0.50*	−0.30*
Support for Dema-gogues	−0.26*	−0.09	0.16	0.07	0.29*	−0.03

* = Significant at 0.05.

TABLE 9.9

DIFFERENCE OF MEANS: THE IMPACT OF GENDER AND PERSONALITY VARIABLES ON PROTEST VOTING AND SUPPORT FOR DEMAGOGUES, CONTROLLING FOR ALIENATION

	Male	Female	Significance Level	High Energy	Low Energy	Significance Level	High Anger	Low Anger	Significance Level
Protest Voting	2.87	2.22	0.001	3.00	2.54	0.037	2.71	2.27	not sig.
Support Demagogues	2.64	2.80	0.001	3.00	2.74	not sig.	2.84	2.58	not sig.

	Invulnerability High	Low	Significance Level	Political Invulnerability High	Low	Significance Level	Level of Conformity High	Low	Significance Level
Protest Voting	2.07	2.72	0.016	2.87	2.22	0.001	2.52	2.60	not sig.
Support Demagogues	2.61	2.80	0.019	2.82	2.68	0.009	2.67	2.81	not sig.

	Psychological Anger High	Low	Significance Level	Evaluation of Alienation High	Low	Significance Level
Protest Voting	2.62	2.34	0.017	2.41	2.58	not sig.
Support Demagogues	2.73	2.81	not sig.	3.0	2.72	0.026

Inspection of Table 9.8 shows that the orientations toward protest voting and toward support for demagogues are both significantly associated with alienation and with nonconformity. Also, significant numbers of our potential revolutionaries found protest voting and support for demagogues to be congenial tactics. Finally, retreatists indicated, in significant numbers, that any voting that they might do would be meant as a protest.

Apparently, then, protest voting and support for demagogues are political positions which are appealing both to radicals and to those alienated people who have withdrawn from ordinary politics but who have not yet radicalized. It may well be that protest voting and support for demagogues are transitional orientations marking the place where withdrawal and radicalization overlap; where the formerly withdrawn individual begins to radicalize and where the radical still uses electoral politics as a signal and symbol of his disaffection.

This interpretation of protest voting and support for demagogues as a kind of half-way house between active and passive alienation, is also lent support by the demographic and personality structures associated with the two orientations (Table 9.9). Comparing Table 9.9 with Table 9.6, we find that all of the personality factors that are associated with protest voting and support for demagogues are consistent with the orientation of conformity, yet women, who are far less conformist than men, predominate among protest voters. Protest voting and voting for a demagogue are, of course, behaviorally indistinguishable from conformity. The secrecy of the voting booth means that only the fact that an individual voted—a conformist and generally valued response—is public knowledge. The person who is alienated can express his alienation at the polls without any fear of social or political sanctions; perhaps this is why people who adopt protest voting or support for demagogues as orientations feel relatively invulnerable to political reprisals.

More concretely, the protest voter is low in psychological comfort with his anger and low in energy. Clearly the rigors of reformism or revolutions are not for him. Withdrawal will not achieve the social changes that his revolutionary orientation bespeaks. Protest voting, requiring little energy or sustained anger, is an ideal behavioral compromise. Similarly, the individual who would support demagogues is relatively satisfied with his alienation, so he has little reason to extend himself. He also tends to feel quite secure in his economic and political positions, and, so long as his political behavior extends only to electoral politics, this pleasant security can easily be maintained.

Conclusion

The basic behavioral orientations to politics that we have been studying are adopted by both alienated and nonalienated people. Accordingly, we cannot expect to explain most of the ways in which individuals adopt their basic behavioral orientation to politics using alienation-relevant variables. Still, alienation and the other variables with which we have been concerned should explain a significant portion of the variance in the basic behavioral orientations. To test this, a multiple regression analysis was performed, allowing us to observe how much of the variance of each behavioral orientation was explained by the variables which we found to be associated with it. Table 9.10 expresses this in the form of five regression equations.

=========== TABLE 9.10 ===========

THE AMOUNT OF VARIANCE OF EACH BASIC BEHAVIORAL ORIENTATION
EXPLAINED BY ALIENATION, SES, GENDER AND PERSONALITY FACTORS

Orientation	*Independent Variables*	R^2 *or Amount of Variance Explained (%)*
Conformity	= Alienation, Anger, Energy, Need Conformity, Economic and Political Invulnerability, Desire to be Reintegrated with Polity, SES and Gender.	48.19
Ritualism	= Alienation, Anger, Psychological Comfort with Anger, Political Invulnerability and SES.	5.17
Reformism	= Alienation, Anger, Psychological Comfort with Anger, Energy, Economic and Political Invulnerability, Need Conformity, SES and Gender.	11.61
Revolutionism	= Alienation, SES and Gender.	27.28
Withdrawal	= Alienation, Anger, Psychological Comfort with Anger, Political Invulnerability and Gender.	6.07

Nonconformity as a political orientation in this university community seems to be rather well explained by the alienation process. It seems clear that the level and the process of alienation, and the interaction between alienation, SES and personality constitute fundamental explanatory factors in the process whereby people adopt a basic behavioral stance toward politics. At least this seems clear enough in this university community. In the next chapter, we explore these processes in another American arena of alienation: the urban ghetto.

10

ALIENATION AND THE ADOPTION
OF BASIC POLITICAL ORIENTATIONS
IN BLACK COMMUNITIES

In general, we have found the process of alienation to be quite similar among blacks and whites, but there are important differences within this essential similarity. The reader will recall our findings that in Newark race was essentially unrelated to the attitude of alienation and that both black and white alienation was significantly associated with TVC, PI and SI. But we also found that black alienation was primarily explicable in terms of TVC, while alienation among whites tended to be far more understandable as a function of SI.*

These differences in the causal process of alienation alerted us to the possibility that similar differences might exist in the process by which the behavioral consequences of alienation take place. More specifically, we hypothesized that (1) for blacks as well as whites, alienation + SES + personality would predict to the individual's basic political orientation which would then be activated into behavior by group and situational variables, but that (2) within this psycho-structural process, the specific orientations that would be adopted and the specific relationships that lead to their adoption might be somewhat different for black people than for whites.

An opportunity to chart the adoption of basic political orientations in black communities was afforded in our sample interview study of Philadelphia's black communities. As described in several earlier chapters, this study involved an area probability sample of the North and West Philadelphia black ghettoes, where a detailed personal interview with 87 residents was attempted by a trained black interviewer. Sixty-nine interviews (79 percent) were successfully completed in the summer of 1969.

---

*This study was conducted by David C. Schwartz and Craig Wynn.

These interviews permitted measurements on the following variables: (1) the five basic orientations to the polity; (2) the attitude of political alienation; (3) the demographic variables of SES and gender; (4) the personality variables of psychological comfort with one's own anger and need for conformity; and (5) group affiliations. In addition, measures were taken of the respondent's (1) behavioral withdrawal of attention from politics; (2) identification with African life and culture ("Negritude"); (3) advocacy of black separatism; and (4) advocacy of the use of public institutions to increase black consciousness.

The indexes which were constructed to measure these variables are reported fully in the Methods Appendix. Here one item for each measure is reported as an example of the kinds of items employed in the interview. It will be noted that, while there is considerable similarity between the items used in this study and those reported in the last chapter, theoretical considerations and problems of access prompted some differences. In the main, however, we regard the two studies as broadly comparable.

Measures

1. *Political alienation:* When I hear about politics and government in America, I feel that I am a part of it.

2. *Ritualism:* You've got to keep trying to get good laws and fairness in politics, but it's really not much use.

3. *Reformism:* We need new political parties so we can change things but do it by politics.

4. *Revolutionism:* We need violent change in both our national goals and in the means we use to accomplish our goals.

5. *Withdrawal:* I don't concern myself about politics anymore. I'm concerned about private things: myself, my family, my friends.

6. *Conformity:* (here, we decided not to use an investigator-defined measure but rather to investigate the respondent's perception of himself as a conformist) I guess I feel about politics the way most people do.

7. *SES:* an index of education and income.

8. *Gender.*

9. *Psychological comfort with one's anger:* Sometimes when I get mad about what's wrong with things, I feel afraid that I won't be able to control myself so I try to put it out of my mind.

10. *Need for Conformity:* I like to go along with people in their views on politics.

11. *Group affiliations.*

12. *Behavioral withdrawal of attention from politics:* I used to pay more attention to politics than I do now.

13. *Negritude* (here, two measures were taken)—

strong negritude: Can you name some of the major tribes in West Africa? Do you speak any African languages? If yes, which ones? Does respondent have natural hair? Does he wear African garb?

weaker negritude: Do you speak any African languages? If not, would you take a course in one if it were offered around here? Does respondent have natural hair? Do you ever wear African clothes?

14. *Black separatism:* One of the political changes that has been proposed by a conference of black people has been a black congress—a legislature to make laws for black people. Would you like to see this come about?

15. *The use of public institutions to achieve increased black consciousness:* Do you believe that African culture should be taught in the schools?

Findings

The first hypotheses in our model are that ritualism, reformism, revolutionism and withdrawal constitute fundamental alternatives to conformity and that they are basically independent of each other. Table 10.1 summarizes the data which afford a test of these hypotheses in the black communities of Philadelphia.

===================== TABLE 10.1 =====================

THE RELATIONSHIPS AMONG THE BASIC POLITICAL ORIENTATIONS IN
THE BLACK COMMUNITIES OF PHILADELPHIA

	Conformity (high to low)	Ritualism (high to low)	Reformism (high to low)	Revolutionism (high to low)	Withdrawal (high to low)
Conformity	—				
Ritualism	−0.36*	—			
Reformism	0.33*	−0.07	—		
Revolutionism	−0.27*	0.22**	0.24*	—	
Withdrawal	0.25*	0.00	−0.21**	−0.01	—

$n = 69$.
* = Significant at 0.01.
** = Significant at 0.05.

Table 10.1 reveals a more complex set of relationships among the basic political orientations adopted by black people than obtained in our study of the predominantly white university community. It is, however, a coherent set of relationships. Here ritualism and revolutionism are the fundamental alternatives to conformity (bearing significant negative relationships to it), while withdrawal and reformism are "conformist responses" (that is, consistent with and positively associated with conformism). Reformism, however, also bears significant positive relationship to revolutionism, probably indicating that reformism in black communities is now often transitional between ordinary politics and more militant orientations. This table seems to suggest that political withdrawal in the black community is not a change-relevant orientation to American national politics but is a conformist response that is negatively associated with revolutionism and unrelated to reformism and to ritual participation. However, we shall see that black people's increasing identification with African life and culture, often interpreted as withdrawal from American society, is also a withdrawal from the American political system. Further, this identification or "identity search" is already having its impact on black people's orientation to politics, as blacks increasingly view public institutions as means to increase black consciousness.

The second proposition in our "alienation-to-behavior" model is that the attitude of political alienation should be significantly associated with nonconformist political orientations. The data presented in Table 10.2 supports this hypothesis.

TABLE 10.2

THE RELATIONSHIP OF ALIENATION TO THE BASIC POLITICAL ORIENTATIONS

	Conformity (High to Low)	Ritualism (High to Low)	Reformism (High to Low)	Revolutionism (High to Low)	Withdrawal (High to Low)
Alienation (Low to high)	0.60*	−0.34*	0.07	−0.43*	0.10

$n = 87$.
* = Significant at 0.055.

As predicted, alienation is strongly associated with nonconformity and significantly correlated with those orientations which are alternatives to conformity: revolutionism and ritualism.

According to the logic of our model, given alienation, social location variables and personality factors should predict to the specific behavioral orientations which different individuals adopt. At least SES and personality should help to distinguish between those individuals who are likely to react passively to thier alienation and those who are likely to be more active in their orientation to politics. To test these hypotheses, analyses of variance were performed on the data, permitting observation of the impact of SES and personality on the behavioral orientations, while holding alienation at a constant, high level (Table 10.3).

TABLE 10.3

DIFFERENCE OF MEANS: THE IMPACT OF SES AND PERSONALITY VARIABLES ON BASIC BEHAVIORAL ORIENTATIONS

	High SES	Low SES	Significance	Male	Female	Significance
Mean Conformity (High to Low)	2.21	1.70	0.51	1.61	2.29	0.07
Mean Ritualism (High to Low)	1.97	2.30	0.30	2.42	1.88	0.96
Mean Reformism (High to Low)	2.92	3.10	0.96	3.31	2.62	0.06
Mean Revolutionism (High to Low)	1.15	1.00	0.07	1.31	1.00	0.03
Mean Withdrawal (High to Low)	2.05	2.00	0.28	1.46	2.41	0.002

	High Psychological Comfort with Anger	Significance	Low Psychological Comfort with Anger	Significance
Mean Conformity	1.87	0.08	2.07	0.53
Mean Ritualism	2.20	0.68	2.11	0.91
Mean Reformism	2.90	0.20	3.07	0.40
Mean Revolutionism	1.13	0.02	1.14	0.04
Mean Withdrawal	2.20	0.03	1.71	0.08

	High Need Conformity	Low Need Conformity	Significance	Low Negritude	High Negritude	Significance
Mean Conformity	2.15	1.70	0.08	1.77	2.56	0.06
Mean Ritualism	1.95	2.45	0.68	2.31	1.67	0.15
Mean Reformism	3.13	2.50	0.20	2.74	3.33	0.70
Mean Revolutionism	1.15	1.10	0.02	1.19	1.00	0.53
Mean Withdrawal	2.20	1.60	0.03	1.67	2.78	0.007

In these black communities, SES has no significant effect on the basic behavioral orientations that alienated people adopt. We shall see that SES does have impact on less fundamental orientations to politics but here the multi-item index of education and income that was our measure of social status bears no significant relationship to any basic political orientation of alienated black people. Gender, on the other hand, does have important associations. As in our study of the university community, alienated women are far more likely to react to their alienation. They are significantly more revolutionary and reformist and significantly less withdrawn in their political orientations than are alienated men. Femininity and active political orientations seem to go hand-in-hand in alienated black populations.

Personality variables also have some predictive power vis-a-vis behavioral orientations. The degree to which an individual feels psychologically comfortable with his own anger, for example, predicts to the activism or passivism of his reactions to alienation. Alienated black people who are relatively comfortable with their own anger are likely to be revolutionary in their orientations to American national politics whereas those who are less able to handle their political rage comfortably tend to become reformers or, especially among black men, to move toward a withdrawn political orientation. Similarly, need for conformity operates in the predicted fashion: alienated black people who are high in need for conformity tend to withdraw their concern from politics, while those who are lower in this need tend to radicalize, that is, to orient themselves to politics as latent revolutionaries. Finally, identification with African life and culture (negritude) is significantly associated with political withdrawal as an orientation among alienated black people.

Again, the broad outlines of the model appear confirmed: alienation is strongly associated with nonconformist orientations toward political behavior and the demographic location and personality structure of the alienated person allows us to predict toward the specific behavior orientation he is likely to adopt.

TABLE 10.4

THE AMOUNT OF VARIANCE IN EACH BEHAVIOR ORIENTATIONS
EXPLAINED BY ALIENATION PROCESS

Behavior Orientation	*Amount of* $R^2 = $ *Variance Explained (%)*
Conformity	37.32
Ritualism	38.36
Reformism	0.00
Revolutionism	24.71
Withdrawal	40.54

Table 10.4 shows the total amount of variance of each of the behavioral orientations explained by this model.

Two aspects of our model remain to be discussed: the role of groups in the process whereby these black people adopted their basic political predispositions; and the operation of group processes in activating these predispositions into political behaviors. We have hypothesized, first, that individuals who become alienated as part of a group are likely to adopt different (but predictable) political orientations than do people who are alienated "alone." Secondly, we reason that, given alienation, individuals with clear group affiliations are more likely to act out their predispositions than are people who lack the reinforcement and stimulation that groups provide.

Both of these formulations seem supported in our data. As Table 10.5 illustrates, alienated individuals who were high in group affiliations tended to be significantly less conformist and less withdrawn in their orientations to politics than were alienated people who lacked group attachments. These findings also indicate that group processes reinforce the affects of alienation. The reinforcement can be seen by comparing Table 10.2 with Table 10.5. In Table 10.2, alienation alone is shown to bear strong negative association with conformity. In Table 10.5, alienation is controlled for, and we observe that alienated individuals who are reinforced by group affiliations are significantly nonconformist in their approach to politics. This latter finding indicates that group affiliation has its own additional impact on conformity. Finally, we have said that group processes do more than merely reinforce alienation, that they also serve to channel the alienation into or away from specific behavior orientations. Again, this hypothesis can be verified by

═══════════════════ TABLE 10.5 ═══════════════════

DIFFERENCE OF MEANS: THE IMPACT OF GROUP AFFILIATION
ON BEHAVIORAL ORIENTATIONS, CONTROLLING FOR ALIENATION

	High Group Affiliation	Low Group Affiliation	Significance
Mean Conformity (High to Low)	2.50	1.25	0.001
Mean Ritualism (High to Low)	1.83	2.54	0.155
Mean Reformism (High to Low)	3.08	2.67	0.810
Mean Revolutionism (High to Low)	1.00	1.33	0.868
Mean Withdrawal (High to Low)	2.33	1.50	0.001

comparing Table 10.2 with Table 10.5. In Table 10.2, some tendency is shown for alienation to be associated with withdrawal. In Table 10.5, we observe that alienated individuals who are reinforced by group affiliation are significantly *less* withdrawn in political orientation than those who are low in group affiliation.

To test the hypothesis that group affiliation has a stimulating effect on basic political predispositions, to show that these processes predict toward behavior, we included a measure on the degree to which the respondent had behaviorally withdrawn his attention from the political arena. Then, controlling for alienation, we compared the mean score on behavioral withdrawal for individuals who scored high on group affiliation with that of those who scored low on group affiliation. The difference of means (0.89, significant at the 0.001 level) indicated that alienated people who are affiliated with political groups actually are less withdrawn, *that their political behavior, and not merely their psychic orientation,* is more active.

Of course, attention to politics and political involvement generally can result in a variety of behaviors and our findings that alienation + group affiliation leads to the behavior of maintaining or increasing of attention to politics needs a great deal of corroboration and extension. Cer-

=== TABLE 10.6 ===

PEARSON PRODUCT-MOMENT CORRELATION COEFFICIENTS OF BLACK
SEPARATISM AND "POLITICS AS CULTURAL CHANGE" WITH
BLACK COMMUNITY STUDY VARIABLES

	Black Separatism (High to Low)	*Politics as Cultural Change* (High to Low)
Conformity	0.12	−0.22*
Ritualism	−0.14	0.24*
Reformism	0.24*	−0.12
Revolutionism	−0.02	−0.20*
Alienation	0.07	−0.29**
Group Affiliation	−0.22*	0.29**
Negritude—Strong	−0.00	0.33**
—Weak	−0.02	0.48**
Psychological Comfort with Anger	0.11	−0.17
Need Conformity	−0.02	−0.06
SES	0.08	−0.07
Withdrawal	−0.10	−0.07

$n = 87$
** = Significant at 0.055.
* = Significant at 0.025.

tain clues as to the likely consequences of attention paid to politics by black people these days, however, may be obtained from our data on two specific orientations to politics: the orientation of black separatism and the orientation which holds that public involvement is useful or even necessary for black people because the institutions of America—schools, churches, etc. —should be used as means of increasing black consciousness. Table 10.6 reports the basic bivariate relationships between these two orientations and our other variables.

Only two of the variables with which we have been working are significantly associated with black separatism: group affiliation and reformism. Black people who are affiliated with national black organizations are, predictably, nonseparatist in orientation. More interesting, though no less predictable, is the finding that reformists tend to be somewhat more separatist in orientation than nonreformists. It will be recalled from Table 10.1 that reformers in the black community may well find themselves psychologically caught between conformity-withdrawal on the one hand and militancy on the other. Note how functional black separatism may be for one caught in this dilemma; in essence, separatism allows him to be "militantly withdrawn."

Involvement in public institutions as a means of increasing black consciousness, however, is associated with a very large number of our variables. It seems essentially to be a response which is neither revolutionary nor conformist on the part of black people who tend to identify with African life and culture and who are affiliated with black political organizations.

These findings highlight the importance of knowing the individual's specific orientations to politics. If two people vote for the same candidate, or even work together politically, but do so out of dramatically different orientations, then their reactions to the political outcome may be very different, and the consequences that their behavior has for the political system may be misunderstood. For example, if Mr. Jones, a black man, works publicly for the election of some candidate because he is hoping thereby to increase the political consciousness of black men, and if Mr. Smith, a white, works for the same candidate as a protest activity, then perhaps neither man's participation should be properly interpreted as primarily supporting of the existing political system. Each man's reactions are likely to be different from the other, whether or not their candidate wins.

People engaged in the same activity, starting with different orientations, tend to learn different things from their experiences and, hence, understand each other less well than one might expect from the fact of their common endeavor. As anyone knows who has been involved in interracial social change efforts in recent years, intense common effort toward seemingly common goals is no guarantee of interracial comity or that the coalition that worked well together on issue A can be put together for issue B.

Accordingly, it becomes important for the political analyst to know not only the individual's general and specific orientations to politics but also to know the specific issue areas or problem contexts in which given individuals will play out their orientations. Can the process model whereby alienation + personal characteristics predict to political orientations also help us to understand the problem areas in which these orientations will be acted upon? Our Newark data, permitting a further comparison of black and white alienation, gives some evidence that it can.

We would expect that the pattern of associations which different issue areas have with both alienation and personal characteristics should help us to predict the issue areas in which an individual's general and specific orientations will be played out. If the individual's perceptions of housing or transportation or foreign policy, for example, are associated with alienation or anger, then we should expect the resulting political orientation to be expressed in these issue areas. A lack of significant associations between specific issue areas and the alienation process should predict to inaction in that issue area, to a more general or diffuse response. Our Newark data permitted us to explore this idea by observing the degree to which alienation and anger were associated with specific perceptions about the public schools and with more general negative attitudes toward the city as a whole (Table 10.7).

The pattern of associations between school variables and alienation are quite similar among blacks and whites. Political alienation is not associated with a negative evaluation of the public schools in either race but *is* associated in both races with: disagreements with school personnel, involvement in school activities, dissatisfaction with school-community spokesmen and with a preference for either a state takeover or local control of schools.

But the pattern of associations that these variables have with anger is appreciably different between the races. First, whites are angry about everything, police, politics, schools and the city as a whole; but black anger is far more focused on schools. Secondly, angry black people are willing to try almost anything to get changes made in public education. They would accept state takeover, local control or political change in the form of a black mayor. Angry whites, however, orient to the schools only in a withdrawn manner; a state takeover is their preferred solution to Newark's school crisis.

From these findings, we would expect that radicalism as an orientation should be located in the school arena for black people but should be a more general or diffuse response in the white community. To test this, we analyzed the differences between the races on a single-item indicator of school radicalism. Predictably, blacks were significantly more radical in orienting to school problems than were whites (p. = 0.0005 or better).

White anger, on the other hand, is primarily associated with threat (0.73) and with dissatisfaction with police services (0.22), so we might predict that white radicalism or predispositions to violence would center upon defensive "law and order" concerns. Taking white orientations together, we would predict that white orientations toward violence would take the form of generalized, threat-oriented self-defense. Our attitudinal data cannot directly show this, but contextual knowledge of Newark testi-

TABLE 10.7

PEARSON PRODUCT-MOMENT CORRELATION COEFFICIENTS OF ALIENATION, ANGER AND SCHOOL-POLITICAL ATTITUDES IN NEWARK

	Alienation		Anger	
	Blacks n = 106	Whites n = 503	Blacks	Whites
1. Evaluation of Newark as a place to live	−0.22*	−0.14*	−0.13	−0.32*
2. Evaluation of Newark's public schools	−0.04	−0.04	−0.19	0.17*
3. Respondents' agreement on school problems				
with teachers	−0.23*	−0.10*	−0.25*	−0.08
with principals	−0.17*	−0.30*	−0.18	−0.43*
with school board	−0.20*	−0.05	−0.34*	−0.01
4. Knowledge of school services	−0.07	−0.05	0.05	−0.03
5. Involvement with school programs	−0.28*	−0.17*	−0.15	−0.15*
6. Satisfaction with school information availability	−0.11	−0.03	0.01	−0.15*
7. School-community spokesman deemed inauthentic	−0.28*	−0.21*	−0.01	0.23*
8. Prefer State takeover of schools	−0.28*	−0.21*	0.22*	0.22*
9. Prefer local control of schools	0.20*	0.14*	0.24*	0.08
10. Prefer Negro mayor to improve schools	0.28*	−0.01	0.22*	0.02
11. Alienation	—	—	0.44*	0.30*
Political Variables				
12. TVC	0.52*	0.45*	0.27*	0.73*
13. PI	0.44*	0.36*	0.28*	0.12
14. SI	0.38*	0.58*	0.30*	0.41*
15. Evaluation of police	−0.14	−0.19*	−0.18	−0.22*

* = Significant at 0.05.

fies that this is precisely true. White predispositions toward violence are almost exclusively manifested in "vigilante" or self-defense organizations and in the purchase of weapons for self-defense against a highly generalized fear of black violence.

Conclusion

We conclude that our general explanatory model of the process whereby people adopt basic political orientations and whereby these orientations are activated into behavior appropriately characterizes the experiences of both blacks and whites in urban and university communities. There are specific differences between the races, to be sure, and these need much more detailed research than they have received heretofore. Nevertheless, there appears to be a general process, operative among both black and white Americans, whereby the individual's alienation level weakens his tendencies to conform to American political norms and combines with demographic and personality factors to produce non-conformist behavioral predispositions.

We tentatively conclude, also, that political behavior emerges out of these basic predispositions by a process of stimulation (often involving political groups). The remaining chapters in this section are attempts to chart this process of behavior stimulation. In the next chapter, we show that alienated people tend to seek stimulation, actively searching for information about radical people and groups.

11

ALIENATION AND COMMUNICATION BEHAVIOR

In order for political predispositions to become activated into overt political behavior, two fundamental preconditions must be met. First, an arousing stimulus must get through the perceptual screen of the predisposed individual and, secondly, that stimulus must facilitate, rather than inhibit, behavior. This chapter is concerned with the first of these processes.

From the extant research on the consequences of alienation, one might be led to believe that very little in the way of political stimulation is likely to be perceived by alienated people. It has been found, for example, that alienation is significantly associated with low political involvement, low interest in politics, blockages to perceiving or learning political information, perceptual distortions of political phenomena and vicarious or escapist use of the mass media.[1] These findings are quite consistent with each other Taken together, they imply that alienated people who withdraw from political involvement seek to maintain their withdrawn orientation by screening out political information which might stimulate involvement.

But withdrawal is only one mode of reacting to alienation, hence there is no reason to believe that screening out political information is the typical consequence of alienation. Indeed, there seems to be every reason to believe exactly the reverse.

An explanation of stimulation-seeking

The idea that alienated individuals should not typically want to screen out political stimulation can be derived by combining our theory of alienation with certain relatively invariant relationships discovered in social psychology. According to our theory, the individual becomes alienated to reduce the threat he feels when his fundamental politicized values seem to be in irreconcilable conflict with those honored in and exhibited by the polity.

190

Withdrawal of his self-identification from the political system brings his cognitive set into greater balance, but it does not ordinarily serve to eliminate the threat entirely. There are several reasons for this. First, devaluing the political system is not the same thing as attaining one's political values; mere withdrawal of self-identification cannot change threatening political realities. Second, alienation itself can be unsatisfying—threatening, lonely, inconsistent with one's own value for participation. Finally, as we will argue below, some evidence that one's cherished political visions remain unfulfilled is likely to filter through to the alienated individual no matter how hard he tries to screen out political stimuli. Accordingly, today, the politically alienated American is very likely to feel at least some political threat, some residual psycho-political disturbance that makes his alienation a potentially unstable state; a state that can be activated and changed by communications stimuli, as in the case of successful appeals by radical or revolutionary groups.

How do people react to such threat? We know that there are three relatively invariant reactions to felt-threat. These are: (1) "heightened vigilance" which takes the form of increased attention to threat-relevant events, scanning for new signs of danger, attending to information about the nature of the threat and thinking about alternative courses of action for dealing with contingencies; (2) seeking reassurances of the individual's ability to handle the threat (or interpretations of the threat); and (3) making judgments about the sources from which to gain the information required by reactions 1 and 2 above.

Very low levels of threat result in little information search, extremely high levels of threat would make for indiscriminate information search; but, for most of the alienated, intermediate degrees of threat produce the need to seek political information selectively. Moderate threat arouses what has been termed "discriminative vigilance".[2]

From this analysis, we would hypothesize that today: (1) political alienation is not significantly associated with a diminution in seeking political information; (2) political alienation is not significantly related to vicarious use of the media; and (3) those alienated individuals who find their alienation to be uncomfortable or threatening will tend to seek significantly more, rather than less, political information.

In short, we would predict that today's alienated individual is not likely to want to screen out political stimuli and, hence, that there is not a behavioral tendency for the alienated individual to perceptually block political communications.

Even if an alienated person did want to screen out the political world, how successful is he likely to be at doing so? The American polity has interpenetrated many social arenas, becoming more relevant and visible to more people. Further, today the media bring the political world into the home, car and office rather insistently and incessantly. Accordingly, it seems inevitable that the alienated individual will receive some political stimuli that will reinforce his felt-threat. This reinforcement, in turn, is likely to send him off looking for more information by which either to reassure himself that he can deal with the threat by normal means or to find out about radical means of dealing with it. This is especially likely to be true of intellectuals and students, who are even more "tied to the media" than are other Americans.

Indeed, the difficulty of successfully withdrawing from our polity is part of the current American political crisis. Many of today's alienated appear to want little more than to withdraw but the seeming omnipresence of the polity prevents this and fosters radicalization. For example, the black leader who wants to withdraw, to "turn inward" into negritude in order to find or build a satisfying black mythology is confronted by the fact that the ghetto is largely dependent upon the white political economy. Youth communes are daily politicized by the police, and, at the other end of the life-cycle, the aged community is powerfully affected by political events, especially social security affairs. Consistent withdrawal into alcohol or drugs brings contact with the polity quickly enough; and today much music, art, theater and business is preeminently political. Conspicuous consumption means tax investigation. Television brings politics home just in time for pre-dinner indigestion. Finally, the academy and the church have become more fully a part of the political system than ever before. In short, for better or worse, we have become a no-exit polity! Today people have to fight to withdraw from American politics.

Again, the difficulty of successful political withdrawal is one of the reasons we hypothesize that withdrawal is not now a typical consequence of political alienation.

If alienation is not associated with withdrawal, but with its opposite, an overt information search, what kind of information search can be expected? The studies cited above as showing alienation to be associated with screening out political stimuli show us exactly what the alienated man's information-search will not be like. All of those studies found that the alienated tend to screen out stimuli from the very political system from which they were alienated or from media which are associated with that polity. This is not surprising. The alienated man can hardly be expected to seek trustworthy information from the very system he has just devalued. He is most unlikely to be looking for alternatives to the political system in information sources he regards as part of, or favorable to, the political system which threatens him.

As Kornhouser puts it: "People become available for mass behavior when they lack attachment to proximate objects. When people are divorced from their community . . . they are free to reunite in new ways. Furthermore [they] are disposed to seek . . . new sources of attachment and allegiance."[3]

The alienated man's information problems can be solved by a search for information from and about radical and revolutionary sources. First, these sources will certainly provide him with alternatives to the distrusted media, which are part of (or associated with) the devalued political system. Second, these sources are likely to provide him with alternative courses of action for dealing with the threat he feels from the alienating polity. Third, radical and revolutionary groups provide at least two possibilities for achieving a sense or community—community in the group and community in the changed society the group is trying to create. Therefore, radical or revolutionary information sources may well provide the alienated individual with a new and satisfying place to reinvest his political identification.

We further hypothesize, therefore, that: (1) political alienation is significantly associated with an active, overt search for information from and about radical and revolutionary sources; (2) alienated individuals who distrust media associated with the regular political system will read significantly more radical material than do alienated people who do not distrust these media; (3) politically alienated individuals who find their alienation to be uncomfortable or threatening will tend to seek significantly more information from and about radical or revolutionary sources.

If our hypothesis that the alienated do not tend to withdraw even from "system media" but use it as a source of information about radical politics is true, then we would expect alienated people to read as much ordinary news as nonalienated people do but, in addition, to read far more news about radical and revolutionary phenomena than do the nonalienated. We would also hypothesize that alienation would constitute a predisposition to read underground or anti-system materials.

These hypotheses, if true, have some important implications. First, if alienated people today do tend to seek political stimulation, then—reasoning from the predisposition-activation theory—more overt alienated behavior can be expected in and against the American polity. Second, if alienated people tend to seek radical information in the regular press and to place themselves in a radical communications network, then the system's ability to "reclaim the alienated" may be quite limited (and, perhaps, declining). If this is so, then the competition between the political system and the various anti-systems for the hearts and minds of the American people may be a most unequal one—a fact that has fundamental import for the future of American politics. If the alienated, in effect, place themselves outside the communications structure reachable by the ordinary polity and inside a communications structure where they hear only reinforcement of their alienation, a perpetual negativity—and perhaps an escalating negativity—is likely. The data reported below suggest that the beginnings of this kind of communications gap is already apparent in America and may produce an increase in revolutionary interest.

An experimental test of these hypotheses

Measures. Two separate tests of these hypotheses were made, a laboratory experiment and a sample interview survey. In the experiment we executed the following post-factum design: Seventy-nine American undergraduate volunteers were employed as subjects and were paid six dollars each to participate in what was described to them as a "mass media experiment."

Measurements of three independent variables, alienation from the American political system, negative evaluation of that alienation and negative evaluation of newspapers were then taken on a pre-experimental questionnaire. Estrangement was tapped by a four-item index composed of such items as: (1) I usually identify myself (feel closely associated) with American politics and government; and (2) In American politics, power is maintained by secrecy and collusion which excludes even the interested citizen. The additional items and index validity (that is, inter-item correlations) of these measures is given in the Methods Appendix. Following conceptual distinctions in the literature, we employed two separate measures of the respondent's tendency to use the media in an escapist or vicarious fashion: (1) Noninformational uses of the media operationalized as a three-item index of items such as: I read the newspaper more for fun than for information, It is facts, not diversion, that I want in a newspaper; (2) Preference for sensationalism in the media, tapped by such statements as: If a newspaper headline doesn't surprise or shock me, I'm less likely to read the article.

Negative evaluation of alienation and negative evaluation of newspapers was tapped respectively by the following single-item indicators, offered here as face-valid: (1) I feel generally alienated from politics and government in the U.S. and find that to be an unpleasant situation; and (2) I think American newspapers report political campaigns rather fairly.

Subjects were then given an experimental newspaper, a 42-page document composed of news articles from the *New York Times, Philadelphia Inquirer* and *Philadelphia Bulletin* (the sources of the articles, except for news services, were not identified). The experimental newspaper differed from a standard quality newspaper in only three basic respects: (1) it was typewritten rather than set in newsprint; (2) it was on 8" x 11" paper rather than newspaper size;[4] (3) it contained five articles on revolution that were not taken from real newspapers but were written, in *New York Times* style, by the experimenter.[5] These articles were about the rise of revolutionary groups in America; an alleged meeting of student revolutionaries; the psychology of revolution (a book review); the revolutionary potential in the U.S. stemming from our urban crises (an editorial); and the idea that planned change, not violent change, is the "real" revolution (an interpretive column). Two of the revolutionary articles were included in the political news section of the paper (at the one-third and two-thirds points in that section to avoid latency or recency effects); one each was placed in the middle of the interpretive political commentary section, the book review section and the editorial section. In addition to these subject sections, the newspaper contained sections on business news, society news, sports, obituaries, ads, fillers and letters to the editor.

Subjects were instructed to read this newspaper just as they would read any other, to read as much or as little as they ordinarily would, to read in whatever order they ordinarily did. Subjects checked each article that they read. In this manner we obtained measures of our dependent variables; total political articles read and total revolutionary articles read. A recall instrument was administered to determine whether subjects were just checking articles without reading them (perhaps in response to latent demand characteristics), but no evidence of this kind of response bias was discovered.

Subjects completed these experimental procedures in approximately one hour.

Findings. The data tend to confirm each of the hypotheses advanced above. Table 11.1 shows that bivariate relationships between political alienation and total political articles read, total revolutionary articles read and self-reported vicarious use of the media.

TABLE 11.1

THE RELATIONSHIPS OF POLITICAL ALIENATION TO TOTAL POLITICAL READING; TOTAL REVOLUTIONARY READING AND VICARIOUS USE OF THE MEDIA.

Total Political Reading	*Total Revolutionary Reading*
0.15	0.28*

Noninformational Use of Media	*Preference for Sensationalism in Media*
—0.07	0.15

* = Significant at 0.01.

The correlation between political alienation and total revolutionary reading is significant at 0.01 or better; those between political alienation and political reading and vicarious uses of the media are not statistically significant. As hypothesized, the alienated did not tend to withdraw from political information, and they did tend to seek revolutionary information.

Our second hypothesis, that the alienated people who have negative evaluations of their alienation will be significantly more interested in radical or revolutionary phenomena, is also supported in our data. The relationship of alienation + negative valuation of alienation to political information seeking can be seen in Table 11.2.

===== TABLE 11.2 =====

DIFFERENCE OF MEANS: THE RELATIONSHIP BETWEEN ALIENATION +
NEGATIVE EVALUATION OF ALIENATION TO TOTAL POLITICAL READING

	Alienation and Negative Evaluation of Alienation	*Alienation Without Negative Evaluation of Alienation*	*Value of +*	*Significance Level*
Mean Number of Political Articles Read	4.89	6.67	0.83	ns
Mean Number of Revolutionary Articles Read	3.29	1.67	1.35	0.01

Inspection of Table 11.2 indicates that even people who are uncomfortable with their alienation do not tend to withdraw from ordinary politics but they seek even more revolutionary information than do people who are satisfied with their alienation.

We also hypothesized that alienation would be significantly and positively related to negative evaluation of newspapers and that the confluence of alienation and negative evaluation of newspapers would be significantly and positively related to revolutionary reading but not to political reading. Both of these hypotheses also appear to be verified in our data.

The correlation coefficient of political alienation with negative evaluation of newspapers was 0.23, significant at the 0.05 level or better. The data summarized in Table 11.3 indicates that alienated individuals who negatively evaluate newspapers tend to read more revolutionary, but not significantly more ordinary political material.

From this study, we conclude that the appeals of reformist, radical and revolutionary organizations probably can get through to politically alienated audiences, because alienation does not predispose men to screen out such appeals, as had been previously hypothesized. In fact, political alienation appears to predispose individuals to be more interested, rather than less interested, in such communications.[6]

TABLE 11.3

THE RELATIONSHIP BETWEEN ALIENATION + NEGATIVE EVALUATION OF NEWSPAPERS TO POLITICAL READING AND REVOLUTIONARY READING

	Alienation (+) Negative Evaluation of Newspapers	*Alienation Without Negative Evaluation of Newspapers*	*+ Score*	*Significance Level*
Mean Number of Political Articles Read	5.21	4.83	0.44	ns
Mean Number of Revolutionary Articles Read	3.58	2.42	7.09	0.0005

A sample survey test of these hypotheses

To determine whether these relationships, operative in the laboratory, were also characteristic of the "real" political worlds of university students, a survey on this subject was conducted at Temple University in Philadelphia during the spring of 1970. Our respondents were 215 students enrolled in the required introductory course in political science. The questionnaires were administered on a voluntary basis in class by the course instructors.

These questionnaires permitted observation on five variables relevant to the communications behavior of alienated students. These were: (1) the attitude of political alienation; (2) a measure of the degree to which respondents read standard "system" sources of political information (for example, *Newsweek, Time*); (3) a measure of the degree to which respondents read underground and radical information sources (for example, *Philadelphia Free Press, Berkeley Barb,* Black Panther publications; (4) the degree to which respondents knew about radical political figures (for example, Bobby Seale, Abbie Hoffman); and (5) the degree to which respondents believed that these radical leaders would be important in the future. Each of these measures were multi-item indexes (items and index-validity are reported in the Methods Appendix).

Our hypotheses, again, were that alienation would not be significantly associated with low degrees of "system-reading" but that alienation would be significantly and positively related to radical reading, knowledge of radical figures and perceptions that radicals would be important in the future of American politics. Table 11.4 shows the relationships on these variables obtained in this data.

═══════════ TABLE 11.4 ═══════════

CORRELATION COEFFICIENTS OF ALIENATION WITH COMMUNICATIONS
VARIABLES AMONG UNIVERSITY STUDENTS

System Reading	Radical Reading	Radical Knowledge	Perception of Radical Future
0.02	0.26*	0.17*	0.10

$n = 79$
* = Significant at 0.05 or better.

As in the laboratory experiment, alienation among these students is not associated with low levels of political information-seeking in "system" sources but is significantly related to the quest for political information in radical sources. Also, the alienated *are* significantly more aware of radical political figures and thus have a broader range of potential reference-groups than do the nonalienated. The particular radicals included in this study, however, do not seem to have succeeded in attracting these alienated students, as the students do not believe in the staying power or the future importance of these particular radicals.

Again, alienation fosters stimulation-seeking, suggesting that—whatever the behavioral predispositions these alienated young people have adopted—it is more likely, rather than less likely, that overt political behavior will result from their alienation. Again, there is some tendency shown here for the alienated to put themselves in a radical communications structure.

Political alienation and communications behavior in adult urban populations

In two studies of alienated college students, our hypotheses appear to be confirmed. Our city-wide sample interview survey of Newark and our study of East Torresdale afford us the opportunity to examine the validity of these ideas among adult urban populations.

In Newark, our interview schedule included items on the degree to which respondents spent their spare time in reading daily newspapers, weekly newsmagazines and "slick" magazines (*Life, Look*). We coded responses to these items into an index of "connectedness to newsmedia." In addition, the Newark survey instrument inquired about the frequency of the respondent's television and radio use and of his reading of non-news printed matter. Responses to these items were aggregated into a general "connectedness to media" index. Finally, both in Newark and in East Torresdale, respondents were asked to give the name of their local representatives (city councilman, etc.) as part of a "political knowledge" measure.

If political alienation were generally associated with a tendency to screen out political stimuli, we should expect significant negative correlation between alienation and our communications and knowledge measures. Of course, our hypothesis was that no such relationship would be evidenced. Table 11.5 shows the relationships among these variables in our data.

TABLE 11.5

CORRELATION COEFFICIENTS OF POLITICAL ALIENATION WITH
COMMUNICATIONS VARIABLES IN NEWARK AND EAST TORRESDALE

News Media Connectedness (Newark)	General Media Connectedness (Newark)	Knowledge (Newark)	Knowledge (East Torresdale)
0.06	0.01	0.01	0.07

We regard these data as rather clear indication that political alienation is not generally associated with a screening out of political stimuli.

But to find that political communications, and especially radical and revolutionary communications, can get through to the information-seeking alienated is not to conclude that these individuals automatically accept these communications, or that they reinvest the identification they have withdrawn from the polity with radical or revolutionary groups. Indeed, in the next chapter, we show that alienation does not, by itself, predict to support for revolutionary organizations. We indicate there some of the relationships which govern the process by which people move from political alienation to revolutionary support.

12

FROM POLITICAL ALIENATION
TO REVOLUTIONARY SUPPORT

By DAVID C. SCHWARTZ and PETER SHUBS

We have seen that alienation is often associated with a predisposition to seek radical and revolutionary stimuli, that radical and revolutionary groups typically *can* communicate with the alienated. To move the individual from alienation to radical and revolutionary behavior, however, such communication must be accepted, must facilitate rather than inhibit behavior. One important process by which this takes place occurs when the radical group obtains the allegiance or support of the alienated individual (and, therefore, directs or at least influences his behavior).

That such support is typically a consequence of alienation is widely accepted in social theory[1] and reasonably well documented in studies of revolutionary movements.[2] The importance of public support to the success of revolutionary movements is almost universally acknowledged by revolutionary writers[3] and scholarly commentators.[4] Yet, despite this general recognition of both the importance of revolutionary support and the importance of alienation in the development of such support, there has been little systematic, empirical research on the processes whereby individuals move from political alienation to revolutionary support. This chapter represents an exploratory effort to address this need.

THEORETICAL CONSIDERATIONS

We know that political alienation is a necessary but clearly insufficient condition for the development of revolutionary support, as alienation is often followed not by revolutionary support but rather by withdrawal from political participation, non-voting, protest voting, reformism, etc. What additional factors are required to channel alienation into revolutionary paths? Almost everyone who has confronted this question has given the answer in terms of a communication or appeal from the revolutionary group to the alienated individual.[5] The alienated individual is depicted as either: newly available to hear revolutionary messages[6] or as actively predisposed to accept them.[7] The revolutionary appeal, then, functions as re-socialization to politics or as the activation of predispositions toward revolutionary behavior. In either case, the revolutionary group—intensely political by its very nature—must appeal to people who are estranged from politics. To do this, revolutionary communications must differentiate the revolutionary group from the rest of the political system, at least on those dimensions which are relevant to alienation. Although this is only implicit in the literature, the revolutionary appeal must manipulate the variables operative in the process of alienation if it is to generate revolutionary support.

Since, in our view, the alienated person is one who views the relationship between himself and the polity as one of threat and futility, we reason that he will give at least tacit support to a revolutionary organization under the condition that it effectively promises contingent reversal of the unsatisfying relationship (reduces or eliminates TVC, PI and SI). More specifically we hypothesize that, given alienation, an individual's self-identification with a revolutionary organization will be a combined function of:

1. a perception that the revolutionary organization is less threatening than the polity (and other anti-systems) because of higher value agreement between the individual and the revolutionary organization;

2. a perception that the revolutionary organization will be efficacious to attain the individual's valued political objects;

3. a perception that the revolutionary organization will make the individual a more effective political actor.

Working with these variables, we hypothesize that:

1. The presence of alienation alone does not produce revolutionary support;

2. Given that an individual is alienated, revolutionary appeals that produce perceptions of *value agreement* between the individual and organization (VA), personal *political efficacy* for the individual (PE) and the *efficacy* of the revolutionary organization in the *system* (SE) will tend to induce him to give higher degrees of support to a revolutionary organization than will appeals which produce VA alone, PE alone, SE alone or any paired combination of these.

Recent findings in social psychology suggest that persuasive appeals that arouse and channel felt-threat are more likely to produce attitude change and behavior than are communications which merely reinforce previously held beliefs.[8] From these findings, we also hypothesize that:

3. Given that an individual is alienated, a revolutionary appeal generating VA, PE and SE will produce higher degrees of revolutionary support than will communications which merely reinforce alienation; but that

4. Given that an individual is alienated, an appeal which reinforces alienation and generates VA, PE and SE will produce higher degrees of revolutionary support than either a reinforcement of alienation alone or an appeal that does not reinforce alienation.

In order to observe individuals moving from political alienation to revolutionary support, under controlled conditions, we chose to test these hypotheses through laboratory experimentation.

The design involved the inducement of alienation in relevant experimental groups, and the generation of an appeal from a revolutionary organization to effect the conversion of alienation to revolutionary support.

The basic experimental design was a multiple "test-experimental treatment-retest" design. Student subjects were randomly assigned to one of five experimental groups: (1) control—no alienation, no reinforcement, no appeal: (2) alienation and reinforcement, VA, SE appeal; (3) alienation and reinforcement, no appeal; (4) alienation, no reinforcement, VA, PE, SE appeal; (5) alienation and reinforcement, VA, PE, SE appeal.

The general procedures of the experiment were as follows: Measures of the independent variables, of alienation, and of the dependent variable, revolutionary support, were recorded prior to experimental stimulation. Then S was given a set of documents designed to induce alienation. A second recordation of TVC, PI, SI, estrangement and revolutionary support was then made. Next, alienation was reinforced in selected experimental samples, and S was given another experimental treatment in the form of the appeal document (a "transcript" of a national television interview with a revolutionary leader), designed to induce differing degrees of the independent variables in the different experimental groups. Final recordations of identification with the revolutionary organization, VA, PE, SE and political estrangement were then made. Table 12.1 summarizes these procedures.

TABLE 12.1

THE ORDER OF EXPERIMENTAL PROCEDURES

---

1. Pre-experimental measurements taken.

2. Treatment 1: Inducement of alienation in all groups except control.

3. Post-treatment measurements taken.

4. Treatment 2: Reinforcement of alienation in selected groups and inducement of independent variables in selected groups.

5. Final measurements taken.

6. Debriefing of subjects.

The character of the experimental measures

The experimental protocols included a series of direct (that is, nondisguised) indicators of the relevant variables: Political Alienation, Value Conflict, TVC, PI, SI, VA, PE, SE, Radicalism as a political orientation and Support for Revolutionary Groups. The specific questions and indices used to tap these variables are reported in the Methods Appendix.

Experimental groupings and form

Given our hypotheses, at least seven basic experimental groupings were possible: (1) VA alone; (2) PE alone; (3) SE alone; (4) VA, PE; (5) SA, SE; (6) PE, SE; (7) VA, PE, SE. In addition, experimental groups with and without reinforcement of alienation were needed, as it is theoretically important to determine whether different levels of reinforced alienation operate to determine degrees of revolutionary support. However, constraints of time and resources necessitated choosing only five groups. Table 12.2 summarizes the experimental conditions for each group.

TABLE 12.2
SUMMARY OF EXPERIMENTAL GROUPINGS

Group	Alienation Treatment	Reinforcement Treatment	VA	PE	SE
1	No	No	No	No	No
2	Yes	Yes	Yes	No	No
3	Yes	Yes	Yes	Yes	No
4	Yes	No	Yes	Yes	Yes
5	Yes	Yes	Yes	Yes	Yes

The form of the experiment was a modified simulation in which subjects were given a hypothetical political situation they were instructed to suppose to exist. S played no artificial or hypothetical role and was instructed to react as he himself honestly felt at any given point in the experiment, so that the simulation aspect of the experiment refers to the political context.

Introduction and reinforcement of stimuli

Alienation was induced in a hypothetical "elitist" change in voter eligibility. This simulated environment has been described above in Chapter 4, so here we note only that S was confronted by a situation he deemed realistic in which he was prospectively disenfranchised by a change in U.S. voter eligibility requirements. Alienation was reinforced, in the relevant experimental subsamples, by presenting S's disenfranchisement as increasingly likely and immediate.

Each of the three variables hypothesized to be operative in the development of revolutionary support were selectively induced in documents reporting the hypothetical appeal of a revolutionary organization (Voters Protection League). VA was induced by presenting the goals of the VPL as the reestablishment of voter eligibility so as to precisely coincide with the values contravened by the system—equality, constitutionality, fairness. Examples of these appeals include the following kinds of statements: "We want to replace this government with a system which will be a government of *all* the people, not the government of some insidious, self-perpetuating small elite. . . . In our new system the government would be responsive and directly responsible to all the people . . . based on the principles of equality, representation, and constitutionality."

SE was induced experimentally in the appeal by presenting the VPL as being potentially effective in achieving its goals. Coalitions, organizations, and influential individuals were reported to have already given support to the VPL, thereby inducing the perception of opening new channels of access. "We have a lot of influential people in our organization; we have the widespread support of those who are as disgusted with the present system as we are. . . . We will forge our own channels to get to [the system], since [the system] won't open up its channels to us."

PE was induced by characterizing the success of the VPL as being dependent upon the support of S. "We need people . . . just as you can't change the system alone; we can't either without help and support. . . . Together we can make waves large enough to sink their ship."

TVC, PI, SI from the system were further reinforced in the appeal: "Congress and the President obviously conspired to push through the (Electoral Reform Law). . . . There are no longer popular controls on those powers. . . . Congress has squeezed us out of the Supreme Court . . . and frankly, this scares the hell out of us. . . . Government officials are completely unresponsive to popular appeals or demands."

The revolutionary character of the VPL was expressed in such statements as: "This is a crisis, *and we are willing to use any and all means necessary to achieve our goals. . . .*"

The control sample received a document of comparable length to the experimental treatments which dealt with the relatively neutral political issue of uniform registration law proposals. This document had been successfully pre-tested for equivalent interest with the experimental treatments and the pre-test had also shown that the document was successful in not affecting TVC, PI or SI.

Sociology of the experiment

All experimental stimuli were pre-tested to ensure that they were inducing the proper effects and to ensure equal interest among the stimuli presented. All protocols were pre-tested against instrument fatigue and for subject involvement. Instrument fatigue was minimal, and extensive debriefing after pre-test indicated no significant relationship between responses and fatigue. High degrees of subject involvement were consistently achieved in the experiment, as observed both in pre-test and in comprehensive experimental debriefing. No time constraints were imposed on S in completing the experiment, since speed of completion was desired to be a function of individual reading rates as well as involvement in the situation. Also, it was felt that the imposition of time constraints might introduce another variable into the situation which was not controlled for, inducing tension or stress from a source other than those theoretically desired. In general, the experiment was completed in approximately two hours.

The experiment was conducted on a sample of American college students. Specifically, the subject sample consisted of student volunteers from the University of Pennsylvania, each subject receiving four dollars for his participation in the experiment. Subjects were allocated at random to provide an equal and known probability of inclusion for any S in each experimental subsample. Total size of the sample was 138; approximately equal subsample sizes obtained in the five experimental groups.

Findings

The data generated in this experiment provides support for each of the hypotheses stated above.

To test our first hypothesis, a comparison was made of the mean change in level of self-identification with the revolutionary organization between the Control Group and Experimental Group 3 (which received reinforced alienation stimuli but no revolutionary appeal).[9] The absence of a signifi-

TABLE 12.3

Group	Mean change in self-identification with the revolutionary organizations	t-score
Control $n = 30$	0.4	
		0.88*
Group 3 $n = 27$	0.5	

*Not significant.

cant difference between these two samples (Table 12.3) indicates that the presence of alienation alone does not produce significant degrees of revolutionary support. This is a finding of some importance, because, if alienation alone predicted to revolutionary support, there would be no need for separate modeling of the support-building process.

Due to the limitations on the number of experimental samples that time and resources permitted us to include in this study, we cannot show unambiguously that a revolutionary appeal inducing the perceptions of VA, PE and SE generates higher levels of revolutionary support than appeals inducing each of these perceptions alone or in every paired combination. We can, however, offer evidence that strongly suggests that this is true by comparing the Control Group with the VA, SE sample, and the VA, SE sample with the VA, PE, SE sample. If our hypothesis is true, then Group 2 (VA, SE) should exhibit significantly higher levels of indentification with the revolutionary organization than did Control, and the VA, PE, SE group should show significantly higher levels of such identification than did the VA, SE sample. These are precisely the relationships which obtained (Table 12.4). Both the mean changes in levels of self-identification and the final levels of self-identification with revolutionary organizations are in the hypothesized direction at statistically significant levels, indicating that, given alienation, the strength of the individual's support for revolutionary organizations is greatest under the full condition of the appeal.

===== TABLE 12.4 =====

IDENTIFICATION WITH REVOLUTIONARY GROUPS: I

	Mean change in self-identification with revolutionary organizations[1]	t-score	Final level of self-identification with revolutionary organizations
Control $n = 30$	0.4	2.00[2]	2.8
Group 2 $n = 20$	1.2		5.8
Group 5 $n = 29$	1.3	2.52[3]	6.2

[1]On a 7-point scale.
[2]Significant at the 0.025 level.
[3]Significant at the 0.01 level.

The third hypothesis, that given alienation a VA, PE, SE appeal would generate higher degrees of support than would a communication which merely reinforced alienation, was tested by comparing mean changes in levels of revolutionary self-identification in Group 3 (alienation + reinforcement, no appeal) and Group 4 (alienation, no reinforcement, VA, PE, SE appeal). Table 12.5 indicates tentative confirmation of this hypothesis. In addition, the mean level of final self-identification with revolutionary organizations is higher in Group 4 than in Group 3, suggesting that the strength of support for revolutionary organizations is more a function of the appeal than of alienation.

TABLE 12.5

IDENTIFICATION WITH REVOLUTIONARY GROUP: II

	Mean change in self-identification with revolutionary organizations[1]	t-score	Final level of self-identification with revolutionary organizations
Group 3 $n = 27$	0.5	3.1[2]	5.6
Group 4 $n = 32$	0.9		6.4

[1]On a 7-point scale.
[2]Significant at the .001 level.

The fourth hypothesis posited a greater support-building potential for the combination of reinforcement of alienation and a VA, PE, SE appeal than for either the appeal or reinforcement alone. This was tested by comparing the mean change in levels of self-identification with revolutionary organizations in Groups 3, 4 and 5 (Table 12.6). As predicted, the relationships which obtained were: (1) the mean change in revolutionary support in Group 4 was significantly greater than that in Group 3; (2) the mean change in Group 5 was significantly greater than that in Group 3; and (3) the change in mean level of self-identification with revolutionary organizations is higher in Group 5 than in Group 4 (though this relationship did not attain statistical significance). Revolutionary appeals that combine a reinforcement of alienation with the inducement of VA, SE and PE are likely to generate higher degrees of revolutionary support than appeals that concentrate on either the alienating situation alone or the revolutionary organization alone. By referring to both in the same appeal, the revolutionary organization distinguishes itself from the political system on the salient, alienation-relevant dimensions.

===== TABLE 12.6 =====

IDENTIFICATION WITH REVOLUTIONARY GROUPS: III

	Mean change in self-identification with revolutionary organizations[1]	t-score mean change	Final level of self identifi-cation	alienation level[4]
Group 3 *n* = 27	0.5	4.0[2]	5.6	1.6
Group 5 *n* = 29	1.3	—	6.2	3.0
Group 4 *n* = 32	0.9	1.17[3]	6.4	2.7

[1]On a 7-point scale.
[2]Significant at the 0.001 level.
[3]Not significant.
[4]On a 7-point scale; the lower the score, the greater the alienation.

Conclusion

It would appear, then, that revolutionary groups can generate support for themselves and thereby move alienated people from passive estrangement toward revolutionary behavior by affecting the variables that produce alienation. In other words, the same factors that account for the individual's withdrawal of self-identification from the politically organized society seem to be crucial in his reinvestment of self-identification with agencies seeking to create a new political order.

People give themselves and their loyalty to a political system and to a revolutionary movement for very similar if not identical reasons: because their dreams are writ large in it, their fundamental values are exhibited by it, their participation is essential to it. If these dignified and dignifying dreams be broken, these values contravened, this participation obviated, they withdraw their hearts and minds from each other and from the collective institutions which no longer seem to be "theirs."

This process seems to be proceeding apace in America today. In acting upon the realization that this is happening, in seeking to "reclaim the alienated", American public leaders have adopted a particularly optimistic, American and social scientific idea: the idea that involvement leads to allegiance. The truth value of this notion as presently operative in urban communities is examined in the next chapter.

13

GET INVOLVED!   AND GET ALIENATED? POLITICAL INVOLVEMENT AND POLITICAL ALIENATION IN URBAN COMMUNITIES

"Get Involved!" "Participate!" "If you're not part of the solution, you're part of the problem." "In a democracy, agreement is not essential, participation is." "Our system works if you work at it." From podium and pulpit, billboard and bus advertisement, and in virtually all of the mass media in America, these messages are transmitted daily.

One assumption which appears to underly these messages is that *political activity leads to identification with the polity*. This assumption seems basic to the American political system's response to the crises of alienation we have been experiencing—leading to programs and policies aimed at increasing citizen participation in governmental decision-making. Judging from both slogans and policy programs, the American political culture seems to include the widespread belief that nonalienated people who get involved in civic and political activity will learn that they can be effective in politics (and hence will not become alienated) and that alienated people who get politically involved will also learn personal and systemic efficacy (and hence have their alienation reversed). By appearing to move decisional power closer to the people, by encouraging local civic action groups and by publicizing these efforts, the system seems to be seeking to reclaim the alienated.

The assumption that political involvement leads to identification with the polity is rather basic to democratic theory, common in middle-class America and generally accepted in modern political science (the latter being strongly influenced by its own predominantly American, middle-class characteristics). Therefore, it is perhaps not very surprising that this assumption has had strong impact on scholarly thinking about political alienation. The hypothesis that social connectedness is inversely related to alienation, an hypothesis that we have already seen to be widespread in the literature, is clearly based upon this assumption; it presumed that the socialization and reinforcement effects of social contacts would induce better connected individuals to identify themselves with the society. Similarly, the argument that interest groups, and especially political parties, link men to the polity, is another example of this assumption in operation. Indeed, the absence of such associational linkages is seen as evidence of mass society, the most distinguishing feature of which is individual alienation.

As we have indicated, this assumption is not restricted to social theory or academic study. Rather, it is increasingly operative in shaping public policies and structural changes in American politics. In recent years, government administrators, seeking to reclaim the alienated and attributing some of the weaknesses of educational, welfare and other social service programs to community apathy, have increasingly sought to involve the community by sponsoring and supporting various local groups. Accordingly, an increasing number of social change programs have come to include a "community involvement" requirement; and a multiplicity of issue-specific community groups have come into existence or grown because of this governmental recognition and support. Social workers, too, have expanded their field of operations from individual case work to a variety of more collective efforts, supporting, and sometimes creating, welfare rights organizations, tenants rights organizations and a variety of *ad hoc* local committees. *The result of popular exhortation and public practice has been the rapid public proliferation of new organizations in the American polity*: new, local organizations of shifting membership and leadership, of various and changing representativeness, of varying sensitivity to the moods of local critics and clientele and of federal funders.

The new and expanding list of political associations and agencies is impressive even in a political culture like America's in which associations abound. A knowledgeable conversation on urban affairs today might well include mention of: model cities, model school districts, CACs, PACs, area-wide councils, local assessment boards, O.E.O., F.A.S.S., W.R.O., H.U.D., the Urban Coalition, Operation Breadbasket—to name only a few groups, agencies and programs which did not even exist a decade ago. Most of these programs and agencies are aimed at, and, to some degree, peopled by, the newly visible poor. In contemporary America this means, of course, that much of this new politics is black politics.

Is the assumption which underlies this vast new arena of participation correct? James Q. Wilson has put the problem aptly. He writes that the "neighborhood civic association is widely regarded as not only a new mechanism for representing citizen wants to the city bureaucracy but as a way of ending the political 'alienation' of those citizens," *but that it is far from clear* "whether such neighborhood groups will provide a means whereby citizens can overcome their alienation or whether they will provide a forum in which citizens can give expression to it."[1] This is another way of asking whether involvement in the new groups and programs leads to identification with, or to alienation from, the major institutions of the American polity. As people acquire familiarity with procedures and styles and strategies in American politics through participation in local civic associations, do they transfer their new found efficacy to the principal agencies of political participation, such as political parties?

These are questions of fundamental import both to the polity and to political science. For the polity, if the political parties do not involve the people and aggregate the interests represented by these new local associations—or are not perceived to be doing an adequate job of this—then we might well expect profound structural change in the American polity in the form of either the semi-permanent institutionalization of these associations or, more likely, their violence-relevant radicalization. In short, unless the political parties do relate to the new organizations, black and poor white Americans will not be integrated for some time to come into the American polity as we have known it. From the scholarly point of view, if involvement does not produce identification, then a good many of our social science notions of the functioning of political systems need basic modification.

Hypotheses

In our view, there is no one invariant effect of involvement on alienation: the effect on political alienation and allegiance will depend upon what is learned as a result of involvement. If one learns that one can be effective, that the polity can be moved, then involvement will lead to allegiance to or identification with the political system. If involvement yields only disappointment and frustration, teaches only that one is inefficacious, then to get involved is to get alienated. Our reasoning runs as follows.

We have seen in Newark and elsewhere that the mere fact that a person is a member of social or political organizations does not, in itself, tend to have a significant impact on the degree of his alienation. Seeman, however, has shown that organizational membership generally does have the impact of reducing perceived powerlessness;[2] and we have shown that perceived powerlessness does usually increase alienation.[3] It seems likely, therefore, that membership in political organizations produces low or reduced levels of alienation if that membership experience teaches the individual that he is politically effective.

Organizational connectedness or involvement can have this effect in at least three possible ways: (1) it can induce in the individual a perception that the organization is politically effective, thereby making him less politically powerless; (2) it can induce the perception that the individual is effective *within* the organization (which might be satisfying irrespective of the group's macro-political efficacy); (3) both of these processes might be operative simultaneously. This suggests that a more comprehensive understanding of the effects of social connectedness would be achieved if we inquired about the individual's satisfactions with such connectedness.

The need to confront these matters of individual satisfaction with political involvement has been recognized in the literature,[4] and there is at least one preliminary finding which indicates the utility of this approach.[5] These matters, moreover, are now of distinct relevance today in both the lower middle class white neighborhoods and the black ghettoes of our cities, for a multiplicity of new groups and agencies are operating in both these settings. In this chapter, we compare the impacts of group processes on political alienation in a white and a black Philadelphia community.

INVOLVEMENT AND
ALIENATION IN EAST TORRESDALE

The white, lower-middle-class area of East Torresdale in Philadelphia was described in Chapter 2 as a modern, middle-aged neighborhood that is anxious to maintain its present character, somewhat status threatened and somewhat status quo in political orientation. It will be recalled that East Torresdale was selected as an interesting research site because of its seeming representativeness of white, lower-middle-class, urban communities in America. It was also a particularly appropriate locus of research for a study of political involvement, as the East Torresdale Civic Association is a well-known, politically energetic community organization that was engaged in several highly visible activities at the time of our study (spring 1969). Accordingly, we could expect to observe, and did in fact observe, a wide range of organizational satisfaction and dissatisfaction in East Torresdale.*

Our sample was composed of 32 members of the Civic Association who completed our questionnaire at a meeting of the Association and 44 non-members, selected on a random-block, random-house basis, who completed the survey instrument in their homes. The 76 men and women comprising our sample represented a response rate of 62.8 percent. Our "average" respondent was 43 years old, a high school graduate earning between eight and twelve thousand dollars per year who perceived himself to be of the lower middle class.

The questionnaire permitted observations to be made on the following variables:

(1) *Urban political alienation*—a three-item index of items such as: When I think about Philadelphia government and politics, I feel like an outsider;

---

*This study was conducted by David C. Schwartz and William Nelsen.

(2) *Organizational connectedness*—(a) member (b) non-member but familiar with organization and its activities (c) nonmember and unfamiliar with the organization;

(3) *Perceived effectiveness of the organization*—a four-item index composed of items such as (a) The East Torresdale Association is effectively making its views known in City Hall and (b) The East Torresdale Civic Association will not be effective in reaching its goals for this neighborhood.

(4) *Perceived political efficacy within the organization*—a four-item index including: (a) I am not able to influence the decisions made by the East Torresdale Civic Association and (b) In general, I feel satisfied with the role I play in the East Torresdale Association.

(5) *Perceived personal political efficacy of the individual in city politics* —a two-item index comprising: (a) There is really very little that I can do to influence decisions in City Hall and (b) My views and those of my neighbors are being heard in City Hall.

(6) *Political knowledge*—a two-item index of items asking respondents to name their local representatives in city government. This variable was included because it was hypothesized that organizational connectedness might function as a socializing phenomenon and thereby affect an individual's perceived efficacy and alienation by increasing his political knowledge.

Findings

These indices were employed in correlational and multiple regression analyses. As we had hypothesized, there is no significant, linear, bivariate relationship between political involvement and urban political alienation ($r = -0.16$). But involvement in political groups does relate to political alienation through the mediation of psychological variables. The line of reasoning stated above, where involvement is hypothesized to affect an individual's perceived political efficacy and where an individual's satisfactions internal to a political group affect his level of alienation, tends to be confirmed in our regression analysis. The following flow diagram represents the pattern of associations which obtained in our data; the strength of each association is stated in terms of its Beta weight.

Figure 13.1 shows two major paths by which organizational involvement functions to produce low levels of alienation. First, involvement seems to work directly upon an individual's sense of personal political efficacy, increasing it; and since perceived inefficacy or powerlessness leads to alienation, involvement operates to produce or maintain low individual alienation. Secondly, organizational involvement seems to function as a political socialization vehicle such that those organizational members who do learn something about politics from the organization tend to see themselves as effective in the organization, to see the organization as politically effective

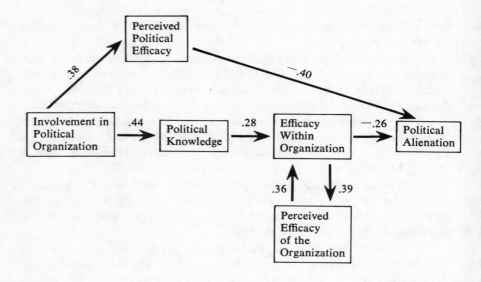

FIGURE 13.1

ORGANIZATIONAL CONNECTEDNESS, ORGANIZATIONAL SATISFACTIONS,
POWERLESSNESS AND POLITICAL ALIENATION

N.B.: Relationships not indicated by arrow and Beta weight tend not to be statistically significant.

in city politics and hence to remain allegiant to the urban polity. Conversely,
those individuals who do not traverse this second path would presumably remain or become more alienated. It appears that political involvement does
function in the alienation process by having impact upon the psychological
variables in that process, and that the degree of an individual's satisfactions
with his political reference group constitutes a basic intervening variable
between political involvement and political disaffection.

Conclusion

Apparently, then, the "involvement-to-allegiance" model holds reasonably
well for Philadelphia's white middle class. But does that model work for
the black Americans to whom it is now being applied in a panoply of programs and exhortations? That question was the subject of a second study,
presented below. In essence, then, we examine here another aspect of
racial differences in alienation.

ALIENATION FROM POLITICAL PARTIES
IN A BLACK GHETTO

The setting and source of data

It is about four miles from East Torresdale to the heart of the North Philadelphia black ghetto, but measured on almost any human dimension, the
distance is enormous. In the white, lower-middle class area, politics is
motivated by status anxieties and fear of neighborhood change. North
Philadelphians are afraid that their neighborhood won't change—and
scared, too, that the sudden violence of kids and cops and the slower violence of drugs and despair will keep on keeping on. Unlike the situation in
East Torresdale, it is not primarily one's social status that is insecure; the
working class and welfarites of North Philadelphia have a status that has
been all too stable—at the bottom of the American status hierarchy.

But gang control of "turf" is a fact of life, and death, in North Philly:
about 40 young people are murdered in gang-related activities every year.
So, while status mobility is desired for the future, it is physical mobility,
the ability for one's kids to walk to school without being killed, that is of
intense concern in the ghetto now. So, too, are the problems of poor sanitation, inadequate housing, limited job opportunities, and the ever-present
abandoned cars, taprooms and drugs. In sum, though they are not yet in
the middle of our society, the black people of North Philadelphia are
troubled in the middle of their struggle to get there and, like so many other
Americans, they, too, have turned to local community development programs, civic organizations, "ad hoc" political associations and the like to
resolve some of their problems.

But, given all of the differences between the two neighborhoods, the
question arises: would the involvement of people in these programs and
associations lead to identification with, or alienation from, more permanent
political institutions, such as political parties?

An opportunity to study this question and to examine some of the general relationships among civic activity, party alienation, value conflict and
perceived inefficacy, was presented to us through the courtesy of one of
North Philadelphia's most active community organizations, the North City
Congress.*

From June 1966 through December 1968, the North City Congress conducted a Police-Community Relations Program in North Philadelphia under
the sponsorship of the Office of Juvenile Delinquency and Youth Development of the United States Department of Health, Education and Welfare.
The purpose of this program was to mitigate some of the sources of tension and to promote cooperation between the police and the communities

---

*This study was conducted by David C. Schwartz and Gerald West.

they served in Philadelphia's largest black neighborhood. *A major aim was to foster and coordinate community organizations of several different types.* To this end, the program sponsored and conducted 830 meetings with a total attendance of 11,791. These meetings were concerned with a wide gamut of topics of local interest—sanitation, housing, abandoned cars, taprooms, youth problems, as well as problems with the police. The majority of these meetings were of two types: community workshops and intergroup sessions.

Community workshops were organized on a neighborhood basis to deal with the community's relations with the police in an informal, mutually educational manner. The workshops normally consisted of two 2½ hour sessions scheduled a week apart. The second session was largely devoted to preparing the group for an intergroup session. The intergroup sessions were designed to bring police and citizens into direct contact with one another in a small group setting to discuss police-community-relations problems.

From lists of the registered citizen participants in these two types of meetings, a random sample ($n = 854$), stratified by police district, was drawn and personally interviewed. By definition, then, the sample population was composed of the more interested, involved, active sector of the North Philadelphia populace. The survey schedule inquired about four major types of data: personal background, evaluation of personal participation in the program, evaluation of the neighborhood conditions in relation to the program, and basic political opinions and attitudes. The schedule was composed of 51 questions, mostly open-ended items.

This schedule was not designed specifically to investigate the relationships of interest here. It did, however, permit the *post-facto* construction of relevant measures for this study. The indices which we constructed were, of course, limited by the nature of the questions asked and their wording. As a result, the comparability of some of these measures to the investigation-designed indices in other of our studies must be interpreted with some caution.

Hypotheses and measures

Indices or indicators of eight relevant variables were constructed: (1) alienation from political parties; (2) degree of activity with police community relations program (PCRP); (3) political interest and participation; (4) political connectedness; (5) social connectedness; (6) expectation of effectiveness of PCRP; (7) perceived value conflict; (8) perceived efficacy of political party personnel.

If civic activity leads to identification with the political party institutions, we should expect a negative relationship between a person's degree of activity in the PCRP and his degree of alienation from the parties. If, however, such activity is seen in the ghetto as a substitute for, or antithetical to, party activity, then a positive relationship should be seen both between civic activity and party alienation and between civic activity and the expectation that the PCRP would be effective.

Similarly, if political interest and connectedness function as we ordinarily expect them to, there should be negative relationships between these variables (3, 4 and 5 above) and alienation from the political parties. But if a concern with public affairs and a firsthand knowledge of local politics only makes the interested ghetto resident more aware of the inadequacies of such politics, then the closer he gets to the local political system, the more alienated he will become.

Finally, we would expect perceived value conflicts to politicize individuals and perceived inefficacy of politics to be alienating, so that we hypothesize the existence of significant relationships between variables 1 and 7 and 1 and 8.

Measures

The measures used to test these hypotheses are presented below. Unless otherwise noted, all indices were constructed by scoring the items, establishing the homogeneity of the index via intercorrelation of index items and averaging the scores.

1. *Alienation from Political Parties*
    (a) In the present attempt to solve North Philadelphia's problems, do you think that community organization like P-CR District or Area Committees are more able or less able than the political party structure to get results?
    (b) Do you think community organizations would be more effective or less effective in solving community problems if they worked directly through the political party structure?
    (c) Do you think community organizations would be more effective or less effective if they attempt to control that structure, for instance, by electing committeemen, etc.?
2. *Degree of Activity with the PCRP* (2 items)
    (a) Would you say you are still active with the PCRP?
    (b) How much time, on the average, have you been spending on activities connected with the program during the last few months?
3. *Political Interest—Participation*
    (a) Generally speaking, how much interest would you say you have in politics: a great deal, a fair amount, only a little, or no interest at all?
    (b) Have you ever done any work for a political party or candidate?
4. *Political Connectedness*
    (a) There are about four political party committeemen in your election district. Are you acquainted with any of them?

(b) If yes, can your acquaintance be described as: personal, casual, or only at election time?

(c) What (political) organizations do you belong to?

5. *Social Connectedness*

(a) What other organizations do you belong to?

(b) How active would you say you are in each of them?

6. *Attitudes and Expectations of Program Efficacy*

(a) Have you gotten anyone to do anything in connection with the program, such as attending meetings, making a complaint, joining a committee?

(b) Have you made further attempts to get people to do something?

(c) If the PCRP were to end, do you think the organized part of it to which you belong would continue by itself?

7. *Perceived Value Conflict*

A single-item indicator, offered here as face-valid: Has there been any general change in your neighborhood since the last interview? Are things getting better, worse or are they about the same? A response of "worse" was taken to indicate a summative value conflict, it being assumed that all respondents would regard neighborhood decline as conflicting with their value 'preference. Note that this is not a direct measure of TVC as there was no indication of the degree of threat which respondent felt as a function of the perceived neighborhood decline. *Accordingly, while we reason that most respondents would feel at least somewhat threatened by this value conflict, we might well expect the relationship between value conflict and alienation to be somewhat weaker here than is true in our other studies of the relationship between TVC and alienation.*

8. *Perceived Inefficacy of Political Party Personnel*

(a) (Filter) What specific roles do you think the politicians (especially your committeemen and ward leaders) should play in solving (housing, employment, education and police community relations) problems? If the answer to the filter question is "direct action" (vs. "indirect action," "can't say," "none"), and the answer to the following question was "no," this was assumed to reflect the respondent's perception of political party personnel as inefficacious.

(b) Have any of these politicians (ward leaders and committeemen) ever been of any help to you?

Findings

The pattern of findings in our data runs counter to the conventional wisdoms regarding the relationships between alienation and civic activity. The more active a person was in the organizations, groups and activities comprising the civic action program (PCRP), the more alienated he tended to be from political parties (Table 13.1). Civic activity in this population led not to identification but to estrangement from political processes.

TABLE 13.1

THE RELATIONSHIP BETWEEN PARTY ALIENATION AND DEGREE OF INVOLVEMENT WITH CIVIC ACTIVITY PROGRAM

| | | *Degree of Activity* | | | |
		0	*1*	*2*	*3*
	0	158	22	13	140
	1	78	13	12	89
Alienation	2	9	1	1	9
	3	72	8	6	73
	4	18	6	0	21

$X^2 = 48.23$; d.f. $= 12$. X^2 is significant at 0.001.

Some of the reasons for this finding become clear from inspection of Tables 13.2 and 13.3. Apparently, the satisfactions of civic activity did not generalize to other political activities but were seen as satisfying substitutes for political involvement. Thus, the more active participants in PCRP also tended to perceive that civic action program to be an effective social change agent, and people sharing that perception—whether highly involved or not—tended to be alienated from the political parties in the ghetto.

TABLE 13.2

THE RELATIONSHIP BETWEEN DEGREE OF ACTIVITY AND PERCEPTION OF PROGRAM EFFICACY

| | | *Degree of Activity* | | | |
		0	*1*	*2*	*3*
	0	1	0	0	0
	1	245	32	23	242
	2	0	0	0	1
Perception	3	0	0	0	1
of	4	25	7	5	97
Efficacy	5	5	0	0	11
	6	1	1	0	4
	7	60	11	4	78

$X^2 = 45.71$; d.f. $= 21$. X^2 is significant at 0.01.

=============== TABLE 13.3 ===============

THE RELATIONSHIP BETWEEN PERCEPTION OF PROGRAM EFFICACY AND
PARTY ALIENATION

		Alienation				
		0	1	2	3	4
	0	0	0	0	0	1
	1	229	110	11	164	24
	2	0	0	1	0	0
Program	3	1	0	0	0	0
Efficacy	4	38	41	2	43	10
	5	4	5	0	6	1
	6	0	0	0	4	2
	7	61	36	6	42	7

$X^2 = 93.60$; d.f. $= 28$. X^2 is significant at 0.001 or better.

Part of the reason for these findings may also derive from the fact that respondents who perceived the civic action program as effective tended also to see the ghetto political party leaders as ineffective (Table 13.4).

=============== TABLE 13.4 ===============

THE RELATIONSHIP BETWEEN EXPECTATION OF PROGRAM EFFICACY AND
INEFFECTIVENESS OF POLITICAL LEADERS

		Inefficacy	
		0	(Low-High)	1
	0	1	0
	1	512	30
Expectation of	2	0	1
Program	3	1	0
Efficacy	4	119	15
(Lo-Hi)	5	10	6
	6	5	1
	7	139	14

$X^2 = 38.46$; d.f. $= 8$. X^2 is significant at 0.001.

The relationships between alienation and political participation and connectedness obtained in our data are also at variance with those typically found or expected in white, middle-class populations. In such populations, persons who express interest in politics, who work for parties or candidates or who belong to social and political organizations might be expected to be less alienated from politics than their less participant, less connected counterparts. In North Philadelphia, this is not so. Political participation, political connectedness and social connectedness are all positively related to alienation. (Tables 13.5, 13.6, 13.7).

TABLE 13.5

THE RELATIONSHIP BETWEEN POLITICAL INTEREST AND PARTY ALIENATION

		Political Interest - Participation		
		0	1	2
	0	250	55	28
	1	110	49	33
Alienation	2	5	10	5
	3	148	87	24
	4	22	15	8

$X^2 = 53.09$; d.f. $= 8$. X^2 is significant at 0.001.

TABLE 13.6

THE RELATIONSHIP BETWEEN POLITICAL CONNECTEDNESS AND ALIENATION

		Political Connectedness				
		0	1	2	3	4
	0	166	31	10	82	44
	1	72	14	10	60	36
Alienation	2	2	3	0	7	8
	3	108	21	17	85	28
	4	9	2	12	11	11

$X^2 = 79.39$; d.f. $= 16$. X^2 is significant at 0.001.

TABLE 13.7

THE RELATIONSHIP BETWEEN SOCIAL CONNECTEDNESS AND ALIENATION

		Social Connectedness		
		0	1	2
	0	233	8	92
	1	108	14	70
Alienation	2	8	3	9
	3	134	21	104
	4	12	8	25

$X^2 = 53.08$; d.f. $= 8$. X^2 is significant at 0.001.

We have seen, then, that both the politically interested ghetto resident and the civically involved ghetto resident tend to be alienated. Thus, the question arises: Are these the same people? Does political interest lead to civic activity which, in turn, leads to alienation? Our data suggests that this is not the case. High degrees of civic activism are essentially unrelated to political interest and political connectedness (Tables 13.8 and 13.9).

=============== TABLE 13.8 ===============

THE RELATIONSHIP BETWEEN POLITICAL INTEREST-PARTICIPATION
AND DEGREE OF CIVIC ACTIVITY

		Degree of Activity in Program			
		0	1	2	3
Political	0	207	29	23	280
Interest-	1	89	14	6	107
Participation	2	42	8	3	47

$X^2 = 3.21$; d.f. $= 6$. X^2 is not statistically significant.

=============== TABLE 13.9 ===============

THE RELATIONSHIP BETWEEN POLITICAL CONNECTEDNESS AND DEGREE
OF CIVIC ACTIVITY

		Degree of Activity in Program			
		0	1	2	3
	0	124	19	16	198
Political	1	32	3	3	35
Connectedness	2	24	2	1	23
	3	103	14	7	123
	4	55	13	3	55

$X^2 = 13.58$; d.f. $= 12$. X^2 is not statistically significant.

The socially connected, however, do tend to be active in civic programs (Table 13.10).

=============== TABLE 13.10 ===============

THE RELATIONSHIP BETWEEN SOCIAL CONNECTEDNESS AND CIVIC ACTIVITY

		Degree of Activity in Program			
		0	1	2	3
Social	0	218	24	22	233
Connectedness	1	15	8	3	28
	2	105	19	7	173

$X^2 = 20.68$; d.f. $= 6$. X^2 is significant at 0.01.

What this means is that there are at least two basic paths to alienation from political parties in the ghetto: (1) from political interest and partici-pation through perceived inefficacy of party personnel to disaffection and (2) from social connectedness to civic activity which substitutes for party involvement or identification. *In short, whether one gets involved in political parties or in social organizations and civic activities, the result in the ghetto is the same—a tendency to become alienated from the political parties.*

As we have suggested above, one reason that political interest, political connectedness and social connectedness all lead to alienation may be that all three of these factors are regularly and significantly associated with the perception that local political party personnel are not effective (Tables 13.11, 13.12 and 13.13).

TABLE 13.11

THE RELATIONSHIP BETWEEN POLITICAL INTEREST AND PERCEPTION
OF PARTY PERSONNEL AS INEFFECTIVE

| | | *Inefficacy* | |
		0	1
	0	519	20
Interest	1	196	20
	2	73	27

$X^2 = 64$; d.f. $= 2$. X^2 is significant at 0.001.

TABLE 13.12

THE RELATIONSHIP BETWEEN POLITICAL CONNECTEDNESS AND PERCEPTION
OF PARTY PERSONNEL AS INEFFECTIVE

| | | *Inefficacy* | |
		0	1
	0	350	5
	1	65	8
Political connectedness	2	49	1
	3	221	26
	4	101	27

$X^2 = 57.46$; d.f. $= 4$. X^2 is significant at 0.001.

===== TABLE 13.13 =====

THE RELATIONSHIP BETWEEN SOCIAL CONNECTEDNESS AND PERCEPTION OF PARTY PERSONNEL AS INEFFECTIVE

| | | *Inefficacy* | |
		0	*1*
	0	474	23
Social Connectedness	1	41	13
	2	273	31

$X^2 = 29.05$; d.f. $= 2$. X^2 is significant at 0.001.

We conclude that a basic social science paradigm of political identification—which runs from social connectedness and political interest, through civic and political involvement, to identification with the polity—seems disconfirmed and even reversed in this ghetto population.

In previous chapters, we have shown that certain psycho-political variables, threat from politicized value conflict and a perception of personal, political inefficacy have strong impact on a person's identification with, or alienation from, political institutions. Is this also true in the ghetto? It must be recalled that this study did not permit measures comparable to those in our previous work. Here we have: (1) indications of an individual's value conflict but not of the degree to which that conflict is threatening and (2) a measure of an individual's perception of the party personnel as ineffective but not of his own sense of political efficacy. Still, from our basic stance which stresses the importance of psycho-political factors, we would expect these variables to have some impact on an individual's identification with political parties. That expectation is borne out in this data. Strong value conflicts tend to be associated with low degrees of activism in the civic action program and with low alienation from the political parties (Tables 13.14 and 13.15).

===== TABLE 13.14 =====

THE RELATIONSHIP BETWEEN VALUE CONFLICT AND CIVIC ACTIVITY

| | | *Degree of Activity in Program* | | | |
		0	*1*	*2*	*3*
	0	8	0	1	5
Value	1	90	20	22	328
Conflict	2	166	23	7	84
	3	74	8	2	17

$X^2 = 200.66$; d.f. $= 9$. X^2 is significant at 0.001.

=== TABLE 13.15 ===

THE RELATIONSHIP BETWEEN VALUE CONFLICT AND PARTY ALIENATION

		0	*1*	*2*	*3*
	0	11	148	138	36
	1	0	98	60	34
Alienation	2	0	11	4	5
	3	2	180	64	13
	4	1	21	11	12

$X^2 = 70.64$; d.f. $= 12$. X^2 is significant at 0.001.

Apparently ghetto residents who see their neighborhood as deteriorating despite all of the efforts to improve it are more likely to perceive a need to work with political parties. Value conflict, in the ghetto as elsewhere, is politicizing. Indeed, so strong is the politicizing effect of such value conflict, that the presence of this variable tends to diminish or destroy the relationships among political interest, political connectedness, social connectedness and party alienation (Tables 13.16, 13.17 and 13.18).

=== TABLE 13.16 ===

MULTIPLE CROSS TABULATION OF INTEREST VERSUS ALIENATION, CONTROLLING FOR VALUE CONFLICT

	Value Conflict		*No Value Conflict*	
	Low Interest	*High Interest*	*Low Interest*	*High Interest*
Low Alienation	64	6	388	54
High Alienation	23	7	272	29
	$X^2 = 4.05$; significance $= 0.05$		$X^2 = 1.19$; not statistically significant	

Original X^2 (value conflict not controlled) of Interest vs. Alienation $= 53.09$ (see Table 13.5).

========== TABLE 13.17 ==========

MULTIPLE CROSS TABULATION OF POLITICAL CONNECTEDNESS
VERSUS ALIENATION, CONTROLLING FOR VALUE CONFLICT

| | *Value Conflict* | | *No Value Conflict* | |
	Low Connectedness	*High* Connectedness	*Low* Connectedness	*High* Connectedness
Low Alienation	24	46	249	195
High Alienation	7	23	137	154
	$X^2 = 1.18$; not statistically significant		$X^2 = 5.69$; significant at 0.05	

Original X^2 (value conflict not controlled) of political connectedness versus alienation = 79.39.

========== TABLE 13.18 ==========

MULTIPLE CROSS TABULATION OF SOCIAL CONNECTEDNESS
VERSUS ALIENATION, CONTROLLING FOR VALUE CONFLICT

| | *Value Conflict* | | *No Value Conflict* | |
	Low *Social* Connectedness	*High* Connectedness	*Low* Connectedness	*High* Connectedness
Low Alienation	47	23	311	134
High Alienation	13	17	172	120
	$X^2 = 2.54$; not statistically significant		$X^2 = 9.45$; significant at 0.01	

Original X^2 (value of conflict not controlled) of social connectedness versus alienation = 53.00.

We have also hypothesized that inefficacy is a block to politicization. Not surprisingly, therefore, a perception that the party personnel are ineffective tends to wipe out the relationship between value conflict and low alienation (Table 13.19). Again the ghetto resident resembles the rest of the polity in finding inefficacy a block to the politicizing impacts of value conflict.

TABLE 13.19

MULTIPLE CROSS TABULATION OF VALUE CONFLICT VERSUS ALIENATION,
CONTROLLING FOR POLITICAL INEFFICACY

| | Political Inefficacy | | No Political Inefficacy | |
	Value Conflict	No Value Conflict	Value Conflict	No Value Conflict
Low Alienation	9	34	61	410
High Alienation	5	18	25	270
	X^2 = not significant		X^2 = 4.48; significant at 0.05	

Original X^2 (political inefficacy not controlled) of value conflict versus alienation = 70.64 (See Table 13.12.)

Conclusion

There is now great and growing concern about the future of the American political party system. The major national political parties have recently conducted widely publicized inquiries, looking toward the restructuring of the parties and nominating conventions to accommodate blacks, women and youth. At about the same time, the Twentieth Century Fund sponsored an official, nationwide study of the future of the political parties. In political science and practical politics, there is much debate about possible party realignments, about fundamental changes in the electorate's response to the parties.

Clearly it would be premature to predict a fundamental restructuring of the political parties or party system in America, but it does seem appropriate and timely to recognize that our political parties are in considerable flux and some trouble. If recent polls are to be believed, the idea that the parties make a difference to the basic problems confronting the polity may now be a minority position.

In the black community, the study reported above suggests that the people who are most interested in politics, and who have worked for political parties and candidates, are most alienated from the parties. Moreover, the same process that, a generation ago, tied people's politicized needs more to the administrative services of the government than to the gift baskets and other services of the local party, is operating in the ghetto today to link men more to civic action, to "the movement" and to federally funded administrative projects than to the political parties. In the short run, at least, those who are most active in such programs think least of the political parties; those who think these programs will work think that the political parties won't. A satisfying relationship with a "surrogate polity" seems to insulate men from the rest of the system.

These relationships hold true among people who think that things in their neighborhood are holding their own or improving; on the other hand, those who see their communities as slipping back, whose values are most in conflict with political reality as they see it, are most likely to want to use the political parties. Such people are likely to be raising the most fundamental political issues in the years ahead. If they, too, get involved and get alienated, the result is unlikely to be happy for them, for the political parties or for the polity as a whole.

Less speculatively, however, we conclude that a fundamental assumption under which much social science and social policy has been operating, that activity leads to identification, needs revision both in theory and application. In Philadelphia's black ghetto—and wherever else in America that people are learning that political involvement does not mean political efficacy or governmental responsiveness—to get involved is, in large measure, to get alienated.

V

Conclusion

14

FROM THE LONELY CROWD
TO THE STRIDENT SOCIETY

Summary of findings and identification of needed research

From our studies, the following conclusions seem warranted:

(1) Political alienation, defined as individual estrangement from the polity, is not now well explained by traditional approaches to its study: specifically, social structural factors and socio-cultural alienation do not bear strong, consistent, direct and linear relationship to political alienation in our data.

(2) Three variables, TVC, PI and SI do account for substantial amounts of the variance in political alienation, across a relatively broad and diverse range of American research settings.

(3) The level of an individual's political alienation and the process by which that level was reached are significantly related to the basic behavioral orientation toward politics that he is likely to adopt—predicting especially well to non-conformist orientations.

(4) SES and personality variables, in confluence with alienation levels, tend to predict toward the specific alienated behavior orientations which given individuals will adopt.

(5) Political alienation tends to be significantly associated with a predisposition to seek information (stimulation) from non-system or anti-system media and groups. Levels of alienation predict to the individual's information-seeking and political communications behavior.

(6) Such media and groups arouse and channel political behavior by activating basic behavioral orientations, and attract support for themselves by manipulating TVC, PI and SI. The extent to which leaders, groups and political communications successfully manipulate the individuals TVC, PI and SI predicts to the individual's acceptance of (allegiance to) those leaders, groups, ideologies, etc. This allegiance predicts the likely directions

231

of his political behavior, if any behavior occurs. The arousal level induced by the communications of the leaders or groups predicts the likelihood of such overt behavior.

(7) Accordingly, the process of political alienation identified in this book seems to constitute an important partial explanation of political behavior.

Naturally, it is hoped that the validity of these generalizations will be tested by other scholars in other research contexts and that they will be modified and refined in that process. Indeed, these findings have already been formalized, as a series of difference equations, by one of my students[1] and applied in a content analysis of revolutionary writings by another.[2] It is also hoped (and expected) that these findings will prove useful in dealing with other social science problems. This process, too, has already begun: TVC, PI and SI have been shown to be significantly related to cohesive behaviors in international alliances[3] and to social deviance in the form of hallucinogenic drug use.[4] In addition, the beginning of obviously needed cross-cultural research is now under way.[5]

Our findings suggest other potentially useful research into the genesis of alienation. As TVC, PI and SI seem to be major determinants of the individual's identification with the polity, we will probably want to know a great deal more about these variables than we presently seem to know. What values do people regard as political? How are values politicized? Which value conflicts most predispose peoples toward alienation? How are political values typically expressed in political systems to maintain moderate to high levels of diffuse support? How do people code their political experiences (and information about other's experiences) to determine their own efficacy and that of the political system? Some work directly related to our theory has been begun on a number of these problems. On the politicization of values, we are looking at folkloristic and mythic expressions in political discourse and, conversely, at political value expressions in popular culture—dance, drama, jokes, songs, etc.[6] The ways in which people interpret their political experiences to determine political efficacy is also a major objective in on-going studies.[7]

Further, it seems clear that we need a far more comprehensive and coherent model of the consequences of alienated attitudes, of the factors which combine with alienation to predict to the basic behavioral orientations that individuals adopt toward politics. Much more refined personality theory and social stratification theories seem called for. Extrapolating from our findings on the importance of perceived personal energy as an intervening variable, we have begun work on the political consequences of a variety of health and physiological factors.[8]

Urgently needed too, is a great deal more explicit concern with the processes whereby behavior issues from individual motivations. Indeed, it is surprising to me that behavioral political science seems to have been so concerned with attitude research that it has rather deemphasized attitude-to-behavior linkages. Here, too, I believe that physiological factors will prove extremely important because the activation of predispositions can be measured (if not defined) in physiological terms. We have started some preliminary work on this problem, too.[9]

No doubt the reader will think of many more research opportunities in the testing and application of these findings than can be listed here. One major problem area which has not been treated in this book, but which deserves very high priority indeed, is the linkages between macro-systemic (political and social) phenomena and micro-political attitudes and behavior. What social and political conditions, events and trends make for alienation? In this book we have given only the partial (that is, micro level) answer: those which create threatening value conflicts and create the perception of personal and systemic inefficacy. To provide a better answer would require both epistemological work on the levels-of-analysis problem and considerable research designed specifically to determine those dimensions of macro-systemic phenomena that are perceived and coded into TVC, PI and SI. In addition, it is very important that we begin to relate the overall level of alienation in a system, and distributions of various alienation levels across social groupings, to macro-political events.

These important tasks have not been attempted in this book. We can, however, offer an interpretation of recent, present and potential American political history in terms of alienation (and revolution), stating a plausible set of interrelationships which, if true, may explain much about the new politics in America.

From the lonely crowd to the strident society

How shall we understand American politics in the 1960s and 1970s? What shall we say of ourselves as a people and a polity in an era of burning cities and bombed campuses, riots, sniper fire, ambushes of police and firemen, political assassinations, alienating scandals signalling almost unprecedented political danger and an arms race in the cities and suburbs. Does our conventional wisdom about American public life account for pitched and deadly battles between soldiers and students or for daylight murders of Presidents, Senators and civic leaders? How shall we explain the whole sequence of radical and violent incidents and movements that has repeatedly and profoundly shocked the American political system in our time? And when certain types of political violence decline sharply, as our urban riots have, at the same time that other types of violence increase, as political assassinations and attacks on police seem to have done, how is this to be understood?

Unless our theories of political behavior can explain the changed frequency, magnitude and social location of the radical and violent behavior we observe in contemporary America, the validity of our models of man (and hence our paradigms of the polity) must be questioned. Unless we can explain the new politics *with the same variables* that we employ to account for older, perhaps more stable politics, the generality of our explanations must be doubted, for if we use one set of theories for political stability but require a very different body of theory for instability, then, at the least, we will confront a very difficult problem of theoretical integration. In sum, unless we understand where we've been and where we are and how we got here, it seems unlikely that we will understand where we are headed or that we will get where any of us wants to go—at least in one piece.

Of course, putative explanations of our politics abound. Americans— the public, politicians and social scientists, too—were surprised, puzzled and shocked by the new politics: for example, by the radicalism of the right,[10] of blacks,[11] and of students.[12] Accordingly, national, state and local investigatory commissions were empanelled again and again to explain our violent politics to us, and their reports, advancing a multiplicity of interpretations, generated extensive discussion and considerable controversy. Because we surprise ourselves, Americans have become explicitly and increasingly introspective about the character of the nation. There are great outpourings of commentary in every media on the crises of our time— alienation, polarization, violence, racism. Public seminars, confrontation meetings, crisis committees and the like proliferate and publicly search their (and our) souls. It is perhaps no exaggeration to say that we are in a period of national identity crisis (and that's what much of the violence is about, too).

The older interpretations of America do not seem to fit us so well any longer. Lord Bryce told us we were a legalistic people, and no doubt there remains some truth to this, but now we find ourselves in an era of massive and mounting civil disobedience and crime. Tocqueville brilliantly stressed our optimism and our equalitarian (however ambivalent) character, but today the national temper appears more uncertain and pessimistic than hopeful, and nonequalitarian ideologies and behavior are plentiful. Myrdal saw us following, or at least seeking, a consistent creed, but presently we are quarreling and killing each other over the quality as well as the application of the creed. The melting pot, if it ever characterized us well, seems less apt a description of America today than is a pressure cooker (or, as will be indicated below, a centrifuge). Riesman thought we were becoming less moralistic in our politics and increasingly seeking "not power but adjustment," whereas on all sides we hear demands for "black power," "student power," "power to the people" and highly moralistic political arguments. The analogies and metaphors of the past remain what they were—analogies and metaphors, not precise descriptions or explanations; they relate to the past but are without sufficient dynamic quality to chart our transition to the present, still less to the future.

Not surprisingly, then, the differences between the 1950s and 1960s in American politics have given rise to a variety of new interpretations. One school of thought has sought to minimize the differences by arguing that most students[13] (or blacks or what have you) aren't violent or radical, implying that our older understandings of ourselves still hold true for most of us. Perhaps, this implication is true (though I doubt it), but even if it is true, it is of limited utility when the radical and violent behaviors are so important, are engaged in by so many people and are approved of by so many more.[14]

Another school of thought seeks to minimize the differences between the 1950s and 1960s by showing that the 1950s weren't so peaceful as all that.[15] This is part of the general, periodic and immensely popular rediscovery of our violent past.[16] There is more than a little movement from thesis to antithesis in this approach, but, more importantly, it too misses the point: our politics have been, by turns, both peaceful and turbulent, *and the problem is to explain both contingencies.* To say that our politics experiences or exhibits periodicity, swinging from quiescence to turmoil like a pendulum, is an engaging metaphor but again fails to explain why (or when) the swings occur. That the roots of today's violent politics lie in the past is true, but this would be equally true if our politics were another "era of good feeling."

The more explicit social science theories of political stability seem not to have been rigorously applied to the contemporary American political system as a whole. Scarcely was the printer's ink dry on the celebration of our polity as stable because of value consensus when the stability was rudely shaken.[17] Did we lose our vaunted consensus so quickly? Did the myth become impotent overnight? If so, why?

Of course, this is not the place for an extended review of the social science literature on American politics and political stability. What follows is a speculative, interpretive summary of what happened in the American political system in the 1950s and 1960s to reinforce alienation and to encourage, in recent years, active rather than passive outplay of that alienation.

I believe that much of the new politics is to be explained as the outplay of political alienation in active modes, encouraged by socio-political trends which formerly inhibited active (and inured toward passive) responses to alienation; that the conditions in, and integration level of, the macro-system led to an increased value on participation among people and population sectors previously somewhat alienated but satisfied with private displacement of that alienation. We have shown that alienated people who place high value on participation tend to radicalize rather than to withdraw. Here I argue that this is precisely what has happened in America generally. More specifically, I will argue that six interrelated mass political processes have operated to restructure the nature of American politics: (1) an increase in alienation; (2) the politicization and activation of that alienation by cultural, economic and communications patterns; (3) an expansion of perceived leaderlessness, whereby the traditional political party leadership was perceived as less relevant to important problems; which led to (4) a fragmentation of our policies into ethnic, racial, sexual and generational movements; some of which reached (5) intense political consciousness and critical mass size; and engaged in (6) a complex process of radicalization (learning-coping, community- and identity-seeking behaviors, in radical fashion).

To begin with, both the 1950s and 1960s witnessed some broadly similar alienating political situations: both saw an unpopular and divisive land war in Asia, and both raised and thwarted fundamental economic and civil rights aspirations. The 1950s brought the 1954 civil rights Supreme Court decision and the failure to implement it and the pattern of prosperity and recessions. The 1960s saw the high hopes of the Kennedy years and the War on Poverty followed by the violent ending of the former and the violence-producing, grudging fits and starts of the latter.

But are substantial portions of the American population alienated from the national polity? Have the socio-political events noted above really given rise to much alienation? There is little available national data on alienation defined as estrangement, but the survey studies do permit some inferences (about estrangement and more about TVC, PI and SI). We conducted secondary analyses of Gallup polls for the 1950-1962 period and found that the percentage of respondents giving answers indicating alienation (on estrangement-type items) jumped from a mean of 4.8 percent, for the 1950s to 16 percent for the 1960-1962 period, and that the mean proportion of Gallup respondents who were estranged from political parties (believing that the parties made no difference to the resolution of policy problems) increased correspondingly from 18 percent to 35 percent. The Gallup data on TVC, in the form of desire for reforms of the polity, also increased from 50.4 percent to 60 percent in the same period.

The SRC data[18] reveals a similar but more detailed picture. The vast majority (63 percent) of Americans do not participate in politics beyond voting! Is this because they are so satisfied with our polity? No! In 1966, 52.5 percent of SRC respondents who reported an opinion believed that they would fail in any effort to influence a local governmental decision, and 70.7 percent believed that any effort they might make to affect the Congress would come to nothing.

Not only do the SRC respondents feel ineffective, they regard their political leaders similarly. Again, according to the 1966 study, 61 percent of the respondents believed that politicians could not help them (or would hurt them) in seeking governmental redress of grievance. Between 1964 and 1966, trust in the beneficence[19] and efficiency of government declined significantly.

Perhaps most important is the dramatic increase in the perception that our political parties make no difference to the resolution of our pressing public policy problems. In 1964, 51 percent of the American public (reflected in the SRC sample) believed that this was true in regard to school integration and related problems, and 48 percent thought that this was so on the question of war. By 1966, only two years later, 67 percent saw no meaningful difference between the parties' ability to handle school matters, and 62 percent believed they had no partisan choice on the overwhelmingly salient matter of war.

The conclusions, I think, are inescapable: The American people, so far from the fat and satisfied herd they have been caricatured (and slandered) as, are in fact in substantial value conflict with the polity (that is, are reformist) and perceive themselves and the polity to be inefficacious. TVC, PI and SI characterize the majority of Americans. From our findings above, I believe that national studies would reveal that alienation is now also a majority position. America, I believe, has become an alienated polity.

But the 1950s were a period in which alienation produced withdrawal, whereas in the 1960s radicalized participation, rather than withdrawal, resulted. Why? Basically, we have been observing the transition from scared to mad in American politics. The politically relevant generations in the 1950s were frightened of political activity: McCarthyism taught many that idealistic political involvement could have profoundly adverse impact on one's personal life even decades later. They remembered the depression only too well and felt economically vulnerable. They were fearful of the bomb, and, when they thought of collective action, they recalled that the major two collective political actions of their lifetime had been war. Fearful and starved for consumer goods, too, they sought the security of private economic well-being.

Of course, the America of the 1960s was different. Today's students have grown up in an era of unprecedented and seemingly automatic prosperity. Their McCarthyism was a largely unrepressed dissent. They are surfeited with economic goods and have lived all of their lives in the nuclear age. Black people are simply sick of being scared and, I think, have found collective and radical action to be less threatening than is anomic, lonely inaction.

At the systemic level, moreover, the increased integration of the American socio-political system makes withdrawal difficult. Most, if not all, great changes in a society's level of integration are accompanied (if not always accomplished) by radical activity and violence. Where can one withdraw from the polity today? Traditionalism is decreasingly attractive and possible. Family life appears to be diminishing as a terminal value (at least in certain social sectors); religion has lost much of its appeal; old people are no longer living in the bosom of the family; the frontier is long since closed. The modern arenas of our society are all politicized: business, labor, universities, the arts. The constant bombardment of the mind by the media almost certainly increases politicization. The decline of tradition makes traditional identities difficult to maintain. The politicization of modern social sectors dramatically increases the number of people with political identities. We are witnessing, then, the politicization of identity and identity crises.

Thus, when the kids decry the university as part of "the war system," they are in some measure complaining about the interpenetration by the polity of their place of withdrawal and identity-search. That is what much of the whole movement for neighborhood or community control (of schools, jobs, etc.) is about, too—an effort to acquire or retain an identity and remain somewhat withdrawn from the alienating polity. Americans have always wanted local control of government; why should black Americans want it less now that we have become a no-exit polity. The functional interdependence of social spheres, the functional interpenetration by the polity of previously nonpolitical social arenas, operates as an alienation-multiplier when policies fail.

We have said, then: (1) that the American public seems characterized by substantial and increasing TVC, PI and SI; (2) that therefore we reason it to be (and that it seems to be) quite alienated; and (3) that the socio-economic trends in the society make for active rather than passive responses to that alienation. If the general public reacts as did our respondents in the studies reported above, we should expect to be witnessing considerable political stimulation-seeking or politicization. The national data on the degree to which Americans are interested in politics and are reading about it or watching it on TV tends to confirm this hypothesis. In the Gallup polls, politicization (responding positively to interest-type items) is up from 56.7 percent in the 1950s to 66.8 percent in the 1960s. The SRC[20] data also show fairly consistent increases in American politicization.

Another aspect of our theory of alienation suggests that, in periods of high alienation, people tend to displace extraordinary degrees of free-floating anxiety on politics. Studies of the frequency, magnitude and social location of psychosomatic illnesses in America indicate that our society is now a place of considerable personal stress,[21] and the rapid increase in psychotherapy, psycho-drama, encounter groups, sensitivity sessions, as well as escapism in the forms of drugs, alcoholism and astrology testify to the truth of this indication. There is certainly plenty of anxiety around to be focused on politics. Politics can be therapeutic or escapist, too, and, while I cannot show that alienated people are increasingly turning to radical politics in part to displace private stress, extensive participant-observation in radical and reformist activity convinces me that this is so.

We have, then, a polity which induces and reinforces considerable alienation, politicizes and activates it and encourages it to be played out in active forms. Why, then, should the radicalism of the present era be surprising? We have seen that the public substantially and increasingly finds the traditional American leadership of the political parties to be irrelevant to their problems and we have known for some time that the nonelite sectors of the American population are considerably less tolerant of others and less committed to "democratic practices" than is the elite. Alienated and politicized, the nonelite participates in politics in our time not vicariously by cheering on the elite, but, finding the elite irrelevant, it participates directly by following its own less tolerant, less procedurally democratic styles. The failure of the elite to be relevant to the great policy questions which touch the lives of Americans directly—like schools and wars—has seen them increasingly swept aside. When men lack or eschew the values, the skills and the resources for stylized peaceful politics and reject the leadership of men who possess these, the result is inevitably some form of social war.

Violence is not the only result of alienated leaderlessness; there is also loneliness, hence the search for intimacy, community and new leaders. In the absence of a genuine community or satisfying polity, men will tend to seek small groups, surrogate-communities, parochial polities. And we have seen this happening all over the nation of late. Ethnic identification in politics has remained high[22] and probably increased recently. Certainly black identification and politicization is up dramatically;[23] the intellectuals have split with the labor movement;[24] politically relevant outre communities based on age, sex, drugs, race, etc. are growing everywhere. They find each other on TV and, as the ad says, in the *New York Times*. The media—both "establishment" and radical—create instant folk-heroes, too. What Riesman calls "the cult of intimacy" paradoxically creates crowds, for, as one perceptive friend put it, "that's what crowds are all about: the desire to touch as many people as possible." So, Woodstock can be reenacted at the Pentagon or White House; or at least one can try to do so, and more than a few have. The fragmentation of the polity, the breaking apart of old coalitions, and the unwillingness of students and blacks to join them, is an effort to have the system shift to a lower level of integration.

Needless to say, people who are aiming at diminutions in systemic integration may find it difficult to get together with other groups (integration for the purpose of seeking less integration does raise some problems) and this accounts, in part, for the highly fragmented character of the "liberal" or "left" movement. On the other hand, new leaders *are* being created (daily), and the coalition potential for a real social movement is not insubstantial. Nonetheless, it does appear that an appreciable parochialization of the polity is occurring. The melting pot has become the centrifuge.

Recent studies have shown that the characteristics of neighborhoods have important effects as stimulants or depressants on the outplay of attitudes,[25] providing some evidence that the more homogeneous a neighborhood is on some attribute, the greater the impact that attribute has on behavior. Riesman[26] and others have made a similar point, stating that radical movements seem to thrive in America only when they can insulate themselves from the divisive effects of the larger society. In this connection, the fragmentation or parochialization of our politics appears especially important, as it means that not only blacks, students, etc., who tend to live in relatively homogeneous communities will have their alienated and radical behaviors reinforced, but that more and more groups and communities will be moving in this direction as well. Of course, student and black activist groups are achieving and some have already achieved critical mass size, but urban ethnics and some suburban groups are not far behind.

A fragmented polity is even harder to understand than a large, complex but integrated one; there are so many possible inputs and coalitions. But confrontation politics simplifies, allowing some activists to psychologically lump all groups (except their own) together, to label all outputs as bad, and to reject reform so they don't have to monitor the polity continuously (which would increase anxiety).

And confrontation *does* simplify, does cut through the red tape, confusing procedures and dilatory studies and get response now! It makes the confronted at least recognize one's existence (a matter of fundamental importance to people seeking an identity).

Confrontation, however, also escalates conflict, generating counterdemonstrations and increasing oppositional thinking and militancy. The movement from parochialization to polarization is a short but terribly crucial one in the history of a polity.

So, the violence! On a hot summer night, a black man confronts a policeman with what the black man perceives to be an injustice (in the absence of trust, men are predisposed to see even ambiguous actions that way; in alienation, the cop becomes an alien intruder). The policeman perceives the confrontation as an attack on his authority (a threat to his identity). A crowd gathers, so the policeman calls for "reinforcements"—which means that his crowd gathers, too. The people in each crowd feel a little bolder, or less scared, because they are touching one another. They are alienated from each other (and from the polity), and both have some weapons (for we are a weapons-saturated society and need an arms control and disarmament agency for America). Identity-acquisition for the black people and identity-retention for the police mean that both crowds are inclined to activism. Add a curse or a rumor or a TV camera, and you have a riot. Put it on the front page and the TV evening news and next week it'll happen in another city.

Similarly, the kids went in a touching parochial crowd to confront a national political convention (another such crowd) and met still a third crowd, the Chicago police. The clothes, beads, beards and buttons of the kids were a source of identity-security, so, like armies, the crowds were in uniform. The students sang a little and chanted some unifying and simplifying slogans. The TV cameras told both crowds "it's instant history time—so do something," and both crowds did their thing.

When it happens on a college campus, with an uptight crowd of mailmen turned National Guard troops for the day, the result is similar if more deadly. When the public's attitudes are those of alienation, mistrust, parochialization, leaderlessness, and activism, and the attitudes of those in authority are the same (*vis-a-vis* the alienated), how can the behaviors be peaceful?

Violence at less than total levels begets violence by imitation, opposition and escalation. "I am the violent one" or, better, "we are the violent ones" is a distinctive identity. Others, seeing that violence "works," imitate it or, if they disagree with the initial violence, become enraged because the conditions they were socialized to accept no longer obtain. "Why should I be peaceful if others aren't?" becomes a relevant question. And "Why should I use only the slow, seemingly uncertain procedures of the polity?" "Why not use private power to obtain my objectives" become equally relevant questions. People who have repressed their anger become doubly enraged when others don't. We have seen the result on ethnic ghetto borders in every city of the land. We know that violence increases alienation."[27]

None of the elements which have made for our new politics is new in human nature or in Americans: until now, we have probably not been observing a characterological change. Men and women, especially young men and women, have always sought to find a satisfying identity. Americans have always wanted dignity and intimacy. Where they once expected to find these values in the American business system, the church and the family, they now expect to find at least some measure of these values in the American political system as well. Also, the schools and the media have been telling the American public for years that politics affects their daily lives and that they ought to care more about it! Why, then, should it be surprising that they are coming increasingly to believe it and acting on those beliefs? Then, too, activism and energy have long been observed to be characteristic American traits, and the absence of community at the national level is not a new phenomenon.

What *is* new is the perceived leaderlessness that makes for direct participation, the expanded scope and depth of alienation, the politicization and fragmentation and therefore the scope, depth, activism and intensity of the radical response.

When individual alienation becomes widespread, a pervasive mood of alienation takes hold in the popular culture, a pervasive public negativity obtains. Alienation in America is now big business, and, for the short run, it seems to be "good politics" (opportunistic politics). So we see the peace symbol co-opted and used in gasoline commercials and a veritable bandwagon of politicians using alienation themes in political campaigns. This not only reinforces the perceptions of the already alienated, it teaches alienation to the unalienated and makes alienation the "goes-without-saying" mood. When talk about revolution becomes fashionable at middle-class cocktail parties and when the underground media become an alternative communications structure, then the mood of alienation is reinforced still more. All of this reinforcement of alienation, all of these rewards for adopting an alienated posture could give rise to a characterological change in Americans—in the direction of a perpetual negativism. I think the beginnings of such a trend are apparent in some quarters.

All of this is frightening to politicians, who then project their fear in political discourse. When political campaigns exacerbate fear, raising the question of whether or not the government can protect the people, then whether you call it "law and order" or "the failure of the elite to fulfill elite functions," the polity is dealing with the most primal question: the politics of survival. Primal politics are unlikely to be peaceful politics, for, when dreams and death are in the streets, the mood of the man in the streets is unlikely to be calm. These conditions obtain here and now, and we are not a people at peace.

The result of reinforced alienation in a parochialized polity can be polarization where each of two sides coalesce to do battle against each other; initially, it is far more likely to be omni-alienation where coalitions fall apart and small groups are invested with the self-identification which has been withdrawn from the polity. Then, any public action creates more alienation, displeases more people than it pleases, and the polity is more a victim of paralysis (and emptiness) than of attack. Some of our cities, in my view, are foundering in this way.

But attacks, in the form of revolutionary organizations offering competitive myths and identities, and not a little violence, are resurgent now, too.

Beyond alienation and anger, the revolutionary identity involves at least the following factors:

(1) total commitment to revolutionary change (for example, one thinks of the kids going to prison and of the black chant "Stokely is a fighter in the army [of blacks]—he has to fight, although he has to die");

(2) desperation occurs (a black militant told me that "If we do the things we have to do, you'll probably have to kill us all—all 20 million black people—but we ain't going like the Jews," and the kids, after Kent State, said "It's not a question now of whether we will mourn for *someone* but of how many");

(3) thus, the enemy becomes inhuman—(for example, "pigs," "white devils," etc.)—justifying any acts the revolutionary commits against him,

(4) and the enemy is viewed as conspiratorial (whether racist, economically imperialistic, or both);

(5) divergent or revisionist interpretations of history are developed (so it appears that the enemy always was inhuman; history becomes a collection of past wrongs, which the revolutionary must right);

(6) accordingly, one is self-righteous because of the purity of one's

motives and the monumental character of one's struggle (for example, "I once was like you"; "You're not there yet"; "You don't understand");

(7) one is also self-righteous (therefore self-confident) because one appeals to higher values than the law and order of the system; one appeals to traditional ambiguous symbols (for example, "Most black violence happens out of *love*"; "We want to realize Christian love of man for man-brother");

(8) this can be said while great bitterness and anger toward the enemy is felt and expressed;

(9) and finally, the enemy of my enemy becomes my friend and the internationalization of the revolutionary movement takes place (for example, "If you try to kill us, what do you think Russia and Red China are going to be doing?").

I am not saying that all of these psychological elements are widespread in America today. I am saying that all of them exist here and now, that some of them are widespread and that the situation deserves to be taken seriously.

I would assert further that the psychology of the ethnic vigilantes and the radical right is not dissimilar. They, too, are threatened—by the rising status of blacks, by the black militancy, by real and imagined Communist victories. They, too, have a revisionist view of history (for the radical right it is one of sell out, for the ethnics it is one that overextends the relevance of their group experience). They, too, see the enemy as inhuman (godless Communists, black apes); they tend to view the world as a conspiracy (whether of Communists, liberals, Easterners, "niggers and nigger-lovers" or whatever); and feel that the system will not work (for the right it is contaminating, for the ethnics it is unprotective). The counter-revolutionaries also appeal to traditional values for legitimacy (free enterprise, private initiative, self-help), hence they, too, feel self-righteous and bitter and angry.

The status-stable (and status-threatened) urban ethnic cannot withdraw from the value conflict into the deceptive suburban calm; hence the virulence of his reaction. He, too, has known where to get weapons of violence and has trained himself to use them. So have the radical right and, I think, an increasing number of suburbanites as well.

The paradox is that all of this has come upon us at or near the threshold of what could be a "golden age in America." We are rich beyond imagination, technically capable of doing almost whatever we want. We are embarking on adventures in space that make previous explorations seem small. Today's kids don't know what polio was, and our work on transdermal hearing, neuro-electric patterning and conscious control of the autonomic nervous system means that much deafness, epilepsy and heart attack may be things of the past, in our lifetime. We are living longer and most of us are living better.

Living longer and more comfortably has also had important effects on our politics. We have been living for a little while now in a period of expanding personal freedom, which has raised aspirations both for more freedom and for improvements in the quality of life. The polity inevitably makes demands on that freedom (laws, taxes, etc.), and people in an increasingly secular age will meet those demands if and only if the polity meets theirs. The political system is not now perceived so much as an end in itself; sacrifices in its name will be made largely on an assessment of its worth. New and integrative political myths will be believed only if and when the policies of governments are perceived to be worthy.

There is in all of this a natural and important blending of rationalism and mythology. The judgment that something is worthy or unworthy is always based on a normative standard—a myth or a value system. Once a value system is accepted, the evaluation of social objects, including political systems, in terms of that standard can proceed quite rationally. Today, we observe a confusion and proliferation of standards concomitant with an increasingly dissatisfied evaluation of our polity. As we come to understand the blend of rationality and myth that is political thought we may better understand the demands we make on our collective institutions.

In this light, it is crucial for us to realize that the demands on the polity to recognize and to satisfy strongly felt needs for identity, dignity and community are new demands on political systems. Such demands used to be made in churches and families but less frequently in politics. It is not surprising, therefore, that political systems falter in responding to these diffuse new demands. When politicians, who enter politics for reasons of identity, stop denying the legitimacy of entering politics to people with different identities, the performance of the polity may well improve. When the demanders come to realize the limitations on the political system's capability to provide these things, we may see modifications (and perhaps some diminutions) in demands.

Presently, however, the diverse demands on the polity seem to far outrun its demand-satisfying capability. Given the competing and contradictory nature of some of the demands from different social sectors, this may be true for some time to come. Such a situation can scarcely be considered a stable state, and neither is America.

Elsewhere,[28] I have conceptualized the development of a revolution as a multi-stage process model, involving *inter alia*: (1) alienation; (2) the formation of revolutionary organization; (3) the revolutionary appeals of those organizations—which create more alienation, reinforce extant alienation and attract the passively alienated to the movement; (4) coalition-building and resource-acquisition; (5) negotiations between the revolutionary movement and the political system; and (6) the outbreak of strategic revolutionary violence. The validity of the behavioral hypotheses and transition rules in this dynamic theory are now being tested, and, therefore, it would be premature to apply this model in detail to contemporary America. Still, we *do* have appreciable political alienation among us, there *are* revolutionary organizations operative in America, and they *are* seeking to make their appeals attractive. The very vagueness of many demands that makes it difficult for the system to meet them is part of the appeal of these demands to those who are at first more interested in the identity of "being a demander" than in the reality of having the demands satisfied. It is also part of the coalition potential of "the movement," for it is far more easy to get people to be for "a complete restructuring of the university" or "a whole new system" than to be for any concrete proposal on how to restructure the system or what in detail to do when it is restructured. Given the alienation, the interest in politics, the loneliness, the leaderlessness and especially the media, the potential for new social movements is enormous. But the co-optational capability of the system and the parochialization of the polity have so far restricted such movements' coalition potential.

This fragmentation of the political system means that different individuals, groups and social sectors are going through the different subprocesses of alienation at different speeds. Some of yesterday's passively alienated are now most active in reform and even revolutionary movements at the same time that some of yesterday's radicals are dropping out and some of yesterday's allegiant population are entering passive alienation. Changes in the social distribution of relevant perceptions create changes in the number and types of people who, at any given moment, are conformists, ritualists, dropouts, reformers, radicals, etc.

Events and outcomes in the national political system are dependent on the level and social distribution of these orientations.

We do not yet fully understand how the changing level of various basic behavioral orientations gets translated into specific political acts or into general levels of political activity. Neither are we clear about how the fact that group X is changing its basic political orientation at some known or knowable rate influences events. Nonetheless, I think that we do sense even short-term changes in the political orientations of important social groups. I think, too, that we are able to discriminate between situations in which basic changes in the orientations of groups are congruent, making for a national mood or tendency, and situations in which strong differences in orientations, across social sectors, make the times seem out of joint. Finally, I believe that we can discern a tendency or drift or direction that our orientations seem to be taking, a tendency toward public negativity and activism and away from positive evaluation of the polity.

So, our politics may now oscillate between periods of intense reform activity, radical action and violence on the one hand and eras of nervous, negative nonaction (but nonpeace) on the other. The action may shift from the ghettos and campuses to the lower-middle-class urban communities and the suburbs. The types of violence and the types of violent people may and do change. The confluences of specific alienation levels and orientations to alienation, across social groupings, may change and thereby change our politics. But the constant overriding fact remains: American politics has become the politics of alienation.

What then of the future? Where do we go from here? I don't know. I do know that much is made in social thought of the ability to discern in advance the coming order of things, and properly so. But no such claim is made here, for, unless there is an inordinate increase in political innovation, I see largely continuing and expanding disorder.

Neither the value conflicts and inefficacy which have made for alienation, nor the social trends which have encouraged the active outplay of that alienation, seem transitory or evanescent. From what we are beginning to know about generational as well as maturational effects in socialization,[29] it appears to me that young people will not wholly outgrow their activism, and that black people will not desist from their search for dignity. I think, further, that the politics of withdrawal would not now result from political repression or economic depression: these would probably lead to increased radicalization. Nor are we likely to become a very patient people.

Thus, the aspirations—for community, identity and dignity—that have become politicized in America are unlikely soon to be depoliticized. Those who hold them, and hold them very dear indeed, are too many and too aware of themselves to be a lonely crowd again. Until those aspirations are realized (whether in a social movement, a restructured polity or a polity that is restructured by a social movement), until the political system reverses alienation, perceived leaderlessness and parochialization and expresses that reversal in a potent myth, and until Americans reinvest their individual identifications collectively, we shall remain a strident society.

NOTES

Preface

1. Herbert McClosky and John H. Schaar, "Psychological Dimensions of Anomy," reprinted in Heinz Eulau (ed.), *Political Behavior in America* (New York: Random House, 1966), pp. 466ff.
2. *Ibid.*

Chapter 1

1. See Gabriel A. Almond, *The Appeals of Communism* (Princeton: Princeton University Press, 1954), p. 215; Hadley Cantril, *The Psychology of Social Movements* (New York: John Wiley and Sons, 1941), p. 69; and *The Politics of Despair* (New York: Basic Books, 1958). Several interesting theoretical discussions are available as to why this relationship should obtain. See especially William Kornhauser, *The Politics of Mass Society* (Glencoe: The Free Press, 1963), pp. 30-33; Robert K. Merton, *Social Theory and Social Structure* (New York: The Free Press, 1957), pp. 155-56; Neil J. Smelser, *A Theory of Collective Behavior* (New York: The Free Press, 1962), p. 333.
2. Ritchie P. Lowry, "The Functions of Alienation in Leadership," *Sociology and Social Research,* Vol. 46, No. 4 (1962), pp. 426ff.
3. Gene L. Mason and Dean Jaros, "Alienation and Support for Demagogues," *Polity* (June 1968).
4. H. Edward Ransford, "Isolation, Powerlessness and Violence: A Study of Attitudes and Participation in the Watts Riot," *American Journal of Sociology,* Vol. 73, No. 5 (March, 1968), pp. 518ff.
5. The classic statement on this relationship is to be found in Charles E. Merriam and Harold F. Gossell, *Non-Voting* (Chicago: University of Chicago Press, 1924). See also Edward L. McDill and Jeanne Claire Ridley, "Status, Anomia, Political Alienation and Political Participation," *American Journal of Sociology,* Vol. 67, No. 2 (1962), pp. 205ff.
6. Among many studies which have arrived at this conclusion, the following represent a wide range of countries and time periods in which the relationship has been observed: Raymond A. Bauer, "Some Trends in Sources of Alienation from the Soviet System," *Public Opinion Quarterly,* Vol. LXIX, No. 3 (1955), pp. 27ff; David Riesman, *The Lonely Crowd* (New Haven: Yale University Press, 1950), pp. 187-190; Morris Rosenberg, "Some Determinants of Political Apathy," *Public*

Opinion Quarterly, Vol. 18 (1954), pp. 349ff; Melvin Seeman, "Alienation, Membership and Political Knowledge," *Public Opinion Quarterly,* Vol. 30 (1966), pp. 353ff; Wayne E. Thompson and John E. Horton, "Political Alienation as a Force in Political Action," *Social Forces,* Vol. 38, No. 3 (1960), pp. 190ff.

7. Jack McLeod, Scott Ward and Karen Tancill, "Alienation and Uses of the Mass Media," *Public Opinion Quarterly,* Vol. 29 (1965), pp. 583ff.

8. Gilbert Abcarian and Sherman M. Stanage, "Alienation and the Radical Right," *Journal of Politics,* Vol. 27, No. 4 (November 1965), pp. 776ff.

9. Marvin E. Olsen, "Two Categories of Political Alienation," *Social Forces,* Vol. 47, No. 3 (March, 1969), pp. 288ff.

10. McDill and Ridley, *op. cit.,* pp. 208ff; see also Marion Roth and G. R. Boyton, "Communal Ideology and Political Support," *Journal of Politics,* Vol. 31, No. 1 (1969), pp. 167ff. and notes 10-16; Marvin E. Olsen, "Alienation and Political Opinions," *Public Opinion Quarterly,* Vol. 29, No. 6 (1965), pp. 202ff.

11. David Easton, *A Systems Analysis of Political Life* (New York: John Wiley and Sons, 1965), pp. 220 and *passim.* Ada W. Finifter makes an excellent point on diminutions in such support for the American polity by referring to the number of recent voluntary renunciations of citizenship; see her "Dimensions of Political Alienation," *American Political Science Review,* Vol. LXIV, No. 2 (June, 1970), p. 389.

12. Gabriel A. Almond and Sidney Verba, *The Civic Culture* (Princeton: Princeton University Press, 1963), p. 242.

13. Perhaps the best-known statement of this proposition is Lucian Pye's *Politics, Personality and Nation Building* (New Haven: Yale University Press, 1962).

14. I refer to a national study undertaken by Twentieth Century Fund in 1969 and to a commission empaneled by the National Committee of the Democratic Party under the chairmanship of Senator McGovern, also in 1969.

15. This has been the recent experience of the Movement for a New Congress in Philadelphia.

16. Richard Flacks, "The Liberated Generation: An Exploration of the Roots of Student Protest," *Journal of Social Issues,* Vol. XXIII, No. 3 (July, 1967), p. 53.

17. Kenneth Kenniston, "Social Change and Youth in America," *Daedalus* (Winter, 1962), p. 165.

18. Department of Justice document, "Report of the Community Relations Service, Student Unrest Survey," September, 1969.

19. *Civil Disorder Digest,* Vol. 1, No. 1 (September 15, 1969), p. 1. It would be very useful, of course, to have data on the incidence of school and university disorders in the preceding period of years, to determine the degree of real increase. As there was little demand for this kind of data in the early 1960s, comparable adequate information on the earlier period is hard to come by.

20. Daniel Bell, *The End of Ideology* (Glencoe, Ill.: The Free Press, 1960), *passim,* and Seymour Martin Lipset, *Political Man* (New York: Doubleday and Company, 1960), p. 453 and *passim.*

21. See Joseph Boskin, "The Revolt of the Urban Ghettos, 1964-1967," *Annals of the American Academy of Political and Social Science* (March, 1968), p. 1; and Louis H. Masotti, et al., *A Time to Burn?* (Chicago: Rand McNally and Company, 1969), pp. 2ff.

22. Flacks, *op. cit.*

23. H. L. Nieburg, *Political Violence* (New York: St. Martin's Press, 1969), p. 4.

24. David Riesman, Nathan Glazer and Reuel Denney, *The Lonely Crowd* (New York: Doubleday and Company, 1965), pp. 190ff.

25. Nieburg, *op cit.,* pp. 113ff.

26. Igor S. Kon, "The Concept of Alienation in Modern Sociology," *Social Research,* Vol. 34, No. 3 (Autumn 1967), pp. 507ff. For another effort at concept clarification, see also Lewis Feuer, "What Is Alienation? The Career of a Concept," *New Politics,* Vol. 1, No. 3 (Spring, 1962), pp. 116ff.

27. Kon, *op. cit.* See also Melvin Seeman, "Alienation: Marx Abandoned It; Shouldn't We," unpublished paper, 1968, pp. 5ff.

28. Robert K. Merton, "Social Structure and Anomie," in his *Social Theory and Social Structure* (Glencoe, Ill.: The Free Press, 1957), pp. 135ff.

29. Leo Srole, "Social Integration and Certain Corollaries," *American Sociological Review,* Vol. 21, No. 6 (1956), pp. 709ff.

30. See Kon, *op. cit.,* and Feuer, *op. cit.*

31. Reported in Srole, *op. cit.*

32. Gwynne Nettler, "A Measure of Alienation," *American Sociological Review,* Vol. 22 (1957), pp. 670ff.

33. Edward L. McDill, "Anomie, Authoritarianism, Prejudice, and Socio-Economic Status," *Social Forces,* Vol. 39, No. 3 (March, 1961), pp. 239ff; Marvin E. Olsen, "Alienation and Political Opinions," *Public Opinion Quarterly,* Vol. 29, No. 6 (1965), pp. 202ff.

34. *American Sociological Review,* Vol. 24, No. 6 (December 1959), pp. 783ff.

35. For the view that alienation should be seen as a general negative *weltanschauung,* see Edward L. McDill, *op. cit.,* and Russell L. Middleton, "Alienation, Race and Education," *American Sociological Review,* Vol. 28, No. 6 (1963), pp. 973ff. For a middle position that one can treat alienation either as a general syndrome or in terms of discrete components, see Dwight G. Dean, "Alienation: Its Measurement and Meaning," *American Sociological Review,* Vol. 26, No. 4 (October, 1961), pp. 753ff., and J. L. Simmons, "Some Inter-correlations Among 'Alienation' Measures," *Social Forces,* Vol. 44, No. 1 (March, 1966), pp. 370ff. The position that alienation should be treated in terms of concrete dimensions which should be kept conceptually distinct is argued on factor-analytic findings in Richard A. Dodder, "A Factor Analysis of Dean's Alienation Scale," *Social Forces,* Vol. 48, No. 4 (December, 1969), pp. 252ff.

36. On the need for dimensionalization, see Kenneth Kenniston, *The Uncommitted* (New York: Harcourt, Brace and World, 1965), pp. 454ff; Joel D. Aberbach, "Alienation and Political Behavior," *American Political Science Review,* Vol. XLIII, No. 1 (March, 1969), pp. 86ff; Marvin E. Olsen (1969), *op. cit.,* pp. 288ff. and Finifter, *loc. cit.*

37. This is not true of the authors cited in note 36, who do tend to make clear which sense of the term "alienation" they are employing.

38. Olsen (1965), *op. cit.*

39. Srole, *op. cit.*

40. Nettler, *op. cit.*

41. Cited in Srole, *op. cit.,* p. 712.

42. Kon, *op. cit.* See also Kenniston, (1965), *op. cit.*

43. I recognize, of course, (1) that individuals can be alienated from only a part of the polity, that is, from a given institution, policy, or process or set of these; and (2) that the behavioral consequences which flow from this more limited alienation will tend to differ from those accruing from general political alienation. Later in this chapter I identify the different conditions under which an individual will become alienated from a part versus all of the system.

44. In the studies reported in this book, no distinction is made between individuals who withdraw voluntarily and those who feel rejected or pushed out of the system, but the conceptual distinction is recognized in the measurement instruments used, and scholars interested in working on this topic might find our data useful.

45. Cited in Kon, *op. cit.*

46. Abcarian and Stanage, *op. cit.*

47. Sheilah R. Koeppen, "The Republican Radical Right," *Annals* (March, 1969), pp. 76ff.

48. Kenneth Kenniston, "The Sources of Student Dissent," *Journal of Social Issues,* Vol. XXII, No. 3 (July, 1967), pp. 190ff. See also Edward E. Sampson, "Student Activism and the Decade of Protest," *Journal of Social Issues,* Vol. XXII, No. 3 (July, 1967), pp. 1ff. and notes.

49. See Herbert McClosky and John H. Schaar, "Psychological Dimensions of Anomy," reprinted from *American Sociological Review,* Vol. 30, No. 2 (February, 1969), pp. 14ff. in Heinz Eulau, ed., *Political Behavior in America* (New York: Random House, 1966), pp. 466ff.

50. *Ibid.*

51. David C. Schwartz and Sara Moore, "Alienation in an Indian Student Community," unpublished paper, University of Pennsylvania, 1969.

52. McClosky and Schaar, *op. cit.*

53. Fredric Templeton, "Alienation and Political Participation," *Public Opinion Quarterly,* Vol. 30 (Summer, 1966), p. 253.

54. McClosky and Schaar, *op. cit.,* p. 470.

55. Dorothy L. Meier and Wendell Bell, "Anomia and Differential Access to the Achievement of Life Goals," *American Sociological Review,* Vol. 24, No. 2 (1959), pp. 189ff.

56. *Ibid.* This literature almost totally ignores the factors of symbolic rewards (and, therefore, of differentials by class in acceptance of political myth). If people accept their lot as either legitimate ("I get what I deserve"; or possibly "whatever happens, happens by luck or fate"), or as nonpolitical (a cognitive compartmentalization between economics and politics), then lower-class status will not lead to a negatively valued political powerlessness.

57. McClosky and Schaar, *op. cit.,* pp. 474ff.

58. Daniel Bell, ed., *The Radical Right* (New York: Doubleday and Company, 1955), pp. 18ff.

59. "Small Businessmen, Political Tolerance and Support for McCarthy," *American Journal of Sociology,* Vol. LXIV (November, 1958), pp. 270ff.

60. Finifter, *op. cit.,* p. 403.

61. Philip Meyer, "The Aftermath of Martyrdom," *Public Opinion Quarterly,* Vol. 32, No. 2 (Summer, 1969), pp. 160ff; Richard Hofstetter, "Political Disengagement and the Death of Martin Luther King" (same journal, pp. 174ff).

62. John G. Robinson, Jerrold G. Rusk and Kendran B. Head, *Measurements of Political Attitudes* (Ann Arbor: Survey Research Center Publication, 1968), pp. 628ff.

63. See Joel I. Nelsen, "Anomie: Comparisons Between the Old and New Middle Class," *American Journal of Sociology,* Vol. 74, No. 2 (September, 1968), pp. 184ff. and notes.

64. William Erbe, "Social Involvement and Political Activity," *American Sociological Review,* Vol. 29, No. 2 (April, 1964), pp. 198ff.

65. Arthur G. Neal and Melvin Seeman, "Organizations and Powerlessness," *American Sociological Review,* Vol. 29, No. 2 (April, 1964), pp. 216ff.

66. See, for example, Anthony M. Orum, "A Reappraisal of the Social and Political Participation of Negroes," *American Journal of Sociology,* Vol. 2, No. 1 (July, 1966), pp. 32ff.

67. Maurice Pinard et al., "Processes of Recruitment in the Sit-In Movement," *Public Opinion Quarterly,* Vol. 33, No. 3 (Fall, 1969), pp. 353ff. and notes.

68. See note 7, *supra.*

69. This definition of inefficacy is adopted from Seeman, 1966, *op. cit.*

70. Almond and Verba, *op. cit.,* pp. 230ff.

71. *Ibid.,* pp. 214ff.

72. The "no response" categories were virtually empty in both studies. Robinson, et al., *op. cit.,* pp. 644 and 648.

73. For an intriguing summary and critique of this view, see Michael Mann, "The Social Cohesion of Liberal Democracy," *American Sociological Review,* Vol. 35, No. 3 (June, 1970), pp. 423ff.

74. Seeman (1966), *op. cit.*

75. In the interests of generality and parsimony, I refer here only to general, summative, fundamental value conflicts, not to the specific values in conflict. No doubt the specifics of a value conflict will have their influence, but here I am interested in *any* fundamental value conflict between the individual and the polity.

76. Riesman, *op. cit.,* p. 213 and pp. 218ff.

77. Robinson, et al., *op. cit.,* pp. 591ff.

78. *Ibid.,* p. 490.

79. The alienation process for persons who have not been socialized to identify with the polity is quite similar. So long as a person is either unaware of the polity or the polity makes no demands on him, alienation will not occur. Once the polity does make such a demand (e.g., taxes, military conscription, etc.), then his local, ethnic, or tribal identification becomes perceived as in conflict with the demands of the polity. If this is a fundamental conflict, and he perceives himself and his group to be inefficacious in the polity, then alienation is likely to result. This process is discussed in greater detail in David C. Schwartz, "A Theory of Revolutionary Behavior," in James C. Davies, *When Men Revolt* (New York: The Free Press, 1970).

80. See, for example, Max F. Millikan and Donald L. M. Blackmer, *The Emerging Nations* (Boston: Little, Brown, 1960), *passim.*

81. Hadley Cantril, *The Pattern of Human Concerns* (New Brunswick: Rutgers University Press, 1965), *passim.*

82. Ted R. Gurr, *Why Men Rebel* (Princeton: Princeton University Press, 1970), *passim.*

83. Ivo K. and Rosalind L. Feierabend, "Aggressive Behavior Within Polities," *Journal of Conflict Resoultions,* Vol. X (September, 1966), pp. 249ff.

84. But see Frederick Frey, "Political Socialization to National Identification: Turkish Peasants," paper presented to 1966 Meetings of the American Political Science Association. To apply a theory of the extinction of response-tendency to alienation would require longitudinal study of the individual's responses to political symbols; the symbols conceived of as conditioned stimuli. Because of the cross-sectional strategy of research followed in this book, and the absence of data matched to this conception, this line of research has not yet been followed.

85. Eric H. Erikson, *Childhood and Society* (New York: W. W. Norton and Company, 1950).

86. The best-known example of this school of thought is Talcott Parsons' *The Social System* (London: Routledge and Kegan Paul, 1951).

87. See, for example, R. Dahrendorf, *Class and Class Conflict in an Industrial Society* (London: Routledge and Kegan Paul, 1959).

88. See Mann, *op. cit.*

89. The reader should consult Hugh David Graham and Ted Robert Gurr, eds., *Violence in America, A Staff Report to the National Commission on the Causes and Prevention of Violence* (June, 1969).

90. See Chapters 9 to 13, *infra.*

91. This statement was heard not infrequently in popular discourse during the most active riot period in 1967. The reader may wish to consult the reports of the Lemberg Center for the Study of Violence, Brandeis University, on this point.

92. Boskin, *op. cit.*

93. "Conformity and Marginality: Two Faces of Alienation," *Journal of Social Issues,* Vol. XXV, No. 2 (Spring, 1969), pp. 39ff.

94. For a more extensive critique of this point of view, see Nieberg, *op cit., passim.*

95. T. George Harris, "The Young Are Captives of Each Other: A Conversation with David Riesman," *Psychology Today,* October, 1969, pp. 28ff.

96. "Current Patterns of a Generational Conflict," *Journal of Social Issues,* Vol. XXV, No. 2 (April, 1969), pp. 21ff.

97. *Ibid.*

98. "Distinctiveness and Thrust in the American Youth Culture," *Journal of Social Issues,* Vol. XXV, No. 2 (April, 1969), pp. 7ff.

99. "Juvenile Delinquency as a Symptom of Alienation," *Journal of Social Issues,* Vol. XXV, No. 2 (April, 1969), pp. 121ff.

100. *Loc. cit.,* 1967.

101. *Loc. cit.*

102. Joseph W. Scott and Mohammed El Assal, "Multiversity, University Quality and Student Protest," *American Sociological Review,* Vol. 34, No. 5 (October, 1969), pp. 702ff.

103. *Loc. cit.*

104. Merton, *op. cit.,* pp. 139ff.

105. Robert Dubin, "Deviant Behavior and Social Structure," *American Sociological Review,* Vol. 24, No. 2 (April, 1959), pp. 147ff.

106. Elinor G. Barber, *The Bourgeoisie in 18th Century France* (Princeton: Princeton University Press, 1967).

107. Dubin, *op. cit.*

108. Merton, *op. cit.*

109. See Flacks (1967) and Kenniston (1967), *op. cit., passim* and notes.

110. Boskin, *op. cit.*

111. McClosky and Schaar, *op. cit.,* pp. 486ff. and, especially, p. 505.

112. Herbert Hendrin, "Black Suicide," *Columbia Forum,* Fall, 1969, excerpted in *Current* (January, 1970), pp. 29ff.

113. Paul Heist, "Intellect and Commitment," in O. W. Knorr and W. J. Mintner, eds., *Order and Freedom on the Campus* (Boulder, Colorado: Western Interstate Commission for Higher Education, 1965).

114. David Whittaker and William A. Watts, "Personality Characteristics of a Nonconformist Youth Subculture," *Journal of Social Issues,* Vol. XXV, No. 2 (April, 1969), pp. 65ff.

115. Kornhauser, *op. cit.,* p. 178; Smelser, *op. cit.,* pp. 337ff; Cantril (1941), *op cit.,* pp. 69ff. See also Lucian W. Pye, *Guerrilla Communism in Malaya* (Princeton: Princeton University Press, 1956), *passim.*

116. Nieburg, *op. cit.,* p. 138 and *passim.*

117. J. Dollard et al., *Frustration and Aggression* (New Haven: Yale University Press, 1939).

118. Konrad Lorenz, *On Aggression.*

119. Robert Ardrey, *The Territorial Imperative* (New York: Atheneum Publishers, 1966).

120. Gurr (1970), *op. cit., passim;* Feierabends, *op. cit.*

121. These topics are treated in some greater detail in Chapter 8. The reader interested in the problem should consult that chapter and notes, the work cited in note 120, *supra,* and especially C. N. Cofer and M. H. Appley, *Motivation: Theory and Research* (New York: John Wiley and Sons, 1964), *passim.*

122. The problem of the activation of predispositions has not been adequately conceptualized in political science. The reader should consult Cofer and Appley, *loc. cit.*

123. See notes 1 and 111, *supra.*

Contexts and Methods of Research

1. Adam Przeworski and Henry Teune, *The Logic of Comparative Social Inquiry* (New York: Wiley-Interscience, 1970), pp. 22-23.

2. See, for example, Bonnie Bullough, "Alienation in the Ghetto," *American Journal of Sociology,* Vol. 72, No. 5 (March, 1967), pp. 469ff. and notes.

3. Przeworski and Teune, *op. cit.,* pp. 34ff.

Chapter 2

1. See, for example, Gabriel A. Almond and James S. Coleman (eds.), *The Politics of the Developing Areas* (Princeton: Princeton University Press, 1960), Introduction; David Easton, *loc. cit., passim.*

2. Riesman, *op. cit.,* pp. 191ff.

3. Pye, *op. cit., passim.*

4. One useful summary of much of this material is in Lester W. Milbrath, *Political Participation* (Chicago: Rand McNally and Company, 1965), *passim*.

5. A good summary of this literature may be found in Lyle G. Warner and Melvin L. DeFleur, "Attitude as an Interactional Concept," *American Sociological Review,* Vol. 34, No. 2 (April, 1969), pp. 153ff and notes.

6. See Samuel A. Stouffer, *Communism, Conformity and Civil Liberties* (Gloucester, Mass.: Peter Smith, 1963), *passim*.

7. I am aware that the converse of this statement is a favorite hypothesis in studies of political socialization and that empirical tests of it are under way at Princeton University's Workshop in Comparative Politics, under the direction of Harry Eckstein. I believe, however, that the findings of these and other studies will be as indicated in the text.

8. Fred Greenstein, *Children and Politics* (New Haven: Yale University Press, 1965), pp. 27ff.; Robert D. Hess and Judith V. Torney, *The Development of Political Attitudes in Children* (Chicago: Aldine Publishing Company, 1967), p. 56.

9. Cecil K. North and Paul K. Hatt, "Jobs and Occupations: A Popular Evaluation," reprinted in Logan Wilson and William L. Kolb, *Sociological Analysis* (New York: Harcourt, Brace and Company, 1949), pp. 464ff.

10. Of course, in all of these historical examples, I am reasoning from allegiant and participatory behavior to nonalienated attitudes—using behavioral indicators in the absence of data on the alienation-relevant attitudes of early immigrants, minority group members, etc. These inferences seem reasonable but, of course, the lack of adequate data makes it impossible to do more than suggest the plausibility of the position I am arguing.

11. Erik H. Erikson, *Childhood and Society* (New York: W. W. Norton and Company, 1950), Chapter 1 and *passim;* Pye, *op. cit.,* pp. 52ff.

12. See, for example, Pye, *op. cit.,* p. 55 and *passim*.

13. *Ibid.,* pp. 584ff.

14. James David Barder, *The Lawmakers* (New Haven: Yale University Press, 1965), pp. 181ff.

15. *Op. cit.*

16. *Op. cit.*

17. *Op. cit.*

18. *Op. cit.*

19. See the Methods Appendix for the matrix of inter-item correlation coefficients of this index. The reader is referred to the appendix for all such matrices.

20. Unless otherwise noted, the correlation coefficients reported in all of our studies are Pearson Product-Moment Correlation Coefficients.

21. As this is the first instance in the book wherein conclusions are drawn from statistical manipulation of our data, a note on the use of significance levels as a means of hypothesis testing is necessary here. In the strictest sense, of course, tests of statistical significance would be maximally meaningful only in the case of a truly random sample of a specified population, where the intellectual objective is to generalize from the sample to the population. Indeed, "randomness" of the sample is one of the assumptions underlying appropriate use of tests of significance. In social science today, however, when investigators are often more interested in generalizing to a process than to a population and where response rates often result in samples which are not truly random, levels of statistical significance are often used as benchmark indications of the strength of relationships, relaxing the assumption of randomness. It is in that sense that we use tests of statistical significance in our studies.

It should also be recognized that measurement differences and difficulties, across indexes, may artificially dampen or increase the magnitude of an observed relationship. In our studies, we have sought to minimize some of these difficulties in typical fashion—by standard scoring the indexes and in general by correlating indexes which had identical numbers of response options on the survey instrument. Given the relative crudeness of attitude measurement in general and the necessary variation in measures used in our studies, the tentative character of our findings must be stressed.

Finally, one substantive point: it will be noted that Srole item a, an item referring to system inefficacy, does intercorrelate with the other Srole indicators of social alienation. This, of course, does not stand in opposition to my conclusion that political alienation and social alienation are essentially unrelated in the East Torresdale sample: inefficacy is not the same thing as alienation.

Also, the different sizes of the commuities we studied (and differences in our access to them) meant that our samples are of different sizes. As tests of statistical significance are sensitive to sample size, the level of significance required to accept or reject the validity of an hypothesis can vary with sample size. Accordingly, we would prefer not to fix upon one particular level of significance (say, 0.05 or 0.01) and reason that any correlation coefficient attaining that level should be regarded as indicating a strong (or theoretically interesting) relationship, confirming or disconfirming an hypothesis. One alternative might be to report the levels of significance which the coefficients in our data actually attained and allow the reader to make his own independent judgment of the degree to which the significance level attained should be interpreted as confirming or disconfirming a given hypothesis. In general, we do that in the studies reported in this book. Nonetheless, we needed to establish a cutting point in order to form our own professional judgment on the hypotheses tested here. For our purposes, in order to "stack the deck" against our own theory, we require only a 0.05 level of significance for the hypotheses deriving from previous literature but, generally, a 0.01 or better level for our own hypotheses.

22. It would seem that the introduction of such controls analytically or by comparing participants with random samples of city or campus residents, while useful, meets fewer of the purposes of the quasi-experimental design.

23. *New York Times,* October 16, 1969.

24. For example, mean age of the demonstrators was 18.74 years compared with 18.86 years for the nondemonstrators. 70.2 percent of the demonstrators were men as were 68.6 percent of the nondemonstrators.

Chapter 3

1. On the general point, see McClosky and Schaar, *op. cit.,* pp. 474ff. A partial listing of studies on point includes: John P. Clark, "Measuring Alienation Within a Social System," *American Sociological Review,* Vol. 24, No. 6 (1959), pp. 849ff.; Dwight G. Dean, "Alienation and Political Apathy," *Social Forces,* Vol. 38, No. 3 (1960), pp. 185ff.; Erse, *op. cit.;* Finifter, *op. cit.;* Meier and Bell, *op. cit.;* McDill and Ridley, *op. cit.;* Middleton, *op. cit.;* Ephraim Harold Mizruchi, "Social Structure and Anomia," *American Sociological Review,* Vol. 25, No. 5 (1960), pp. 645ff; Olsen (1955 and 1969), *op. cit.*

2. See Chapter 1, note 5, *supra.*

3. *Ibid.,* note 7, *supra.*

4. An extensive review of this literature is in David C. Schwartz, "Political Recruitment: A Comparative Essay in Theory and Research," unpublished Ph.D. dissertation (M.I.T., 1965), Chapter 4.

5. At least the social background variables typically employed are relatively easy to observe. But as social scientists refine their notions of social stratification and, hopefully, move toward a "political life history" approach—we may find that relevant social background variables can only be studied through intensive biographical interviewing.

6. See Chapter 1, notes 35 to 40 and 63, *supra.*

7. See Chapter 1, notes 73 and 74, *supra.*

8. *Newark in the Seventies: College and Community,* Graduate Planning Studies (New Brunswick: Rutgers University Press, 1968).

9. Jack Chernick, *et al., Newark: Population and Labor Force* (New Brunswick: Rutgers University Press, December, 1967).

10. Norton E. Long, "The Local Community as an Ecology of Games," *American Journal of Sociology,* Vol. 64 (1958), pp. 251ff.

11. $n = 60$ respondents; derived from a mailed questionnaire study conducted during the winter of 1969. The response rate to this mailing was a disappointing 30 percent so that the relationships discussed here should be interpreted with considerable caution.

12. To this point the analysis of all of our data has been of a correlational nature. Most of the data analysis in the book is of this character. Where, however, our measures did not yield interval-type data (or data that is routinely treated in social science as interval in character), the form of analysis typically used herein includes difference of means tests and/or analyses of variance.

13. See Sandra J. Kenyon, "The Development of Political Cynicism in Negro and White Children," paper presented to the 1969 Meetings of the American Political Science Association.

14. Amitai Etzioni, "Basic Human Needs, Alienation and Inauthenticity," *American Sociological Review,* Vol. 33, No. 6 (1968), pp. 870ff.

15. See, for example, S. M. Lipset, "Student Opposition in the United States," *Governmental Opposition,* Vol. 1, No. 3 (1966), pp. 366ff. and "Students and Politics in comparative Perspective," *Daedalus* (Winter, 1968), pp. 3ff. and *passim.*

16. *Ibid.,* 1968

17. Subsequently, Drexel changed its name and, to some extent its program. It is now Drexel University.

18. See, for example, Reinhard Bendix and Seymour M. Lipset, "Karl Marx's Theory of Social Classes," intheir *Class, Status and Power* (New York: The Free Press, (1966), pp. 6ff.

19. David M. Riesman, *The Lonely Crowd* (New Haven: Yale University Press, 1950), *passim.*

20. Seymour Martin Lipset, "Students and Politics in a Comparative Perspective," *Daedalus* (Winter, 1968), pp. 2ff.

21. Jules Pfeiffer, *Challenge Magazine,* 1968.

22. See note 3.

23. *Ibid.,* p. 15.

24. S. M. Lipset, "Student Opposition in the United States," *Government and Opposition,* Vol. 1, No. 3 (1966), p. 367.

25. Lipset (1968), *op. cit.,* p. 5.

26. Lipset (1966), *op cit.*

27. See notes 3 and 7. See also, Seymour Martin Lipset and Philip G. Altbach, "Student Politics and Higher Education in the United States," in Seymour Martin Lipset, (ed.), *Student Politics* (New York: Basic Books, 1967), pp. 207ff.

28. Lipset (1968), *op. cit.,* pp. 18ff.

29. See, for example, Lewis A. Froman, Jr., *People and Politics* (Englewood Cliffs, N.J.; Prentice-Hall, 1962), p. 96.

30. David J. Armor, et al., "Professor's Attitudes Toward the Viet-Nam War," *Public Opinion Quarterly,* Vol. XXXI (Summer, 1967), pp. 159-175.

Chapter 4

1. See Melvin Seeman, "Alienation and Social Learning in a Reformatory," *American Journal of Sociology,* Vol. LXI, No. 3 (1963), pp. 270ff. and Seeman, "Alienation, Membership and Political Knowledge," *loc. cit.*

2. *Ibid.*

3. Note that in this view, cognitive conflict need be perceived to be threatening. We have shown, in Chapter 2, that individuals are capable of considerable cognitively compartmentalized action about politics. The compartmentalized areas and the individual's different orientations to them are not threatening because they are not perceived as conflicting.

4. Note that the order in time is specified here but is not the actual time it takes to go through the states. This real-time aspect varies with individuals, with variable magnitudes and ranges from seconds to years.

5. David C. Schwartz, "A Theory of Revolutionary Behavior" in James C. Davies, *When Men Revolt* (New York: The Free Press, 1970).

6. Judson S. Brown, "Principles of Intrapersonal Conflict," *Journal of Conflict Resolution*, Vol. 1, No. 2, pp. 143ff.

7. We are referring here to what, in practical situations, are basic, self-defining values. For example, "I'm black but the system discriminates against blacks." Race, religion, philosophy, class—important aspects of the self—are what we are considering here.

8. Sigmund Freud, *Civilization and Its Discontents* (New York: W. W. Norton and Company, 1961), *passim*.

Chapter 5

1. The relatively few studies that do focus on alienation from urban politics tend to concentrate more on the consequences of alienation and rather less on its causes. See John E. Horton and Wayne E. Thompson, "Powerlessness and Political Negativism," *American Journal of Sociology*, Vol. 67, No. 5 (1962), pp. 485ff; McDill and Ridley, *op. cit.*; Thompson and Horton, *op. cit.*

2. See, for example, Jan Hajda, "Alienation and Integration of Student Intellectuals," *American Sociological Review*, Vol. 26, No. 5 (1961), pp. 758ff; Neal and Rettig, *op. cit.*; Meier and Bell, *op. cit.*; Mizruchi, *op. cit.*; Srole, *op. cit.*; Templeton, *op. cit.*

3. Nettler, *op. cit.*; Dean (1960 and 1961), *op. cit.*

4. Ransford, *op. cit.*

5. Lowry, *op. cit.*

6. *Ibid.*

7. *Ibid.*, notes 5, 10 and 11.

8. *Ibid.*

9. M. Kent Jennings and Richard G. Niemi, "Party Identification at Multiple Levels of Government," *American Journal of Sociology*, Vol. 72, No. 1 (July, 1960), pp. 86ff; and M. Kent Jennings, "Pre-Adult Orientations to Multiple Levels of Government," *Midwest Journal of Political Science*, Vol. XI, No. 3 (August, 1967), pp. 291ff.

10. Jennings, *op. cit.*, pp. 306-312.

11. In those other studies, the items purporting to measure the same variable are also substantially more highly intercorrelated with each other than with other variables — indicating the conceptually distinct character of the independent variables more clearly than is possible with single-item indicators. (See the listings of TVC, PI. SI and alienation indexes for Chapter 5 in the Methods Appendix.)

12. See note 9.

13. Possible conceptual differences between "threat from value conflict" and "threat from perceived inefficacy" must be kept in mind. For upper SES populations of the character being studied here, it seems reasonable to suspect that inefficacy is a value conflict but, ultimately, this must be demonstrated, not merely suspected. The data presented here are offered within the clear limitations imposed by the conceptual distinction between TVC and threat from perceived inefficacy.

14. Differences in the level of government inquired about in these studies (national government in the black communities, urban government in the white communities) may also be involved here — although our findings in Newark and the Mainline make this relatively unlikely in our view.

Chapter 6

1. See, for example, Seymour Martin Lipset, "Students and Politics in Comparative Perspective," in *Daedalus* (Winter, 1968), pp. 1ff.; and, for an appreciation of the size of the empirical literature on student political behavior, consult: Philip G. Altbach (ed.), *Select Bibliography on Students, Politics and Higher Education,* (Cambridge, Center for International Affairs, Harvard, 1967).

2. Contrast the public positions of Bruno Bettelheim and/or S. I. Hayakawa with those of Flacks, *op. cit.,* or of Christian Bay, "Political and Apolitical Students," *Journal of Social Issues,* XXIII, No. 3 (1967), pp. 76ff.

3. See, for example, Gary C. Byrne, "Minority Problems, Value Inconsistency and Student Protest Behavior," paper read to the 1969 Meetings of the APSA, pp. 6ff.; Flacks, *op. cit.;* and Lipset (1966), *op. cit.*

4. For a comparative summary on this point and an assertion that campus-relevant variables will predominate over SES variables, see Lipset (1968), pp. 3ff.

5. See Lipset (1968), *op. cit., passim.*

6. See notes 3-6.

Lipset (1966), *op. cit.,* pp. 388ff.

8. *Ibid.*

9. Byrne, *op. cit., passim.*

10. Lipset (1966), *op. cit.,* Kenniston (1967), *op cit.*

11. The Washington Monument, the Boston Common, etc.

12. Philip Converse, reporting on Survey Research Center data (Speech at Haverford College, April 28, 1970).

Chapter 7

1. See Chapter 3 notes and *passim.*

2. See, for example, Seymour Martin Lipset, "Student and Politics in Comparative Perspective," *Daedalus* (Winter, 1968), pp. 18ff.

3. See, for example, Marshall Windmuller, "International Relations: The New Mandarins" in Theodore Roszak (ed.), *The Dissenting Academy* (New York: Random House, 1966), pp. 110-111.

4. The relative oversampling of political scientists no doubt represented the unconscious biases of the author; corrected, in part, by the response rates.

5. Perhaps the single most clear assertion of the importance of region can be found in V. O. Key, Jr., and Frank Munger, "Social Determinism and Electoral Decision," reprinted in Frank Munger and Douglas Price, *Readings in Political Parties and Pressure Groups* (New York: Cromwell, 1964), p. 382.

6. All of the voting studies are on point. For what is perhaps the benchmark study, see George Belknap and Angus Campbell, "Political Party Identification . . .," *Public Opinion Quarterly,* XV (1951-1952), pp. 601ff.

7. See, for example, Daniel Bell, *The End of Ideology* (1960), *op. cit., passim.*

Chapter 8

1. I believe that the general paradigm expressed here is useful in the explanation of most political behavior whether or not the behavior to be explained issues out of alienation. As already has been said, other factors beside alienation account for the behavior orientation which a given individual adopts so that nonalienated people can adopt conformist, reformist, withdrawn and ritualist orientations (but probably not revolutionary orientations). Clearly, too, the SES and personality variables identified here to account for the behavior orientations adopted by alienated men should also help to explain those adopted by nonalienated individuals. In addition,

the processes whereby behavior orientations are aroused and channeled into political behavior by media and group processes should also help to explain nonalienated behavior. In this sense, much of this chapter presents a schema which may be useful as a general model of human political behavior and not merely an explanation of alienated political behavior.

Chapter 11

1. See notes 5, 6 and 7 of Chapter 1, *supra*.
2. Irving L. Janis, "Effects of Fear Arousal on Attitude Change," in Leonard Berkowitz (ed.), *Advances in Experimental Social Psychology* (New York: Academic Press, 1967), pp. 170ff.
3. Kornhauser, *op. cit.*, p. 60. (Italics added)
4. Pre-test subjects reported no disturbance in reading patterns associated with these differences.
5. Pre-test subjects did not differentiate between these articles and the articles taken from the real newspapers; they accepted these as part of the newspaper.
6. We recognize, of course, that this conclusion must be interpreted narrowly, especially in light of the characteristics of the subject samples. College students are higher in verbal skills and are more predisposed to read than are less well educated samples. Research on the revolutionary interests and communications behavior of less educated, alienated population sectors is an obvious and necessary next step.

Chapter 12

1. See, for example: Kornhauser, *op. cit.*, pp. 30-33; Merton, *op. cit.*, pp. 155-56; and Smelser, *op. cit.*, p. 333.
2. Gabriel A. Almond (1954), *op. cit.*, p. 215; Cantril (1941), *op. cit.*, p. 69; and *The Politics of Despair* (New York, Basic Books, 1958), *passim*.
3. See, for example, V. I. Lenin, "Partisan Warfare," translated in *ORBIS*, Vol. II, No. 2 (1958), pp. 149ff.; Mao Tse-Tung, *On Guerilla Warfare*, Samuel P. Griffith (ed.) (New York: Praeger, 1961), pp. 43ff.; Regis Debray, *Revolution in the Revolution?* reprinted in *Monthly Review*, Vol. 19, No. 3 (1967), *passim*.
4. A partial listing includes: Franklin M. Osanka, *Modern Guerrilla Warfare* (New York: The Free Press, 1962); Lucian W. Pye, *Guerrilla Communism in Malaya* (Princeton: Princeton University Press, 1956); T. E. Lawrence, "Guerrilla Warfare,' *Encyclopedia Britannica* (London, 1950), Vol. X: Ralph Sanders, "Mass Support and Communist Insurrection," *ORBIS*, Vol. IX, No. 1, 1965, pp. 214ff.
5. "The . . . appeal has to be forthcoming . . . before available people may be mobilized." Kornhauser, *op. cit.*, p. 178; ". . . The spread of a . . . movement depends on the possibility of disseminating a generalized belief," Smelser, *op. cit.*, p. 337. See also Cantril (1941), *op. cit.*, p. 69.
6. Almond (1954), *op. cit.*, pp. 230ff.
7. Eric Hoffer, *The True Believer* (New York: Harper & Row, 1958), *passim;* Kornhauser, *op. cit.*, p. 32; Hannah Arendt sees both processes operative, distinguishing between masses who are available and mobs who are predisposed. See *The Origins of Totalitarianism*, (New York: Meridian Books, 1958), pp. 341ff.
8. See, for example, Irving L. Janis, "Effects of Fear Arousal on Attitude Change," in Leonard Berkowitz (ed.), *Advances in Experimental Social Psychology* (New York: Academic Press, 1967), pp. 167ff.
9. Control and Group 3 were asked to what extent they identified with revolutionary organizations, since no specific revolutionary organization was presented to them in the simulation. In effect, for these groups, we were measuring S's cognitive predisposition to support a revolutionary organization.

Chapter 13

1. James T. Wilson, "Planning and Politics: Citizen Participation in Urban Renewal" in Jewel Bellush and Murray Hans Knech (eds.), *Urban Renewal: People, Politics and Planning* (Garden City, New York: Anchor Books, 1967), pp. 299-300.

2. See Erbe, *op. cit.,* and Neal and Seeman, *op. cit.*

3. *Ibid.*

4. See note 2.

5. *Ibid.*

Chapter 14

1. Susanne DiVincenzo, unpublished manuscript, 1969.

2. Peter Shubs, "Revolutionary Symbology," paper read to the 1969 Meetings of the American Political Science Association.

3. David C. Schwartz, *Alliance Processes and International Politics* (Philadelphia: Foreign Policy Research Institute, 1967).

4. Studies by Stanley Renshon, University of Pennsylvania, 1971.

5. Schwartz and Moore, *op. cit.*

6. We expect an edited volume *Folklore and Politics* to issue from a faculty-graduate seminar conducted at the University of Pennsylvania jointly by Kenneth Goldstein and David C. Schwartz.

7. David C. Schwartz, "How People Interpret Political Experiences," forthcoming.

8. See, for example, David C. Schwartz, "Perceptions of Personal Energy and the Adoption of Basic Political Orientations," paper read to the 1970 Meetings of the International and American Political Science Associations.

9. David C. Schwartz and Nicholas Zill, "Psycho-physiological Arousal as a Predictor of Political Participation," paper read to the 1971 Meetings of the Amercan Political Science Association.

10. On the puzzlement of social scientists about the resurgence of the radical right, see Bell (1963), *op. cit.,* pp. 55 and *passim.*

11. On the shock produced by the black ghetto riots, see Massotti, et al., *op cit.,* Introduction.

12. We have already discussed the surprise of the scholarly community concerning student radicalism. See Flacks, *op. cit.*

13. See, for example, Kenniston (1967), *op. cit.*

14. Boskin, *op. cit.*

15. See Scott and El Assall, *op. cit.*

16. Graham and Gurr, *op. cit., passim.*

17. Almond and Verba (1963), *op. cit.;* Lipset (1964), *op. cit.* One can find these assertions as late as 1967, too. See Robert A. Dahl, *Pluralist Democracy in the United States* (Chicago: Rand McNally).

18. This discussion is based upon Robinson et al., *op. cit.,* pp. 591ff.

19. The consequences of mistrust are, of course, enormous. See both Erikson and Almond and Verba, *op. cit.*

20. Robinson et al., *op. cit.*

21. See, for example, "A Report of the Health Problems of the Poor," *Sources,* November 1968.

22. This is the burden of a number of recent studies. See, for example, Raymond E. Wolfinger, "The Development and Persistence of Ethnic Voting," *American Political Science Review,* Vol. LIX, No. 4, pp. 896-898.

23. Orum, *op. cit.*

24. See *The Annals of the American Academy of Political and Social Science* (November, 1963), *passim*.

25. R. Alford and H. Scoble, "Sources of Political Involvement," *American Political Science Review,* Vol. LXII, No. 4 (December 1968). See also Irving S. Foladere, "The Effect of Neighborhood on Voting," *Political Science Quarterly,* Vol. 83, No. 4 (December, 1968).

26. Cited in Chapter 1, *Psychology Today, op. cit.*

27. Philip Meyer, "The Aftermath of Martyrdom," *Public Opinion Quarterly,* Vol. 32, No. 2 (Summer, 1969), pp. 160ff.; Richard Hofstetter, "Political Disengagement and the Death of Martin Luther King," *Public Opinion Quarterly,* Vol. 32, No. 2 (Summer, 1969).

28. Schwartz, in Davies, *op. cit.*

29. Neal E. Cutler, "Generation, Maturation and Party Affiliation," *Public Opinion Quarterly,* Vol. 33 (Winter 1969), pp. 583ff.

METHODS APPENDIX

This appendix follows the organization of this book. The items used to measure each attitudinal variable introduced in the text of a chapter are reported here, along with the matrix of inter-item correlation coefficients (Pearson's r) for every index constructed to measure attitudinal variables. Unless otherwise noted, all items are "agree-disagree" type items (either dichotomous or Likert scale-type formats).* Indexes were constructed by aggregating standard scores on each indicator in the index.

Chapter 2

Political Alienation from *Municipal Government:*	*East Torresdale*	*a*	*b*	*c*
(a) I generally think of myself as a part of Philadelphia government and politics.		—		
(b) When I think about Philadelphia government and politics, I generally feel like an outsider.		0.43	—	
(c) Many people feel they used to be part of Philadelphia government and politics, but no longer. I feel the same way.		0.14	0.62	—

Social Alienation (Srole Scale)		East Torresdale			
	a	*b*	*c*	*d*	*e*
(a) There's little use writing to public officials — local, state, or national — because often they aren't really interested in the problems of the average man.	—				

*In general, we did not intercorrelate items that had different response formats.

(b) Nowadays a person has to live pretty much for today and let tomorrow take care of itself. 0.53   —

(c) In spite of what some people say, the lot of the average man is getting worse, not better. 0.61   0.40   —

(d) It's hardly fair to bring children into the world with the way things look for the future. 0.48   0.46   0.70   —

(e) These days a person doesn't really know whom he can count on. 0.58   0.45   0.70   0.68   —

Social Alienation (Srole Scale)	University of Pennsylvania			
	a	*b*	*c*	*d*	*e*
(a) It's hardly fair to bring children into the world the way things look for the future.	––				
(b) These days a person really doesn't know whom he can count on.	0.08	—			
(c) Nowadays, a person has to live pretty much for today and let tomorrow take care of itself.	0.08	0.18	—		
(d) There's little use in writing to public officials because often they aren't interested in the problems of the average man.	0.05	0.01	0.14	—	
(e) In spite of what some people say, the lot of the average man is getting worse, not better.	0.11	0.24	0.03	0.18	—

N.B. As indicated in the text, this "scale" was not treated as an index because of the low level of inter-item correlation.

Political Srole Scale	University of Pennsylvania			
	a	*b*	*c*	*d*	*e*
(a) When I think of the direction things are going in the government, I feel frightened for the kids growing up.	—				
(b) I'm just not sure I can rely on representatives in government.	0.40				
(c) One never knows what the government is going to do next.	0.25	0.22	—		
(d) Most public officials are concerned with the interests of the average man.	0.34	0.11	0.36	—	
(e) Public officials come and go but government seems to keep getting worse.	0.33	0.25	0.45	0.29	—

Cultural Alienation (Nettler Scale)

	1	2	3	4	5	6	7	8	9	10	11	12	13	14	15	16	17
1	—																
2	0.15	—															
3	-0.02	0.07	—														
4	0.24	0.16	0.70	—													
5	0.14	0.18	0.06	0.05	—												
6	0.06	0.30	-0.03	-0.04	0.30	—											
7	0.08	0.16	0.09	0.19	0.05	0.06	—										
8	-0.08	0.10	0.02	0.17	-0.13	-0.07	0.11	—									
9	-0.01	0.21	0.24	0.17	-0.08	0.02	0.19	0.15	—								
10	0.25	0.23	0.15	0.13	0.24	0.20	0.30	0.10	-0.03	—							
11	-0.01	0.15	0.03	0.01	0.22	0.46	0.09	0.04	-0.15	0.18	—						
12	0.40	0.21	0.04	0.50	-0.08	-0.07	0.30	0.20	0.22	0.31	0.07	—					
13	0.14	0.06	0.01	0.16	-0.11	0.00	0.01	0.11	0.15	0.14	0.03	0.19	—				
14	0.06	0.11	0.13	0.19	0.08	-0.01	0.28	0.26	0.18	0.27	0.16	0.17	0.15	—			
15	-0.13	0.15	0.03	0.12	0.02	0.09	0.16	0.13	0.09	0.15	0.07	0.17	0.13	0.19	—		
16	0.15	0.10	-0.25	0.15	-0.04	0.11	0.08	-0.01	-0.08	0.02	0.05	0.19	-0.09	0.10	0.03	—	
17	-0.01	0.08	0.24	0.02	0.05	-0.07	0.11	0.07	0.13	0.13	-0.04	-0.04	0.06	0.34	0.29	-0.16	—

Political Alienation from National Polity	University of Pennsylvania				
	a	*b*	*c*	*d*	*e*
(a) When I think about politics and government in America, I consider myself an outsider.	—				
(b) In American politics and government, power is maintained by secrecy and collusion which excludes people like me.	0.34	—			
(c) The way things are in government now, people like me are no longer represented.	0.50	0.32	—		
(d) I tend to identify myself (feel closely associated) with American politics and government.	0.33	0.22	0.24	—	
(e) When I hear or read about the politics and governmental system of the United States, I feel that I am a part of that system.	0.47	0.12	0.30	0.37	—

Cultural Alienation (Nettler Scale)

1. Do national spectator sports (football, baseball) interest you?
2. Do you think most politicians are sincerely interested in the public welfare, rather than being more interested in themselves?
3. Do you think children are generally a nuisance to their parents?
4. Do you like the new model American automobiles?
5. Although some people say human life is an expression of divine purpose, it is really only the result of chance and evolution.
6. Religion is mostly truth, rather than mostly myth.
7. Most people live lives of quiet desperation.
8. Were you interested in the recent national elections?
9. Do you vote in national elections (or would you if of voting age)?
10. Life, as most men live it, is meaningless.
11. Do you like to participate in church activities?
12. Do you enjoy TV?
13. Do you think you could just as easily live in another society — past or present?
14. Do you think most married people lead trapped (frustrated) lives?
15. For yourself, assuming you could carry out your decision or do things over again, do you think a married life would be more satisfactory than a single life?
16. Do you read *Reader's Digest?*
17. Are you interested in having children?

Political Alienation from National Polity	University of Pennsylvania experiment			
	a	*b*	*c*	*d*
(a) I generally share the basic values exhibited in the policies and processes of American politics.	—			
(b) I usually identify myself (feel closely associated) with American politics and government.	0.30	—		
(c) In American politics, power is maintained by secrecy and collusion which excludes even the interested citizen.	—0.26	—0.21	—	
(d) The way things are going in our society, my friends and I aren't really represented anymore.	—0.23	—0.23	.23	—

Interpersonal Estrangement—Vietnam Moratorium (r = 0.35)
  I find the basic things of value are not generally valued by other people; and the projective item, It is almost impossible for people to really understand each other.

Interpersonal Mistrust—Vietnam Moratorium (r = 0.37)
  If you don't watch yourself, people will take advantage of you; Some people say that most people can be trusted, others say you can't be too careful in your dealings with other people. How do you feel?

Value on Group Identification—Vietnam Moratorium (r = 0.33)
  A person truly finds himself when he joins with others to achieve common goals; Humans don't really fulfill their potential unless they involve themselves deeply in some group.

Preference for Interpersonal Cohesion—Vietnam Moratorium (r=0.31)
  It doesn't pay to be too different from your friends; In general, I'd rather agree with people than argue with them.

Social Obligation—Vietnam Moratorium	*a*	*b*	*c*	*d*
(a) Not only does everyone have the right of life, liberty and the pursuit of happiness, he also has an equal moral obligation to protect others from having these rights taken away from them.	—			
(b) Acting to protect the rights and interests of other members of one's community is a major obligation of all people.	0.51	—		
(c) An individual who has not caused another's misfortune has no moral obligation to help the other person.	—0.41	—0.48	—	
(d) An individual's responsibility for the welfare of others doesn't extend past his intimate circle of friends and relatives.	—0.35	—0.43	0.59	—

Political Alienation from	*a*	*b*	*c*
National Polity—Vietnam Moratorium			
(a) The government no longer seems to represent people like me.	—		
(b) In American politics, power is maintained in secret, shutting out even interested citizens.	.40	—	
(c) The government seems to be unwilling to do the things I think need to be done.	.55	.37	—

Chapter 3

Political Alienation from Municipality—Newark (Single-item Indicator)
When I think about the political system in Newark, I feel like an outsider.

Political Alienation from National Polity—Philadelphia black communities (r=0.64)
When I hear about politics and government in America, I feel that I am a part of it; I feel that my friends and I are still really represented in our government.

Political Alienation from National Polity—Philadelphia suburbs

	a	*b*	*c*
(a) When I think about the politics in Washington, I feel like an outsider.	—		
(b) When I think about the government in Washington, I don't feel as if it's my government.	0.52	—	
(c) People like me aren't represented in Washington.	0.50	0.66	—

Policial Alienation from State Polity

	a	*b*	*c*
(a) When I think about the politics in Harrisburg (the state capitol), I feel like an outsider.	—		
(b) When I think about the government in Harrisburg, I don't feel as if it's my government.	0.56	—	
(c) People like me aren't represented in Harrisburg.	0.60	0.64	—

Political Alienation from Local Polity

	a	*b*	*c*
(a) When I think about the politics in my town, I feel like an outsider.	—		
(b) When I think about the government in my town, I don't feel as if it's my government.	0.64	—	
(c) People like me aren't represented in my town.	0.58	0.68	—

Political Alienation from National Polity—Temple University (r = .52)
(a) When I hear about politics and government in America, I feel that I am a part of it.
(b) I feel that my friends and I are still really represented in our government.

Political Alienation from National Polity—Penn Sit-In
When I think about public affairs in America, I feel like an outsider, a single-item indicator.

Chapter 4

TVC—Experimental Protocols
Value Conflict: Do you think that the major institutions of the American political system agree with your values about politics? Yes . . . . . . No . . . . . .
Threat from Value Conflict: If not, how threatened do you feel by this apparent discrepancy? (Rank on a scale from 1 to 7; 7 meaning most threatened.)

PI —Experimental protocols
Please rate, on a scale from 1 to 7, how effective you feel you can be, *at this time,* in influencing American politics. (7 meaning most effective)

SI —Experimental Protocols
Please rate, on the same scale, how effective you feel that American politics is, *at this time,* in inflecting the needs and wishes of the American people.

Political Alienation from National Polity—Experimental Protocols
To what extent do you identify with (feel closely associated with) the American political system *at this time?* (Rate on a scale from 1 to 7, 7 meaning most positive identification.)

Chapter 5

TVC—Newark
When I think about the future of kids in Newark, I get very scared.

PI —Newark ($r=.22$)
(a) "Sometimes politics and government in Newark are too complicated for people like me to understand."
(b) "Voting is the only way people like me can ever do anything about what goes on in Newark."

SI —Newark
"The politicians and administrators in Newark don't really care about people like me."

Threat from Inefficacy at All Levels of Government—Philadelphia suburbs
"When I think of how basically helpless I am to affect the decision in _____ (Washington, Harrisburg, my town), I get scared."

PI, All Levels of Government—Philadelphia suburbs ($r = 0.53$ National,
$r = 0.52$ State,
$r = 0.60$ Local)
(a) It is really impossible for one man to make his voice heard in _____ (Washington, Harrisburg, my town); (b) Only large groups like big business and labor unions can get what they want in _____ (Washington, Harrisburg, my town).

SI, All Levels of Government—Philadelphia suburbs
There is at least one group in _____ (Washington, Harrisburg, my town) that seems to speak for my interests.

TVC—Philadelphia black communities
 When I think about the difference between what I want for people and what American politics is doing to people, I feel scared.

PI —Philadelphia black communities
 There is just about nothing that I can do to get the laws and policies I favor adopted in America.

SI—Philadelphia black communities	*a*	*b*	*c*
(a) There is at least one political group in America that effectively represents my views.	—		
(b) Today, in American politics, leaders seem unable or unwilling to do what I most want to see done.	−0.36	—	
(c) There don't seem to be any people or groups in American politics that can accomplish what I think needs doing.	−0.20	0.35	—

TVC—Philadelphia's white community ($r = 0.50$)
 (a) City officials and people in this neighborhood have little or no contact with each other; (b) City officials and people in other neighborhoods also have little or no contacts with each other.

PI —Philadelphia's white community ($r = -0.33$)
 (a) There is really very little that I can do to influence decisions in City Hall; (b) My views . . . are being heard in City Hall.

SI —Philadelphia's white community ($r = 0.38$)
 (a) City officials . . . don't care about neighborhood concerns; (b) I don't believe my views are being well represented in City Hall through my elected representatives.

Chapter 6

TVC—University of Pennsylvania (1969)	*a*	*b*	*c*
(a) Unlike some of the prophets of gloom, I don't feel frightened about what the government does.	—		
(b) When I compare my values to those exhibited by the government, I get scared.	0.61	—	
(c) When I think about the differences between what I want in the world and what the government does, I get scared.	0.58	0.76	—

PI —University of Pennsylvania (1969)
 (a) It's almost impossible for a person to make his voice heard in government.

SI —University of Pennsylvania (1969)
 (a) Only large groups like labor unions and big business can get what they want from the government.

TVC—University of Pennsylvania (1970) (r = 0.55)
(a) When I think about the difference between what I want for people and what American politics is doing to people, I feel scared.
(b) When I think about the way our government is running things, I'm often frightened.

PI —University of Pennsylvania (1970)
There is just about nothing I can do to get the laws and policies I favor adopted in America.

SI —University of Pennsylvania (1970) (r = 0.46)
(a) Today, in American politics, leaders seem unable or unwilling to do what I most want to see done.
(b) The way things are going in America, it's frightening because the politicians do what they want, not what we want.

Political Alienation from National Polity—University of Pennsylvania (1970)

	a	*b*	*c*
(a) In American politics, power is maintained in secret, shutting out even interested citizens.	—		
(b) I feel that my friends and I are still really represented in our government.	−0.44	—	
(c) When I hear about politics and government in America, I feel that I am a part of it.	−0.37	0.50	—

TVC—Temple University (r = 0.64)
(a) When I think about the difference between what I want for people and what American politics is doing to people, I feel scared.
(b) When I think about the way our government is running things, I'm often frightened.

PI —Temple
There is just about nothing I can do to get the laws and policies I favor adopted.

SI —Temple
Today, in American politics, leaders seem unable or unwilling to do what I most want to see done.

TVC, PI, SI—Drexel
(a) How threatened do you feel by _____ [the discrepancy between the values expressed by respondent and the values he perceived as operative in the major institutions of American politics] (Respondent self-ranked on seven-point scale);
(b) People like me don't have much say about how the government runs things (Ranked on seven-point scale);
(c) How optimistic are you that the American political system can solve the problems facing this country? (TVC, PI and SI, thus were all self-ranked by respondents on a seven-point scale.)

Political Alienation from National Polity—Drexel (r = 0.49)
(a) To what extent do you identify with (feel closely associated with) the American political system? (rated on a seven-point scale);
(b) How much do you like the American political system? (rated on a seven-point scale).

TVC—Atlantic County Community College	*a*	*b*	*c*
(a) When I think of the difference between what I want for the world and what American policies are doing in the world, I feel scared.	—		
(b) I find that the basic things I value for people are not generally valued in American public life and that is frightening.	0.34	—	
(c) Unlike some of the gloom and doom prophets, I don't feel afraid about the future of American politics.	−0.40	−0.19	—

PI   —Atlantic County Community College ($r = -0.41$)
(a) People like me don't have much say about how the government runs things.
(b) I feel that I can be effective in getting the laws and policies I favor adopted in American politics.

SI   —Atlantic County Community College ($r = -0.58$)
(a) There is at least one political group in America that effectively represents my views.
(b) There don't seem to be any persons or groups active in American politics that can accomplish what I want to see done.

Political Alienation from National Polity—Atlantic County Community College	*a*	*b*	*c*
(a) I usually identify myself (feel closely associated) with American politics and government.	—		
(b) In American politics, power is maintained by secrecy and collusion, which excludes even the interested citizen.	−0.48	—	
(c) The way things are going in our society, my friends and I aren't really represented any more.	0.22	0.57	—

TVC—Penn Sit-In ($r = 0.58$)
(a) Do you feel generally threatened by the policies or structures of American government?
(b) When I think about public affairs in America, I feel threatened.

PI   —Penn Sit-In
Do you personally feel that you can be effective in changing (the) policies or structures (of American government) via the ordinary institutions of American government?

SI   —Penn Sit-In
(a) Do you think President Nixon can improve our foreign policy?
(b) Do you think that desirable change is possible within our present political system?
(c) Do you think Nixon administration *can* solve the problems of the black community?
(d) Do you think the present political system would allow the black people to solve their own problems?

	a	b	c	d
(a)	—			
(b)	0.24	—		
(c)	0.46	0.31	—	
(d)	0.36	0.35	0.25	—

Political Alienation—Penn Sit-In
Comparable to that used in almost all of our studies and achieving high inter-item correlation in previous studies, viz: When I think about public affairs in America, I feel like an outsider.

Threat from Value Conflict with the University—Penn Sit-In
Do you feel generally threatened by the policies or structure of this university?

Political Inefficacy in the University—Penn Sit-In
Do you personally feel that you can be effective in changing (university) policies or structures via the ordinary institutions and processes of this university?

University Linkage with Political System—Penn Sit-In
To be interested in school is to be interested in politics because today politics controls education.

Comparisons of Anxiety About Personal Relationships Versus Political Relationships
—Penn Sit-In (r = 0.23)
(a) Political activity is less tensionful than the classes and school work at college.
(b) I get into more unpleasant conflicts with my parents or teachers or friends than I do with political opponents.

Liberalism Versus Conservatism—Penn Sit-In
On national issues, which of the following general positions most describes where you stand? (Rated 1-5, strong liberal to strong conservative.)

Revolutionism—Penn Sit-In
Do you think our present political system must be destroyed and replaced with another one?

Course Work Versus Political Activity—Penn Sit-In
Compared to your experience in courses, how satisfying have you found your political experience? Rated 1-5, much more—much less satisfying than course experience.)

Threat-Anger from Value Conflict—Vietnam Moratorium (r = 0.54)
(a) When I think about the way our government is running things, I'm often frightened.
(b) When I think of the difference between what I want and what the government is doing, I get angry.

SI —Vietnam Moratorium (r = −0.50)
(a) There is at least one political group that effectively represents my views.
(b) There don't seem to be any groups in American politics that can accomplish what I think needs doing.

PI —Vietnam Moratorium
People like me don't have much say in how the government runs things.

Political Cynicism—Vietnam Moratorium (r = 0.38)
(a) Politicians spend most of their time getting reelected or reappointed.
(b) Money is the most important factor influencing public policies.

Radical Reformism—Vietnam Moratorium

	a	*b*	*c*
(a) It is the direct form of political action (like marches and sit-ins, etc.) that brings results.	—		
(b) It will probably be necessary to break some laws in order to bring about ... the ideals that people like me hold.	0.34	—	
(c) Voting just isn't effective; it is the direct forms of political action that bring results.	−0.31	−0.34	—

Revolutionism or Acceptance of Violence as a Tactic—Vietnam Moratorium

	a	*b*	*c*	*d*
(a) It seems as if only violent incidents really produce the kinds of change that I would like to see happen.	—			
(b) The chance that direct political action . . . may result in violence is a chance we just have to take.	0.34	—		
(c) It will probably be necessary to resort to some sort of violence to . . . produce the values . . . that people like me hold.	0.47	0.39	—	
(d) Violence is never an acceptable tactic to bring about social-political change.	−0.48	−0.24	−0.49	—

Political Obligation—Vietnam Moratorium ($r = 0.58$)

(a) A person should . . . cooperate with democratically elected leaders, even though they were not the ones he personally preferred.

(b) Conformity to ... policies that you don't agree with is wrong, even if they were arrived at democratically.

Chapter 7

Political Alienation from National Polity—National Sample of Social Scientists ($r = 0.56$)

(a) I usually identify myself closely with American politics and government.

(b) When I hear about politics in America, I feel part of it.

TVC—National Sample of Social Scientists

	a	*b*	*c*
(a) When I think of the difference between what I want for the world and what American politics are doing in the world, I often feel scared.	—		

(b) Unlike some of the gloom and doom prophets, I don't feel afraid about the future of American politics.   −0.41   —

(c) The basic things I value for people are not generally shared in American public life (and this is frightening).   −0.40   −0.27   —

PI   —National Sample of Social Scientists (r = 0.44)

(a) I feel that I can be effective in getting the policies and laws I favor adopted in American politics.

(b) I probably could never have any effective influence on public policy.

SI   —National Sample of Social Scientists

There is at least one group in America that effectively represents my views.

Ideology—National Sample of Social Scientists (r = 0.78 for Political Scientists, r = 0.38 for Sociologists)

(a) A seven-point "semantic differential" type item—"Left 1 2 3 4 5 6 7 Right" —asking the respondent to indicate the place best describing his position on the American political spectrum.

(b) A direct item asking the respondent which of the following ideological positions best described his position: conservatism, liberalism, socialism, other.

Chapter 9

All indexes in Chapter 9 were used in a study at the University of Pennsylvania (1970).

Conformity—Acceptance of American National Polity

	a	b	c	d
(a) If people would only use the laws and institutions of our political system, they would find that the system really works quite well.	—			
(b) I use (or plan to use) only the regular ordinary channels of political activity in this country: voting, lobbying, writing letters to Congressman, testifying before legislative and administrative agencies, working through the courts.	0.47	—		
(c) I used to accept the American political system more fully than I do now. Today, I feel highly critical of it.	−0.34	−0.44	—	
(d) My feelings of respect and affection for American political institutions have not diminished over what they were.	0.30	−0.33	0.53	—

Ritualism

There are some public policies which I still advocate because I used to believe that they would work, even though now I am not very convinced that they would work.

Reformism (r = 0.41)

(a) In order to get new and better public policies we still probably have to make some reforms of our political structures. I'd support such structural reform if it comes about without violence.

(b) I'd like to help bring about major changes in American politics—a peaceful revolution in our attitudes, priorities, policies and institutions.

Revolutionism	a	b	c
(a) We need violent change in our politics.	—		
(b) I would support a social movement in this country which would bring about an end to slums, poverty, pollution and prejudice in public life — even if considerable violence were necessary to carry out that program.	0.50	—	
(c) I would not support a revolutionary movement in this country.	−0.43	−0.52	—

Withdrawal	a	b	c
(a) I intend to vote in the next Presidential election — or would if I were old enough.	—		
(b) I don't feel a part of this political system, so I don't (or won't) vote.	−0.67	—	
(c) (As a consistency check, we repeated Item *a* 72 items later.)	0.86	−0.57	—

Political Alienation, TVC, PI and *SI* have already been given in this appendix (Chapter 6).

Perception of Personal Energy (r = 0.64)

(a) I get tired faster than most people.

(b) I think of myself as being low in energy. I'm often physically listless, or tired or run down.

Anger	a	b	c
(a) Politics in America often makes me angry.	—		
(b) When I think about how unfair our political system is to so many people, I feel angered.	0.43	—	
(c) When I think about the negative impacts of United States policies at home and abroad, my response is to get mad.	0.29	0.36	—

Psychological Comfort with Anger

When I think about mean and unfair things, like the murders of John Kennedy, Robert Kennedy, and Martin Luther King, my own anger makes me scared.

Perception of Economic Invulnerability (r = −0.30)

(a) I think of myself as very vulnerable to economic changes in this country.

(b) I'm certain that I'll do all right financially, no matter what political stands I may take.

Perception of Political Invulnerability (r = 0.33)
(a) I don't like to sign petitions because you never know how government officials might use it against you later.
(b) If I were to get very involved in reformist politics, I'd be afraid of being followed, spied on, having my phone tapped, etc.

Need for Conformity (r = 0.40)
(a) I like to agree with my friends about politics.
(b) I like to go along with people in their views on politics.

Desire to Be Reintegrated with the Polity (r = 0.51)
(a) I keep hoping that things will change in America soon so that I can feel a part of our public life again.
(b) I feel alienated from American politics but I don't feel quite differently.

Protest Voting Orientation (r = 0.68)
(a) When I think about myself as performing the act of voting, I think of it as a protest.
(b) My vote is usually cast (or would usually be cast) mostly as a protest against American politics, policies and politicians.

Support for Demagogues Orientation (r = 0.55)
(a) Today, our problems are so great that I would even favor a political leader who was something of a demagogue if he could change things for the better.
(b) If a demagogue or extremist could get America to give real racial justice, end poverty and pollution and bring us peace—I'd support a demagogue.

Group Versus Individual Process of Alienation
I became alienated because I got friendly with some people who were alienated.

Chapter 10

All indexes reported here were used in our study of Philadelphia's black communities.

Perceived Conformity
I guess I feel about politics the way most people do.

Ritualism (r=0.35)
(a) I vote, you have to use the vote to get social changes, but I don't expect it to do any good.
(b) You've got to keep trying to get good laws and fairness in politics, but it's really not much use.

Ritualism (r = 0.35)
(a) When it comes to politics, I think we need new parties and new institutions.
(b) We need new political parties so we can change things but do it by politics.

Revolutionism
We need violent change in both our national goals and in the means we use to accomplish our goals.

Attitudinal or Cognitive Withdrawal (Our two measures of withdrawal intercorrelate at 0.54 but were treated separately for theoretical purposes.)
I don't concern myself about politics any more. I'm concerned about private things: myself, my family, my friends.

Behavioral Withdrawal
I used to pay more attention to politics than I do now.

Political Alienation from National Polity (r = 0.64)
(a) When I hear about politics and government in America, I feel that I am a part of it.
(b) I feel that my friends and I are still really represented in our government.

Psychological Comfort with Anger (r = 0.43)
(a) Sometimes, when I get mad about what's wrong with things, I feel afraid that I won't be able to control myself so I try to put it out of my mind.
(b) I wouldn't want to be a Congressman or city councilor because the responsibility for all those decisions and all those people would put me too uptight.

Need for Conformity	a	b	c
(a) I like to agree with my friends about politics.	—		
(b) I'd rather be in a group where people agree on their politics than one where they disagree.	0.72	—	
(c) I like to go along with people in their views on politics.	0.48	0.46	—

Black Separatist Orientation (r = 0.48)
(a) Some black people have suggested that whites and blacks should be two separate governments. Would you agree with this as a goal?
(b) One of the political changes that has been proposed by a conference of black people has been a black congress—a legislature to make laws for black people. Would you like to see this come about?

Orientation Toward Using Public Institutions to Achieve Black Consciousness (r = 0.60)
(a) Do you believe that African culture should be taught in the schools?
(b) Several religions—like Jews, Catholics and Protestants—have a released time arrangement with the public schools so that kids can leave public schools and go to separate schools of religious study in the community. Would you like to see such an arrangement for the teaching of black studies?

Chapter 11

Political Alienation from National Polity—Experimental Protocols

	a	b	c	d
(a) I usually identify myself (feel closely associated) with American politics and governments.	—			
(b) In American politics, power is maintained by secrecy and collusion which excludes even the interested citizen.	−0.21	—		

(c) The way things are going in American society, my friends and I aren't really represented any more.   −0.23   0.23   —

(d) I generally share the basic values exhibited in the policies and processes of American politics.   0.30   −0.26   −.23   —

Negative Evaluation of Alienation—Experimental Protocols
I feel generally alienated from politics and government in the U.S. and find that to be an unpleasant situation.

A Measure of Negative Evaluation of Newspaper Reporting—Experimental Protocols
I think American newspapers report political campaigns rather fairly.

Political Alienation from National Polity—Temple University (r = 0.52)
(a) When I hear about politics and government in America, I feel that I am a part of it.
(b) I feel that my friends and I are still really represented in our government.

Chapter 12

Space restrictions and the fact that all variables had to be measured repeatedly in the experiment necessitated the use of single-item indicators for all variables in this study. Accordingly, we chose direct (nondisguised, nonprojective) items, offered here as face-valid.

Political Alienation from National Polity
To what extent do you identify with (feel closely associated with) the American political system *at this time?* (Rate on a scale from 1 to 7, 7 meaning most positive identification.)

Value Conflict
Do you think that the major institutions of the American political system agree with your values about politics? Yes_____ No_____

TVC
If not, how threatened do you feel by the apparent discrepancy? (Rank on a scale from 1 to 7, 7 meaning most threatened.)

PI
Please rate, on a scale from 1 to 7, how effective you feel you can be, *at this time,* in influencing American politics. (7 meaning most effective.)

SI
Please rate, on the same scale, how effective you feel that American politics is, at this time, in reflecting the needs and wishes of the American people.

Radical Identification
To what extent do you identify with or are you attracted to what you would consider radical groups, *at this time?* (Rate on a scale from 1 to 7, 7 meaning most positive identification or attraction.)

Identification with Revolutionary Group
To what extent (rated on a seven-point scale) do you identify with (feel closely associated with or positively attracted to) the VPL (Voters Protection League)?

VA
To what extent are the goals of the Voters Protection League (VPL) compatible with your own values?

PE
To what extent do you believe that you could be effective politically as a supporter of the VPL?

SE
Without your support, to what extent do you believe that the VPL is likely to achieve its political goals?

Chapter 13

Political Alienation from Municipal Polity—East Torresdale
(See this Appendix, Chapter 1.)

Perceived Effectiveness of the Organization—East Torresdale

	a	b	c	d
(a) The East Torresdale Civic Association is effectively making its views known in City Hall.	—			
(b) City Hall officials will have to listen to East Torresdale Civic Association, especially if its members stick together.	0.53	—		
(c) The East Torresdale Civic Association is *not* effectively representing the views of most of the people in this neighborhood to City Hall officials.	−0.44	−0.41	—	
(d) The East Torresdale Civic Association will *not* be effective in reaching its goals for this neighborhood.	−0.41	−0.38	0.72	—

Perceived Effectiveness of the Individual Within Organization—East Torresdale

	a	b	c	d
(a) I am able to make my views heard in the East Torresdale Civic Association.	—			
(b) The East Torresdale Civic Association represents my best interests most of the time.	0.59	—		

(c) I am *not* able to influence the decisions made by the East Torresdale Civic Association.   −0.25   −0.41   —

(d) In general I feel satisfied with the role I play in the East Torresdale Civic Association.   0.79   0.59   −0.22   —

PI —East Torresdale (r = 0.33)
    (See this Appendix, Chapter 1.)

North Philadelphia Study

Much of these data were in nominal form. Aggregation, therefore, was decided upon solely on face-validity and theoretical bases.

Alienation from Political Parties
(a) In the present attempt to solve North Philadelphia's problems, do you think that community organizations like P-CR District or Area Committees are more able or less able than the political party structure to get results?
(b) Do you think community organizations would be more effective or less effective in solving community problems if they worked directly through the political party structure?
(c) Do you think community organizations would be more effective or less effective if they attempted to control that structure, for instance, by electing committeemen, etc.?

Degree of Activity with the PCRP
(a) Would you say you are still active with the PCRP?
(b) How much time, on the average, have you been spending on activities connected wtih the program during the last few months?

Political Interest—Participation
(a) Generally speaking, how much interest would you say you have in politics: a great deal, a fair amount, only a little, or no interest at all?
(b) Have you, yourself, ever done any work for a political party or candidate?

Political Connectedness
(a)There are about four political party committeemen in your election district. Are you acquainted with any of them?
(b) If yes, can your acquaintance be described as: personal, casual or only at election time?
(c) What (political) organizations do you belong to?

Social Connectedness
(a) What other organizations do you belong to?
(b) How active would you say you are in each of them?

Attitudes and Expectations of Program Efficacy
(a) Have you gotten anyone to do anything in connection with the program, such as attending meetings, making a complaint, joining a committee?
(b) Have you made further attempts to get people to do something?
(c) If the PCRP were to end, do you think the organized part of it to which you belong (area committee, district committee, etc.) would continue by itself?

Perceived Value Conflict

A single-item indicator, offered here as face-valid:

Has there been any general change in your neighborhood since the last interview? Are things getting better, worse, or are they about the same? A response of "worse" was taken to indicate a summative value conflict; it being assumed that all respondents would regard neighborhood decline as conflicting with their value preference. Note that this is not a direct measure of TVC as there was no indication of the degree of threat which respondent felt as a function of the perceived neighborhood decline.

Perceived Inefficacy of Political Party Personnel

(a) (Filter) What specific roles do you think the politicians (especially your committeemen and ward leaders) should play in solving (housing, employment, education and police-community-relations) problems? If the answer to the filter question is "direct action" (versus indirect action . . . can't say or none) and the answer to the following question was "no," this was assumed to reflect the respondent's perception of political party personnel as inefficacious.

(b) Have any of these politicians (ward leaders and committeemen) ever been of any help to you?

NAME INDEX

SUBJECT INDEX

283